MW00827371

COMING TO PALESTINE

Sheldon Richman

The

LIBERTARIAN

INSTITUTE

Coming to Palestine
Sheldon Richman

First Edition, 2019

Edited by Scott Horton

Cover picture by krystianwin

Cover design by TheBumperSticker.com

Published in the United States of America by

The Libertarian Institute
612 W. 34th St.
Austin, TX 78705

LibertarianInstitute.org

ISBN-13: 978-1-7336473-2-8
ISBN-10: 1-7336473-2-5

To Palestinians everywhere and to all who wish for freedom, justice, toleration, and peace in Palestine.

And in loving memory of my grandfather Samuel Richman.

Contents

Foreword

From the outset, the creation of Israel on the ruins of historic Palestine was accompanied by a distorted historical narrative, one that labored to mask the true nature of the colonial Zionist project. For that to happen, the Zionists constructed the myth of the miraculous birth of Israel in an arid, empty desert.

Sheldon Richman has been aware of the Zionist falsification of history for many years, and has, capably and thoroughly, challenged the oft-repeated Israeli myths in his many well-written essays. In the chapter "The 'Jordan Option' Is Based Upon Blatant Falsification of History," Richman dissects parts of the Israeli political discourse aimed at erasing the Palestinian people. He directs the reader to the infamous remarks by Israeli Prime Minister Golda Meir (1969–1974), who told the British *Sunday Times* newspaper in June 1969 that "it is not as though there was a Palestinian people in Palestine considering itself as a Palestinian people and we came and threw them out and took their country away from them. They did not exist."

Golda Meir's comments, however, must not be viewed in isolation from the deeply-rooted Israeli Zionist trajectory that plotted to eradicate the Palestinians, their historical claim to Palestine, their culture, their identity and, needless to say, their political rights. That erasure is still central to the Zionist agenda in Palestine. Indeed, the notion that Palestinians are not a people with a collective sense of nationhood has remained a defining concept of Zionism until this day, and has spread well beyond Israel's borders. American Christian evangelicals are particularly avid supporters of this idea, which has led some American politicians to publicly embrace it. In 2011, for example, then U.S. presidential candidate Newt Gingrich told the Jewish Channel that the Palestinians were an "invented people."

"I think that we've had an invented Palestinian people who are in fact Arabs and who were historically part of the Arab community. And they had a chance to go many places, and for a variety of political reasons they have sustained this war against Israel now since the 1940s, and it's tragic," Gingrich said, quoted by the British *Guardian* newspaper on December 10, 2011.

The ongoing falsification of history has greater objectives than erasing the Palestinian people and their collective claim to human rights and dignity. It also aims at normalizing Israeli military occupation, apartheid, and colonialism. It provides a historical amnesty for all the crimes that Israel has committed and will continue to commit.

Of the many tools intended to normalize apartheid in Israel was the long, painful and ultimately failed "peace process," which rebranded Israel as a peace-seeking party in an American-led noble endeavor aimed at resolving the decades-long tragedy.

Oslo was achieved through U.S.-styled negotiations, which operated largely outside the framework of international law. Talks that began in Madrid in 1991, followed by the Oslo Peace Accord in 1993, the Paris Protocol in 1994, the Hebron Protocol in 1997, Wye River in 1998, Camp David in 2000, and other agreements and understandings only led to the cementing of the Israeli occupation, a tripling in the number of illegal Jewish settlers and the vast expansion of the illegal Israeli settlement network in the Occupied Territories.

"What the Palestinians won't accept," wrote Richman, "is a 'state' that is little more than a few uncontiguous villages separated by a wall, a 'state' over which Israel asserts ultimate control in the name of security. But even that is too much for most Israelis. They have no objection to the Palestinian Authority exerting authoritarian control over the Palestinians — that's all the Oslo Accords accomplished, relieving Israelis of the bad-PR dirty work — but they will not accept Palestinians in charge of their own security against Israel, which means not only the Israeli military but also the fanatical settlers, many of them Americans, who think nothing of killing, bashing, and humiliating the goyische Palestinians with impunity."

That, too, is an outcome of Israel's relentless attempt at erasing Palestinians, marginalizing them at every turn and negating their most basic human rights. But no matter what Israel does, the truth cannot be forever altered. The story of Palestine is the story of the Palestinian people, for they are the victims of oppression and the main channel of resistance since the *Nakba* — the creation of Israel on the ruins of Palestinian towns and villages in 1948.

This book is far more than a deserved celebration of Richman's intellectual wisdom and astute political and historical analyses throughout the years. It is, first and foremost, a serious and convincing challenge to the protracted Zionist deception and lies that predate the establishment of Israel itself. According to Zionist propaganda, supported by successive U.S. administrations, Israel is a peace-loving, progressive, democratic country that is facing hordes of warring, "anti-Semitic" Arabs.

"In the rich mythology of the Middle East, no myth has more malign effects on current affairs than the one which says that (for decades) Israel has stood ready to negotiate peace," wrote Richman, and that "the Arab leadership has been committed (and remains committed) to Israel's destruction."

In truth, Israel needs more to survive in its current undemocratic, racist, colonial form than a powerful army, nuclear arms, and blind U.S. support. It also needs to sustain, for as long as possible, the myth that it is a democratic haven in a tumultuous sea of authoritarian and violent Arabs, who are a threat not only to the Jewish people (all of them) but to Western civilization as well.

Richman's is a book of political myth-busting, a craft that the author has mastered through many years of morally guided scholarship, painstaking research and an eloquent writing style. And, ultimately, this is the kind of unapologetic truth-telling that Israel fears most.

Ramzy Baroud
PalestineChronicle.com

Introduction

Anyone who seeks to understand the complexities of the Middle East, the manner in which Zionism, or Jewish nationalism, has corrupted Judaism and the Jewish moral and ethical tradition, would do well to consult the thoughtful essays in this collection. The author, Sheldon Richman, has made a notable contribution to the study of this subject and, over the years, he and I have had the opportunity to work together.

In my role as editor of *Issues*, the quarterly journal of the American Council for Judaism, I have tried to advance a view of Judaism which predates Zionism — as a religion of universal values, not a nationality. While Israeli leaders claim that Israel is the "homeland" of all Jews, it is our belief that Americans of the Jewish faith are American by nationality and Jews by religion, just as other Americans are Protestant, Catholic or Muslim. The homeland of American Jews is the United States.

This has been the belief of the vast majority of American Jews all through our history. In his dedication of America's first Reform synagogue in Charleston, South Carolina, Rabbi Gustav Poznanski declared: "This happy country is our Palestine, this city our Jerusalem, this house of God our temple. As our father's defended with their lives that Temple, that city and that land, so will their sons defend this temple, this city, and this land."

Theodore Herzl, the late founder of modern Zionism, did not believe in God or in Judaism. The state he sought to create would be secular, based on the idea of Jewish "national" and "ethnic" identity and incorporating those features he found most attractive in Europe, particularly Germany. This immediately brought opposition from Jews of a variety of viewpoints, including the Orthodox and those Jews who considered themselves full members of the societies in which they were born and lived.

The chief rabbi of Vienna, Moritz Gudemann denounced the mirage of Jewish nationalism: "Belief in One God was the unifying factor for Jews," he declared, and said that Zionism was incompatible with Judaism's teaching.

For Reform Jews, the idea of Zionism contradicted almost completely their belief in a universal, prophetic Judaism. The first Reform prayer book eliminated references to Jews being in exile and to a Messiah who would miraculously restore Jews throughout the world to the historic land of Israel and who would rebuild the Temple in Jerusalem. The most articulate spokesman for the Reform movement emerging in Europe, the distinguished Rabbi Abraham Geiger, argued that revelation was progressive and new truth became available to every generation. The Jewish people were a religious community destined to carry out the mission to "serve as a light to the nation's" — to bear witness to His moral law. The dispersion of the Jews was not a punishment for their sins, but part of God's plan whereby they were to disseminate the universal message of ethical monotheism.

In 1885, Reform rabbis meeting in Pittsburgh wrote a platform that declared, "We recognize in the era of universal culture of heart and intellect, the approaching of Messianic hope for the establishment of the kingdom of truth, justice, and peace among all men. We consider ourselves no longer a nation, but a religious community and therefore expect neither a return to Palestine nor a sacrificial worship . . . nor the laws . . . concerning the Jewish state." It is this vision of America's original Reform Jews that the American Council for Judaism has sought to preserve and advance.

In his book *What Is Modern Israel?* Professor Yakov Rabkin of the University of Montreal, an Orthodox Jew, shows that Zionism was conceived as a clear break with Judaism and the Jewish religious tradition. He believes it must be seen in the context of European ethnic nationalism and geopolitical interests rather than as an incarnation of biblical prophecies or a culmination of Jewish history. The religious idea of a Jewish return to Palestine had nothing to do with the political enterprise of Zionism. "Jewish tradition," writes Rabkin, "holds that the idea of return must be part of a messianic project rather than human initiative of migration to the Holy Land. There was little room for Jewish tradition in the Zionist scheme. . . . It is not the physical geography of the biblical land of Israel that is essential for Jews but the obligation to follow the commandments of the Torah."

The early Zionists not only turned away from the Jewish religious tradition but, in their disregard for the indigenous population of Palestine, Jewish moral and ethical values as well. They spoke of "a land without people for a people without a land." In fact, Palestine was fully occupied. In his book, *Israel: A Colonial-Settler State*, the French Jewish historian Maxime Rodinson writes that, "Wanting to create a purely Jewish or predominantly Jewish state in Arab Palestine in the 20th century could not help but lead to a colonial-type situation and the development of a racist state of mind and in the final analysis to a military confrontation."

Only with the rise of anti-Semitism in Russia and Eastern Europe in the early 20th century, followed by the rise of Nazism and the Holocaust did sympathy for Zionism and the creation of a Jewish state in Palestine begin to grow. Even then, many Jewish voices warned against the rise of nationalism. Albert Einstein, alluding to Nazism, in 1938 warned an audience of Zionist activists against the temptation to create a state with "a narrow nationalism within our own ranks against which we have already had to fight strongly even without a Jewish state."

Another prominent German Jewish philosopher, Martin Buber, spoke out in 1942 against the "aim of the minority to 'conquer' territory by means of international maneuvers." From Jerusalem, in the midst of the hostilities that broke out after Israel unilaterally declared independence in May 1948, Buber cried with despair, "This sort of Zionism blasphemes the name of Zion; it is nothing more than one of the cruel forms of nationalism."

After Israel's creation, the organized Jewish community embraced it and made it "central" to Jewish identity. Israeli flags were displayed in synagogues, lobbying groups were created to promote Israel's interests, making it the largest recipient of U.S. aid in the world. The Palestinians were displaced and, in 1967, their land was occupied. In reality, the Palestinians have become the last victims of the Holocaust, for which they bear no responsibility whatever.

What we have witnessed since 1948 can only be considered a form of idolatry, making the State of Israel, not God and the Jewish moral and ethical tradition, "central" to Jewish identity. This is reminiscent of the story of the Golden Calf in the Bible.

During all these years, the older Jewish tradition of universal values and a rejection of nationalism has been kept alive by, among others, the American Council for Judaism, as well as independent voices from many sectors of the Jewish community. Sheldon Richman has been one such important and eloquent voice. His contribution has been vital and those who read these essays will recognize the breadth of his vision and his understanding.

This book arrives at a hopeful time. American Jews are increasingly disillusioned with Israel and its 51-year occupation of the West Bank and East Jerusalem. They used to believe Israel's claim that it was a Western-style democracy. They now understand that Israel is a theocracy, with no separation of church and state. Non-Orthodox rabbis cannot perform weddings or funerals or conduct conversions. Jews and non-Jews who wish to marry must leave the country to do so. Millions of Palestinians under occupation have no political rights at all.

It is a positive sign that many Israelis recognize what is happening to their country. Professor David Shulman of the Hebrew University in Jerusalem, notes that, "No matter how we look at it . . . unless our minds have been poisoned by the ideologies of the religious right, the occupation is a crime. It is first of all based on the permanent disenfranchisement of a huge population. . . . In the end, it is the ongoing moral failure of the country as a whole that is most consequential. . . . The failure weighs heavily on our humanity. We are, so we claim, the children of the prophets.

. . . Once, they say, we were slaves in Egypt. We know all that can be known about slavery, prejudice, ghettos, hate, expulsion, exile. I find it astonishing that we, of all people, have reinvented apartheid in the West Bank."

The essays collected together here show how Zionism has altered and distorted the humane Jewish tradition and shows, as well, how Zionist political efforts have altered U.S. foreign policy and made us, in effect, participants in Israel's occupation. Israel has been the recipient of more U.S. foreign aid than any country in the world. As these essays show us, the interests of the U.S. and of peace and justice in the region have been ill-served by this enterprise.

Where the future will lead is impossible to predict. One hopeful possibility is that the movement toward universalism and the rejection of nationalism which proceeded dramatically in the nineteenth and early twentieth centuries — and was interrupted by the rise of Nazism, World War II, and the creation of a Jewish state in Palestine — will once again move forward in the future. There is now every indication that this will be the case. The current divisions in American Judaism certainly point in this direction.

When people look back at the time when narrow nationalism replaced Judaism's historic religious contribution, a belief in ethical monotheism and in a God who created men and women of all races and nations in His image, those who worked to maintain that tradition will be honored. Sheldon Richman, although a self-described Spinozan, will surely be one of these.

Sheldon grew up in a period when, in the wake of the Holocaust, many Jews believed that Palestine was indeed a land without people, as Zionists proclaimed. Desperate to find a place for the survivors, they embraced a policy that displaced another people. Some Jews understood the reality of what was happening. Many did not. Sheldon was lucky to have a paternal grandfather who was skeptical of Zionist claims. I always liked Sheldon's recollection of his grandfather presiding over the annual family Seder at Passover and proclaiming, "Next year in Philadelphia" rather than the traditional "Next year in Jerusalem." This must have gotten Sheldon thinking about these things, which he has done for the rest of his life.

This collection of essays is an essential contribution to understanding Judaism, Zionism, and the continuing conflict in the Middle East. If anyone wonders why Palestine matters, this important book provides an answer.

Allan C. Brownfeld
American Council for Judaism

"He who knows only his own side of the case, knows little of that."

— John Stuart Mill, *On Liberty*

1

Why Palestine Matters

The Libertarian Institute, June 29, 2018

Why does Palestine matter? It's a question I ask myself nearly every day. Another way to put it is, "Is the devotion of major attention to the plight of the Palestinians an obsession worthy of suspicion or an appropriate response to a grave historic and continuing injustice?"

No one will be surprised when I reply that major attention is an appropriate response. Palestine matters and should matter. I will try to explain why.

First, perhaps most basically, the sheer cruelty — the scope of the violation of human, i.e., natural individual rights — of Israel's treatment of the Palestinians warrants the concern of all who favor freedom and other (classical) liberal values: justice, social cooperation, free exchange, and peace.

Let's start with the Occupied Palestinian Territories. As B'Tselem, the Israeli Information Center for Human Rights in the Occupied Territories, says front and center on its website: "Israel's regime of occupation is inextricably bound up in human rights violations." No one who sheds the blinders of the Official Narrative can help but feel pain over the institutional barriers to normal life, not to mention the literal destruction of life, that are regular features of Israel's rule in the West Bank (with nearly three million Palestinians), East Jerusalem (over 300,000), and the Gaza Strip (nearly two million). It is no exaggeration to describe the system as an instance of apartheid, which is the word used by Israeli human-rights organizations and former government officials. (Then-Prime Minister Yitzhak Rabin used the word in a warning as far back as 1976. So did Israel's first prime minister, David Ben-Gurion, when he was out of office after the 1967 war.)

The Palestinians in the West Bank and East Jerusalem have lived under harsh military rule for over half a century. This rule consists of "low-level" repression such as checkpoints (even for ambulances), travel permits, and Jewish-only roads that subject Palestinians to daily humiliation, disruption, and the arbitrary whim of soldiers charged with the task of controlling an occupied population.

Imagine trying to live a normal life — making a living, caring for your children — when you don't know how long you will be delayed en route from Point A to Point B because you are stopped, questioned, and searched by unaccountable, heavily armed government officers who don't like you because of your race, ethnicity, or religion or who are suspicious of people who naturally resent being dominated. Imagine, further, a life of poverty in which water (in the arid Middle East!), electricity, and education are scarce and unreliable simply because the government provider of those services favors the subsidized, comfortable Jewish settlers (many from America) living nearby. The juxtaposition of water shortages for Palestinians with swimming pools for Jews is too obvious an outrage to require comment.

This daily mistreatment is frequently accentuated by outright violence at the hands of the military rulers: bone-breaking beatings, torture, killings, house demolitions for reasons of collective punishment and ethnic cleansing, indefinite detention without charge or trial, and the like. These measures are intensified whenever Palestinians stage largely nonviolent intifadas (uprisings) and mass civil disobedience. Any of this would be regarded (one hopes) as intolerable in America or anywhere else in the West.

Add to this, Israel's continuing de facto annexation of the West Bank (East Jerusalem has been annexed de jure) through the expansion of illegal (by international law) Jewish-only settlements and a wall that snakes through the West Bank, isolating Palestinian towns, separating communities from each other and their farmland, and making a mockery of the "two-state solution." (Not that Israel's leaders ever intended to vacate the lands conquered in 1967 during an expansionist war of choice against four Arab nations during which the Israeli air force also attacked a U.S. intelligence ship, the USS *Liberty*, killing 34 sailors and wounding more than 170.)

But that horror doesn't begin to describe how the nearly two million people, more than half of them children, in the densely populated Gaza Strip live every day. Their territory has been described — even by Israelis — as an open-air prison or ghetto. Israel's defenders claim that the Jewish State "withdrew" from Gaza more than a decade ago without any resulting peace dividend, but this is misleading. Yes, the military left, and the settlers went with them. But that is like cheering guards for withdrawing from a prison to positions just outside the walls. Under the decade-old blockade, the state determines who and what can enter and leave Gaza. As Norman Finkelstein points out in his exhaustive research on Gaza, even toys, chocolate, and potato chips are barred. Drinking water is contaminated because of the ban on supplies needed to repair facilities destroyed by the Israeli military.

Palestinians who get too close to the fence separating Gaza and the rest of Israel and Palestine risk being shot by soldiers. Peaceful demonstrators far from the fence face the same risk. Israel controls Gaza's Mediterranean coast as well, including the crucial ability to fish beyond a certain point. Closer in the fish are likely to be contaminated by sewage for the reason already noted.

This daily hardship (to use a grossly mild noun) is underscored by periodic massacres — indistinguishable from terrorism, according to international law — committed by Israeli warplanes, drones, and ground troops, incredibly brutal assaults that have left many civilians (including children) dead or maimed, tens of thousands of homes destroyed, and tons and tons of rubble in their wake. These regular violent onslaughts against the people of Gaza — a level of brutality that shocks even people who have been in the world's worst war zones — serve two purposes: to demonstrate Israel's deterrent power to others (after humiliating defeats by Hezbollah in southern Lebanon) and to "mow the lawn," that is, to maintain the people at a certain low level of nutrition and morale, thereby limiting their ability to resist even nonviolently. "Israel's evolving modus operandi for restoring its deterrence capacity," Finkelstein writes, "described a curve steadily regressing into barbarism." With many experts predicting that Gaza will soon be "unlivable," this is a campaign of genocidal proportions.

"But Hamas. . ." is no counterargument to the foregoing. Israel helped nurture Muslim Hamas in the 1980s in a divide-and-conquer move, that is, as a rival to the secular Fatah and PLO, which had already recognized Israel as a state, thereby conceding 78 percent of historic Palestine to the Zionists. Hamas's influence is a direct result of Israel's refusal to talk to the moderate Palestinian leadership in good faith. In other words, Hamas is a "threat" of Israel's own making.

Moreover, Israel on several occasions violated ceasefires that Hamas had been honoring. When Hamas responded with what are misleadingly called "rockets," Israel has countered with monstrous force, killing many noncombatants, including children, and leaving Gaza buried in rubble.

Further, the Palestinians in Gaza, sick of the West Bank Palestinian leadership's corruption and fecklessness, elected Hamas in a monitored and fair election during the George W. Bush years (2006), for which the Gazans were punished with harsh U.S. and European Union sanctions and a U.S.-backed failed coup attempt by the Palestinian Authority, Israel's subcontractor for internal security in the occupied territories. (The bankrupt PLO leadership took on that lucrative quisling assignment under the deceptive Oslo Accord.)

Bush officials had demanded an election in Gaza, then regretted it when they saw the results. Indeed, Bush critic Sen. Hillary Clinton

3

commented after the balloting, "I do not think we should have pushed for an election in the Palestinian territories. I think that was a big mistake. And if we were going to push for an election, then *we should have made sure that we did something to determine who was going to win.*" [Emphasis added.] (What's that she now says about alleged Russian meddling to keep her from winning the presidency?)

But most crucial, Hamas has changed its inflammatory charter to accept, unlike successive Israeli governments, Israel's 1967 borders, i.e., the two-state solution, which entails a complete Israeli withdrawal — settlements and separation wall — from the West Bank and Gaza in accordance with international law. But no matter. Hamas has been too convenient an excuse for Israel to claim it has no unified partner for peace. But when Hamas joined with the West Bank Palestinian Administration, Israel claimed it can't talk to anyone who would partner with Hamas — even though the partner has conceded 78 percent of Palestine to Israel, as the PLO did 30 years ago. (Israel has built settlements for 600,000 Jews on — and otherwise directly controls — more than half of the remaining 22 percent the Palestinians were willing to settle for.)

At any rate, Hamas must be judged against the larger context: namely, the Israeli occupation and de facto annexation of Palestinian property and the total subjugation of the Palestinian people. Killing noncombatants is of course immoral, but Israel, which routinely targets civilian neighborhoods in Gaza and the West Bank, hardly has clean hands in that regard.

The 1.5 million Palestinian "citizens" inside Israel (20 percent of the citizen population) have it better than their counterparts in the occupied territories, but only somewhat. After being under military rule from 1948 to 1966, the Palestinians inside Israel settled into second- or rather third-class citizenship. As the self-proclaimed State of the Jewish People (everywhere in the world), Israel does not treat non-Jewish citizens the way it treats Jewish citizens. (This is an ethno-national, rather than a religious, designation, although there is no Jewish ethnicity or race.) While Palestinians (i.e., those who managed to survive the ethnic cleansing of 1947–1948) can vote, form political parties, and hold office, they nevertheless may not change Israel into a democratic republic for all its citizens. A recent attempt in the Knesset to do that was quashed without debate or vote. Nor can they end the systemic discrimination against Palestinians in access to land (most land is either officially or unofficially off-limits to non-Jews; see Ben White's *Palestinians in Israel: Segregation, Discrimination and Democracy*) and in the allocation of government-provided services like utilities and schooling. In addition, Palestinians driven from their homes in 1947–1948, that is, the *Nakba*, may not return, yet anyone born anywhere and living anywhere who has a Jewish mother or who was converted by an approved rabbi can become an Israeli citizen automatically no matter where he was born or is now living.

In light of all this, note the significance of the recent Israeli demand that the Palestinians in the West Bank and in Gaza recognize Israel not just as a legitimate state, but as a Jewish State. Such a concession would betray the non-Jewish citizens of Israel.

The second reason why Palestine matters is that American taxpayers are forced to underwrite this system of injustice and repression. The U.S. government gives Israel, the Middle East's only nuclear state, over $3 billion a year in military aid on the most favorable terms. Even the allegedly anti-Israel Obama administration set records in giving military aid to Israel, which violates U.S. law (and international law) by using the weapons to repress the Palestinians and to wage war against civilians. Obama never once penalized Israel for expanding West Bank and East Jerusalem settlements even though the U.S. government has always officially regarded them as in violation of international law.

Some justify this unstinting and unique support for Israel on grounds that Israel is an American "strategic asset," and Israeli leaders cynically talk in those terms. But this makes no sense. For one thing, as many American political and military leaders have acknowledged since 9/11, rather than being an asset, Israel has been a liability. A big reason for the Muslim terrorism directed at Americans is precisely the unconditional U.S. military assistance to, not to mention the diplomatic support of, Israel. What goes a long way toward explaining the huge sums given to Israel each year — over $10 million a day — is the influential Israel Lobby, which brags about its power over U.S. politicians. AIPAC and other organizations have created an environment in which criticism of Israel or Zionism is smeared as anti-Semitism, although this baseless association has finally begun to wear thin. It's worth pointing out that some of the first and most incisive anti-Zionists were Jewish.

Would things change drastically if U.S. aid ended? It's hard to say; ending the aid would be a big blow to the pocketbook, but the ideological commitment to keeping the Palestinians down is strong. Nevertheless, Americans' forced complicity in this injustice must end.

The third reason I want to point to is the threat of a wider war, one that could reach beyond Palestine and Israel and even beyond the Middle East. Analysts have long warned that the region could be a flashpoint for a war involving Iran, a long-standing regional power, and Russia. We need only look at Syria, where Russia and Iran have intervened on behalf of their ally President Bashar al-Assad, whom the U.S. and Israel are trying to undermine — and assisting groups related to al Qaeda, the perpetrators of the 9/11 attacks. It is not far-fetched to envision a clash between U.S. and Russian forces in that country. Moreover, the U.S. and Israel have conducted covert warfare and sponsored terrorist acts against Iran, which Israeli politicians have found useful for distracting attention from their oppression of the Palestinians. A U.S. war against Iran, which would be virtually inevitable should Israel attack the Islamic Republic, would be a regional if not larger catastrophe.

The Trump administration's so-called peace initiative, led by his patently unqualified and biased son-in-law Jared Kushner and other unabashedly pro-Israel figures, has shaped up as nothing more than an effort to unite Israel and the Arab countries (especially the illiberal regimes in Saudi Arabia and Egypt) against Iran — with the Palestinians being sacrificed in the process. The Saudis are expected to "deliver the Palestinians," a phrase that drips with condescension, for a deal that essentially enshrines Israel's domination and crushes Palestinian hopes for self-determination.

The attempt to subordinate the Palestinians' grievances to the reckless anti-Iran campaign will only make things worse, both by provoking Iran, which is surrounded by U.S. military facilities, and dashing any remaining hope that the Palestinians will at last see some justice. Even on pragmatic grounds, why leave it to Iran alone to champion the long-suffering Palestinians?

In light of my personal background, it has not been easy for me to write this; it's been enervating and even painful. But as Finkelstein shows in heavily documented books and YouTube lectures, the Palestine-Israel "conflict" is really not complicated. Contrary to those solemn pundits who, seeking to discourage people from looking at the matter closely, write about the "clash of civilizations," the ancient religious feud, and other such rubbish, widespread agreement exists among historians (including Israelis) that Palestinian enmity toward the Zionists was based on a justified fear of land theft and that Israel was founded through ethnic cleansing — what can the establishment of a Jewish State entail if not the removal of non-Jews? Before the rise of Zionism, Arabs got along reasonably well with Jews, far better than the European Christians did.

Israeli historians reported on the incriminating official documents more than 30 years ago. The leader in this effort was Benny Morris, who acknowledges and documents the wholesale removal and killing of Palestinians while approving of it. Indeed, he writes, "The fear of territorial displacement and dispossession was to be the chief motor of Arab antagonism to Zionism." Morris also wrote that "transfer [of the Palestinians out of Palestine] was inevitable and inbuilt into Zionism — because it sought to transform a land which was 'Arab' into a 'Jewish' state and a Jewish state could not have arisen without a major displacement of Arab population." This is from a defender of Israel's founding, one who laments that the ethnic cleansing was incomplete.

The point is that the facts are not seriously disputed.

Further, unanimous agreement exists among all respected human-rights organizations (including Israeli organizations) that since the state's founding, Israel has routinely treated the Palestinians brutally and discriminatorily, with the most egregious cases being the West Bank, East Jerusalem, and Gaza, which were acquired by war contrary to international law. Still further, the International Court of Justice has ruled (14–1, with the one "dissenter," who did not call his opinion a dissent, agreeing with much of the majority position) that the separation wall in the West Bank is illegal because the occupation of and settlements in the West Bank are illegal.

So where is the controversy among people who bother to study the matter? On every major moral and legal question, it doesn't exist. Contrary to what some Israel defenders suggest, the same moral and legal principles that identify the Nazi Holocaust as unspeakably evil also apply to Jews. (A few political controversies, such as whether the right of return for the six million Palestinian refugees is feasible, remain.)

The reasonable minimal steps toward a just remediation therefore follow: complete Israeli withdrawal from the West Bank, including dismantling of the settlements; removal of the wall and compensation for those whose property was damaged by its construction; the liberation of Gaza, permitting the Palestinians full "self-government" (alas, libertarianism isn't on the menu today); the right of return for Palestinian refugees driven from their homes 70 years ago (although monetary compensation may figure in lieu of this), and full rights for the Palestinian citizens of Israel.

This sounds like the famous two-state solution, but an alternative focusing on one democratic state with equal rights for all citizens has gained prominence. (This is what PLO chief Yasser Arafat called for in his UN General Assembly address 44 years ago.) It comes down to a debate over what is realistically achievable in the near term.

On one side are those who say it's too late for two states because since 1967, a de facto single state has existed between the Mediterranean Sea and the River Jordan. Thus, the only remaining question, they argue, is what kind of state shall this be: democratic or apartheid?

After all, this side adds, when the UN General Assembly in 1947 recommended partition of Palestine into Jewish and Arab states — the UN never partitioned Palestine and did not have the power to do so — the Jews were assigned 56 percent of the territory, the Arabs 44 percent, even though the Arab Muslims and Christians were the overwhelming majority and Jewish land purchases amounted to less than 7 percent of Palestine (much of that of dubious legitimacy because of Ottoman feudalism). But after the ethnic cleansing, and after the neighboring Arab governments feebly attempted to defend the overrun Palestinians (the so-called War of Independence), Israel expanded into nearly 80 percent. (The Palestinians had rejected the partition recommendation; from the time that Great Britain first contemplated ruling the Middle East and then conquered Palestine during World War I, the Palestinians were deemed unworthy of consultation about the fate of their own land.)

Then, when the occupied territories were acquired in 1967, Israel methodically established "facts on the ground" — Jewish-only settlements, roads, the separation wall, etc. — precisely to guarantee that the territories would never have to be given up. The hoped-for Palestinian state thus shrunk from the original 44 percent to 22 percent, which consists of communities cut off from each other and Gaza miles away. What kind of state is that, ask the advocates of a single democratic state? Better, they say, to declare equal rights for all throughout Israel-Palestine and let reforms flow from the new democratic environment.

The two-state advocates respond that it will be much easier (however difficult) to persuade Israel to withdraw from the Territories than to persuade it to change from a Jewish state to a secular liberal democratic state in which Jews would soon be the minority. (In the whole of Israel-Palestine today the population split is roughly 50–50.)

As tempting as it is to weigh in on this debate, I think Norman Finkelstein put it best in 2014:

> I don't advocate anything. It's not my place to advocate. First of all, I'm not a Palestinian. Second of all, I'm not Israeli. . . . I don't live anywhere near the affected regions. . . . Anyone who's involved in politics knows that politics is not about personal preferences. If you ask my personal preference, I would say that I don't believe in two states; I don't believe in one state; I happen not to believe in any states. I'm an old-fashioned leftist in that regard. But politics is not about what you prefer; it's not about what I prefer. Politics is about a realistic assessment of the balances of forces in the world.

I would add, as Finkelstein has on many occasions, that the best we can do is to work to build broad public support for a solution rooted in justice, liberty, and peace for all, enlisting sound moral intuitions and established liberal legal principles in the service of reasonably achievable ends.

2

Depopulating Palestine,
Dehumanizing the Palestinians

The Libertarian Institute, July 27, 2018

One might have thought that, in the wake of the Nazi regime's systematic crimes against humanity last century, dehumanization would have become unthinkable once and for all. Unfortunately, this has not been the case. It has shamefully continued unabated, the assorted perpetrators including, with tragic irony, those who themselves were victims of Nazi dehumanization.

Dehumanization is an apt term because it consists of more than merely murder, massacre, torture, blockade, dispossession, humiliation, and the like. It consists of the very denial of the *humanity* of the victims and their cultures; it may include attempts to wipe them from the archives and from anyone's memory. This denial makes simple physical destruction easier: cruel treatment on a mass scale would seem to require that the victimizer view the victim as subhuman, as verminous, as something that infests the surroundings, as something unworthy of the consideration one normally gives even strangers about whom one knows nothing.

The case of the Palestinians is hardly the only case of dehumanization in the post-World War II era. Off the top of my head, I think of the African victims of the European powers (the mistreatment of whom got underway well before the 1930s), of Maoist China, of South Africa, of Rwanda, of Darfur, of Cambodia, of the Central African Republic. What seems to distinguish the Palestinian case (which of course began before World War II) is the sophistication, duration, and outside support of the effort to deny the very existence of people, Muslims and Christians, who have lived for a long time south of Syria and Lebanon and north of Saudi Arabia between the Mediterranean Sea and the Jordan River.

No one vocalized this denial better than a former Israeli prime minister, Golda Meir, who famously said:

> There were no such thing as Palestinians. When was there an independent Palestinian people with a Palestinian state? It was either southern Syria before the First World War, and then it was a Palestine

9

including Jordan. It was not as though there was a Palestinian people in Palestine considering itself as a Palestinian people and we came and threw them out and took their country away from them. They did not exist.

A libertarian approach to this matter offers a perspective that tends to get overlooked by conventional analysis. Examining whether the Palestinians as a group constitute a "people" deserving of "national" self-determination or liberation can yield useful information, but that question cannot be fundamental because whether or not "Palestinians" qua communally conscious people lived in "Palestine" before the Israeli statehood movement (Zionism) got underway, we do know this: *individual human beings* who were not recent European Jewish immigrants legitimately owned property there.

We have no good alternative to methodological individualism; human beings come in individual units. So the individual and his or her rights — including the right to land justly acquired — must have primacy. However important a person's identification with an ethnic, racial, or national group, or lack thereof, may be, it has no bearing on the question of rights. A "Palestinian" can have no more rights than an unattached atomistic individual or one who identifies as an Asian, an Arab, or a Nabulsi. Therefore, individual self-determination must precede communal self-determination if the latter is to be valid because group rights make sense only if they extend from and are consistent with *members' individual rights.*

Morally, we have rights by virtue of our personhood, not by virtue of our inclusion in a subgroup of persons. The idea of rights not rooted in the individual literally is nonsense. Among other things, this means there is no *Jewish* land, *Palestinian* land, or land with any other ethnic, racial, or religious qualifier. There is only legitimately and illegitimately acquired land. (In this connection, see Chapter 37 about Khaled Sabawi, which focuses on his attempt to reestablish individual property rights in the West Bank through formal registration.)

Thus, even had Golda Meir been right, the establishment of Israel as it took place would have been no less a crime against the territory's indigenous inhabitants. Likewise, even if one could show that the non-Jews driven from Palestine at gunpoint in 1948 had only recently migrated from elsewhere in the Middle East (which one cannot), this in itself could not justify their expulsion.

But in fact, notwithstanding fabricated and wholly discredited "histories" of Palestine and Israel, it is now uncontroversial to state that the establishment of Israel saw hundreds of thousands of indigenous individuals driven from their ancestral homes and hundreds of others massacred by recent European immigrants (many of them atheists yet nevertheless claiming to be Jewish) with a tenuous connection to Palestine or ancient Israel. H. G. Wells posed a reasonable question: "If it is proper to 'reconstitute' a Jewish state which has not existed for two thousand years, why not go back another thousand years and reconstitute the Canaanite state? The Canaanites, unlike the Jews, are still there." (Quoted in Ian Gilmour and David Gilmour, "Pseudo-Travellers," *London Review of Books*, February 1985.) What did Wells mean? The Gilmours explain:

> The modern Palestinians are a people of various ethnic origins, descended from the conquerors of Palestine since early biblical times. Their ancestors are the Canaanites and Philistines who, unlike the Jews, were never deported. They remained in Palestine (which took its name from the Philistines) and their descendants formed, and still form, the core of the indigenous population. In the seventh century, the Muhammadan Arabs brought with them their government, their language and their religion, and a majority of the inhabitants accepted all three. Palestine and its people became Arabised. Yet they remained the same people. There was little racial change in the population because the Arab conquerors were so few in number.

Evidence for this comes from an interesting source, David Ben-Gurion, Israel's first prime minister, and Itzhak Ben-Zvi, Israel's second president (and also a historian), in their 1918 book, *Eretz Israel in the Past and in the Present*. As quoted in Shlomo Sand's *The Invention of the Jewish People*, Ben-Gurion and Ben-Zvi wrote:

> The fellahin [Palestinian farmers] are not descendants of the Arab conquerors, who captured Eretz Israel and Syria in the seventh century CE. The Arab victors did not destroy the agricultural population they found in the country. They expelled only the alien Byzantine rulers, and did not touch the local population. Nor did the Arabs go in for settlement. Even in their former habitations, the Arabians did not engage in farming. . . . They did not seek new lands on which to settle their peasantry, which hardly existed. Their whole interest in the new countries was political, religious and material: to rule, to propagate Islam and to collect taxes.

Sand tells us that "historical reason indicates that the population that survived since the seventh century had originated from the Judean farming class that the Muslim conquerors had found when they reached the country." He then continues with Ben-Gurion and Ben-Zvi's text:

> To argue that after the conquest of Jerusalem by Titus and the failure of the Bar Kokhba revolt Jews altogether ceased to cultivate the land of Eretz Israel is to demonstrate complete ignorance of history and the contemporary literature of Israel. . . . The Jewish farmer, like any other farmer, was not easily torn from his soil, which had been watered

with his sweat and the sweat of his forebears. . . . Despite the
repression and suffering, the rural population remained unchanged.

Sand comments that "this was written thirty years before Israel's
Proclamation of Independence, which asserts that the whole people was
forcibly uprooted. . . . Although the ancient Judean peasants converted to
Islam, they had done so for material reasons — chiefly to avoid taxation
— which were in no way treasonous. Indeed, by clinging to their soil they
remained loyal to their homeland."

Sand notes that Ben-Zvi's 1929 book *Our Population in the Country* took
a more "moderate" position on who the fellahin were: "Obviously it would
be mistaken to say that all the fellahin are descendants of the ancient Jews,
but it can be said of most of them, or their core." Ben-Zvi also added a
second reason for their religious conversion: in Sand's words, the "fear of
being displaced from the soil." Sand writes that Ben-Zvi's later book:

> maintained that immigrants arrived from many places, and the local
> population was fairly heterogeneous, but the traces left in the language,
> place-names, legal customs, popular festivals such as that of Nebi
> Musa (the prophet Moses), and other cultural practices left almost no
> doubt that "the great majority of the fellahin do not descend from the
> Arab conquerors but before that, from the Jewish fellahin, who were
> the foundation of this country before its conquest by Islam."

History supports this thesis. Sand's book documents that neither the
Romans in the first century CE nor the Arab Muslims six centuries later
exiled the Jews:

> It must first be emphasized that the Romans never deported entire
> peoples. . . . It did not pay to uproot the people of the land, the
> cultivators of produce, the taxpayers. . . . They definitely did not deport
> whole populations in the countries they conquered in the East, nor did
> they have the means to do so — none of the trucks, trains or great
> ships available to the modern world.

This stunning fact, support for which Sand found among historians
specializing in the area, undermines the official narrative that the modern
state of Israel was founded and peopled by long-wandering exiles who
finally returned home. Sand explains in various lectures that when he was
researching his book, he was shocked to find no histories of the Roman
exile in the Tel Aviv University library. When he consulted the experts in
the university's department of Jewish history, he said he was told, "It
wasn't exactly an exile." Thus was vindicated the American Reform Jewish
movement, which declared in 1885 that it did not regard the Jews outside
of Palestine as constituting a diaspora longing to return "home": "We
consider ourselves no longer a nation, but a religious community, and

therefore expect neither a return to Palestine, nor a sacrificial worship under the sons of Aaron, nor the restoration of any of the laws concerning the Jewish state." In 1841, Allan Brownfeld of the American Council for Judaism reports, Rabbi Gustav Poznanski of Temple Beth Elohim in Charleston, South Carolina, spoke for his co-religionists when he said, "This country is our Palestine, this city our Jerusalem, this house of God our temple." In our time, the idea of a diaspora is disappearing. Jane Eisner, in the Jewish publication *The Forward*, says "the negative connotation of 'Diaspora' formulated in classic Zionism is fading — with so many Israelis living in Los Angeles and Berlin, how could it not?" She's pro-Israel, yet she writes, "Let's leave behind the outdated notion of 'Diaspora.'" (A few years ago the Israeli newspaper *Haaretz* reported that Berlin had the "world's fastest growing Jewish community.")

The early Zionist affinity for the indigenous population of Palestine faded, Sand writes, when it began to resist the encroachments by the European Jewish newcomers. Sand writes:

> From that moment on, the descendants of the Judean peasantry vanished from the Jewish national consciousness and were cast into oblivion. Very soon the modern Palestinian fellahin became, in the eyes of the authorized agents of memory, Arabian immigrants who came in the nineteenth century to an almost empty country and continued to arrive in the twentieth century as the developing Zionist economy, according to the new myth, attracted many thousands of non-Jewish laborers.

The upshot is that since before biblical times, people have lived continuously in Palestine. Every emissary who scouted the area for Theodor Herzl and his new Zionist project reported the same thing: Palestine was not "a land without a people," contrary to the claim made in the 1948 Declaration of the Establishment of the State of Israel.

As the Gilmours point out, Ahad Ha'am, a "spiritual Zionist" who had spent time there, reported in 1891, "'Palestine is not an uninhabited country,' and has room 'for only a very small proportion of Jews,' since there was little untilled soil except for stony hills or sand dunes." Ha'am and others warned the Zionist movement to respect the indigenous population. They were not heeded.

Thus if there was to be a Jewish state, most if not all of the non-Jews would have to go. "'Only in a very few places in our colonialisation were we not forced [sic] to transfer the earlier residents,' Ben-Gurion told the 1937 Zionist Congress" (Gilmours). His militias would "be forced" to transfer many more a decade later.

To repeat, it's a secondary matter whether these individuals thought of themselves as "Palestinians" or whether they perceived themselves to be living in a country called Palestine. They were individuals with rights, and they were dispossessed and made into refugees when they weren't murdered.

As individual human beings, they obviously cared about their homes and communities, whether rural or urban, and thus could be counted on to resist proposals that they be "transferred" — expelled — from their homes to somewhere else — even to places where people spoke a similar language (though the dialects might differ) and practiced the same religion. To assume otherwise is to see these individuals as less than human.

In fact, though, we can find signs of "national" (for lack of a better term in the context of anti-colonial resistance) self-consciousness at different times and in different stages of development. "Islam and the Ottoman Empire were the broadest and most meaningful socio-cultural and political entities, but there developed a type of proto-national sense regarding Filastin, as it was termed, from the seventeenth century on," writes Khaled M. Safi, a historian at Al-Aqsa University. Safi quotes a distinguished historian of the Arab world, Albert Hourani ("The Fertile Crescent in the Eighteenth Century" in *A Vision of History: Near Eastern and Other Essays*, 1961):

> Since the central [Ottoman] Government could no longer control the Empire, it could no longer serve as the focus of loyalty and solidarity. Thus we can observe in the course of the eighteenth century a strengthening of the communal loyalties which had always formed the basis of Ottoman society, and a regrouping of the peoples of the Empire around those authorities which could give them what the Imperial Government no longer gave: a defense against disorder and a system of law regulating the relations of man and man.

Hourani continued: "It was the pressure of these local forces which gave a new form to the relationship between the Ottoman Government and the provinces. All over the Empire, there arose local ruling groups loyal to the Sultan but possessing a force, a stability and to some degree an autonomy of their own. It was only through the mediation of these groups that the Ottoman Empire was still able to keep some sort of moral and material hold on its subjects."

Palestinian consciousness, however, seems to have preceded the 17th century. The famous 10th-century Arab geographer Al-Muqaddasi, who was born in Jerusalem, describes Palestine (or Filastin) in great detail, including its lush farmland and nourishing natural waters, in his book, *Description of Syria, Including Palestine*. Nazmi Al-Ju'beh, a historian at Birzeit University, writes in "Palestinian Identity and Cultural Heritage" that Al-Muqaddasi "uses the terminology 'Palestine' and 'Palestinian' with the clear-cut meaning of geographic belonging and identity."

Later, inhabitants of Palestine resisted Napoleon's army and in 1834, peasants there rebelled, unsuccessfully, against the taxes and conscription imposed by the Egyptian Ibrahim Pasha. Such threats from perceived foreigners tend to create a communal consciousness. Safi concludes, "The revolt [against the Egyptians, that is, against other Arab Muslims] indicates the presence of an embryonic territorial and therefore social and political awareness."

In the early 1920s, after the French (under the Sykes-Picot Agreement) forbade independent Arab rule of greater Syria, of which Palestine was regarded as the southern province, Arab leaders were determined to defend the independence of Palestine. The British of course would have none of that; it ruled Palestine under the League of Nations mandate system that incorporated the 1917 Balfour Declaration's endorsement of the "establishment in Palestine of a national home for the Jewish people." The victims of British and French duplicity, like their forebears, tended to develop, or rather increase, a communal identity. This identity was already solidifying as the Zionist plan for an exclusivist state became a reality on the ground through the eviction of fellahin and city dwellers from properties purchased by Jewish individuals and organizations; in Zionists' eyes these were Jewish lands that had to be redeemed after their defilement by non-Jews. (Stephen Halbrook's valuable "The Alienation of a Homeland" shows that only a small percentage of those properties were purchased from individual tillers of the soil. Most were acquired from absentee feudal landlords in Beirut and elsewhere who had never established ownership in a Lockean manner, that is, by mixing their labor with the land.)

The dehumanization of the Palestinians was manifest in the Western attitude that these individuals saw themselves merely as undifferentiated members of an Arab horde, indifferent to their immediate surroundings, that is, to their homes, towns, villages, farming communities, market relations, and ultimately their larger homeland, and thus would accept "transfer" to other Arab areas. No westerner ever thought of himself in such nonhuman terms, but thinking of Palestinians that way came easy. That's the stuff of mass injustice, of literal and cultural genocide.

Realization of the dream of a Jewish state logically entailed the dispossession and expulsion of the Palestinians, who by the common standard of justice were legitimate owners of their land. Those who remained were made third-class citizens or even worse in an apartheid state. The countless micro offenses against those individuals were compounded by a macro offense: the destruction of their flourishing culture, communities, and country.

3

On Israel's 'Right to Exist'

Free Association, May 20, 2012

When I posted Sharmine Narwani's provocative article "Excuse Me, But Israel Has No Right to Exist" on Facebook, I got an inappropriate reaction from libertarians. It was summed up by one comment this way:

> No territorial State has the right to exist. They are all organizations against individual rights and liberties.

This answer is true but inappropriate. Why?

Narwani was not tendering a general proposition in political philosophy. She had no intention of operating in the realm of abstraction on this occasion. Rather, she was making a point that seems to elude people, including many (most?) libertarians. Narwani was drawing attention to the fact that invocation of the Jewish State of Israel's "right to exist" is intended to derail any effort to focus on the right of Palestinian *individuals* to live on and work the land they and their families have inhabited for more than a thousand years (and perhaps much further back.) Changing the subject to the State of Israel's alleged right to exist — and that's what this move is, a *change of subject* — is designed to make sure that the rights of Palestinians are never discussed.

Imagine you caught a burglar in your home pilfering your silverware. Now imagine that when you demanded he put your property down, he responded, "Wait. Before we talk about that, I demand that you first acknowledge my right to exist *on this spot with these things in my hands.*" You would not regard that demand as legitimate.

To proclaim Israel's right to exist is to proclaim that a political entity founded by a group of individuals on an ideology of ethno-racial chauvinism has a moral right to land it obtained through brutal ethnic cleansing. The Zionist movement had (and has) as its premise that Palestine is "Jewish land" and that non-Jews are unfit for it. Thus it had (has) to be "redeemed." The outcome was what the Palestinians call the *Nakba*, or catastrophe. The political entity known as Israel thus occupies land stolen from Palestinian people.

That is the context from which to judge all that goes on in

16

Palestine/Israel today. This is no "dispute" or "conflict" in the sense that two sides have roughly equal claims to the same land and resources. The claims are no more equal than those of my hypothetical homeowner and burglar.

David Ben-Gurion, Israel's first prime minister, was quoted in Nahum Goldman's *The Jewish Paradox* asking, "Why should the Arabs make peace? If I was an Arab leader, I would never make terms with Israel. That is natural: we have taken their country. . . . We have come here and stolen their country. Why should they accept that?"

Contrition therefore belongs on the Jewish, not the Palestinian, side. (I hope no one will say that the UN General Assembly recommendation of partition made this all morally acceptable.)

(For details see Jeremy Hammond's excellent brief introduction, *The Rejection of Palestinian Self-Determination*. For a close examination of the Zionists' alleged purchases of land see Stephen P. Halbrook's "The Alienation of a Homeland." On the systematic efforts to cleanse the *Nakba* from history see Neve Gordon's "Erasing the Nakba." For the Jewish case against Zionism, rooted in the Prophetic tradition, see Jack Ross's biography, *Rabbi Outcast: Elmer Berger and American Jewish Anti-Zionism*. But you need not take their word for it. Consult an Israeli historian, Benny Morris, who thinks ethnic cleansing was a good thing but did not go far enough.)

We may put it another way: Israel is the only country I can think of that, *de jure*, does not belong to *all its citizens*. (I am not saying that other countries actually operate as though they belonged to their citizens.) As the self-proclaimed "Jewish State," Israel is said to belong not to its citizens but to the Jewish People *worldwide*. Under the "Law of Return," anyone who qualifies as a Jew (that is, has a Jewish mother and hasn't converted to another religion or was converted to Judaism by an approved rabbi) may become a full citizen merely by moving to Israel. Note the word "return." A Jewish person who "makes aliyah" need not have *ever lived* in Israel, so she would not literally be returning. (It's merely assumed, despite reasons for assuming otherwise, that her ancient ancestors might have once lived in Palestine.)

On the other hand, a Palestinian who was one of the million-plus Arabs driven from their villages in 1948 (or even earlier) and 1967 and who *could* therefore actually return to her home is *prohibited from doing so*. Her home has long been confiscated, perhaps demolished. In fact her entire village may have been leveled to make way for an exclusively Jewish town. (Over 400 such villages were destroyed following the declaration of Israeli independence.)

Yes, the Muslim, Christian, and secular Arabs who were not among the 750,000 who fled what became Israel in 1948 were allowed to become citizens of the Jewish State, with the vote and representation in the Knesset. But there's less here than meets the eye. Non-Jews are second (third?)-class citizens who get inferior government services and who have no power to change Israel's official designation as the state of the Jewish People. Indeed, any political party that aspires to change that designation is outlawed. A recent law requires new non-Jewish citizens to pledge allegiance to Israel as a "Jewish, democratic [sic] state." In 2010 Prime Minister Benjamin Netanyahu proposed, as a condition for progress in negotiations, that Palestinian leaders acknowledge Israel as "the national state of the Jewish People." It is worth noting that until a 2005 legal challenge, the Israeli identity card identified citizens *not* as Israeli but as Jewish, Arab, Druze and Circassian, and so on. Citizens are still so designated in government records.

Thus, in this context, when libertarians say, "all states are illegitimate," they blur a critical distinction and give those who occupy Palestinian property and otherwise oppress Palestinian individuals an undeserved pass. I imagine that an ardent Zionist would much rather hear that response than one that perceives and exposes the real intent behind the proclamation of Israel's right to exist: the negation of the rights of Palestinians.

I shouldn't have to mention this, but I will: To say that the state of Israel has no right to exist is *not* to say that the *individuals* living in Israel have no right to exist — quite the contrary — and the Palestinians would agree. That raises the question of how best to proceed in achieving justice for the long-suffering Palestinians. This is a complicated question to which there is no easy answer. But here's one thing advocates of universal freedom and justice can say: The rights of the Palestinians must not be plastered over by irrelevant claims about the Jewish State's right to exist.

4

The Abused Jews of Iraq

The Libertarian Institute, May 25, 2018

From April 1950, nearly two years after the Zionists in Palestine unilaterally declared independence for the state of Israel, to March 1951, three bombs exploded among Jews in Baghdad, Iraq: one each outside a cafe on Abu Nawwas Street; at the U.S. Information Centre, a popular reading place for young Jewish Iraqis; and outside the Mas'uda Shemtov synagogue, where Kurdish Jews were awaiting transit to Israel. Fortunately, only one person, a boy, was killed and one, an old man, injured. Suspicion was immediately directed at "an extremist Iraqi organization," David Hirst writes in *The Gun and the Olive Branch: The Roots of Violence in the Middle East*. In fear for their security, most members of the old Jewish community prepared to emigrate to the new state of Israel. The Iraqi government did not forbid this, but "the Iraqi parliament passed a law confiscating the property of all Jews who renounced their citizenship. No one was allowed to take more than £70 out of the country." (This immoral act of parliament carried a revealing message: we don't want you to go.)

Those acts of terrorism, however, "were the work not of Arab extremists," Hirst continues, "but the very people who sought to rescue [the Jewish Iraqis]" — that is, "a clandestine [pro-Israel] organization called 'The Movement.'" In fact, "the bombs which terrorized the Jewish community had been Zionist bombs."

The startling revelation came from Yehudah Tajjar, an Israeli agent, whose arrest in Baghdad made possible the arrest of 15 members of a covert Zionist organization in Iraq. "Shalom Salih, a youngster in charge of Haganah arms caches, broke down during interrogation and took the police from synagogue to synagogue, showing them where weapons, smuggled in since World War II, were hidden," Hirst writes. "During the trial, the prosecution charged that the accused were members of the Zionist underground. Their primary aim — to which the throwing of three bombs had so devastatingly contributed — was to frighten the Jews into emigrating [to Israel] as soon as possible. Two were sentenced to death, the rest to long prison terms." (Tajjar faced life in prison, but was freed 10 years later and returned to Israel.)

Over a decade later, a detailed account of the operation began to make its way into Israeli magazines. "Then on 9 November 1972," Hirst writes, "the *Black Panther*, the militant voice of Israel's Oriental Jews, published the full story. The *Black Panther* account includes the testimony of two Israeli citizens who were in Baghdad at the time."

Comments Hirst:

> It is often forgotten that the "safeguard" clause of the Balfour Declaration — "it being clearly understood that nothing shall be done which may prejudice the civil and religious rights of the existing non-Jewish communities in Palestine, or the rights and political status enjoyed by Jews in any other country" — was designed to cover Diaspora Jews as well as native Arabs. But the uprooting of a million "Oriental" Jews showed that, for the Zionists, it was a clause to be ignored in both its parts. *Everywhere they applied the same essential techniques, but nowhere, perhaps, with such thoroughness as they did in Iraq. "Cruel Zionism," someone called it.* [Emphasis added.]

Why? Hirst supplies an answer direct from a writer in the Israeli labor movement's publication, *Davar*:

> I shall not be ashamed to confess that if I had the power, as I have the will, I would select a score of efficient young men — intelligent, decent, devoted to our ideal and burning with the desire to help redeem the Jews — and I would send them to the countries *where Jews are absorbed in sinful self-satisfaction.* The task of these young men would be to disguise themselves as non-Jews and plague Jews with anti-Semitic slogans such as "Bloody Jew," "Jews go to Palestine" and similar intimacies. I can vouch that the results in terms of a considerable immigration to Israel from these countries would be ten thousand times larger than the results brought by thousands of emissaries who have been preaching for decades to *deaf ears.* [Emphasis added.]

Hirst adds the crucial context:

> Zionism had much less appeal to Oriental Jews than it did to European Jews. In the pre-State period only 10.4 percent of Jewish immigrants came from "Africa and Asia." In their vast majority, the Oriental Jews were actually Arab Jews, and the reason for their indifference was simply that, historically, they had not suffered anything like the persecution and discrimination of their brethren in European Christendom. Prejudice did exist, but their lives were on the whole comfortable, and their roots were deep [going back to the Babylonian exile]. They were nowhere more at home than in Iraq, and a government official conceded — tongue in cheek — that their

Mesopotamian pedigree was much superior to that of the Muslim majority.

Zionist agitation in the Arab world outside Palestine began long before the declaration of Israeli independence:

> Zionist activities in Iraq and other Arab countries date from the beginning of the [20th] century. . . . At first, it was the British, rather than local Jews, who bore the brunt of Arab animosity. In 1928, there were riots when British Zionist Sir Alfred Mond visited Baghdad. The following year demonstrations in mosques and streets, a two-minute silence in Parliament, black-edged newspapers and telegrams to London marked "Iraqi disapproval of the pro-Jewish policy of Great Britain." It was not until the mid-thirties, when the troubles of Palestine were reverberating round the world, that Arab Jews began to excite suspicion and resentment. In Iraq these emotions came to a head in 1941 when, in a two-day rampage, the mob killed some 170 to 180 Jews and injured several hundred more. It was terrible. But it was the first pogrom in Iraqi history. . . .
>
> There was no more such violence.

The Iraqi Jews were to be "ingathered," to use the Zionist lingo. "'Ingathered' for what?" Hirst asks.

> The Iraqi Jews soon learned; those of them, that is, who actually went to Israel, or, having gone, remained there. For by no means all of uprooted Oriental Jewry did so. A great many of them — particularly the ones with money, connections, education and initiative — succeeded in making their way to Europe or America. But what the irretrievably "ingathered" learned was the cruelest and most enduring irony of all: Oriental Jewry was no more than despised cannon-fodder for the European creed of Zionism.

So much for the much-believed tale of how Iraq uprooted its ancient Jewish community and drove the Jews to Israel.

5

The Middle East Harvests
Bitter Imperialist Fruit

The Future of Freedom Foundation, June 20, 2014

The wall-to-wall coverage of the disintegration of Iraq ought to carry this credit: This bloodshed was made possible by the generosity of British and French imperialists.

The stomach-wrenching violence in Iraq — not to mention the horrendous civil war in Syria, the chronic unrest in Palestine/Israel, and problems elsewhere in the Middle East — are direct consequences of the imperialist acts of the British and French governments at the end of World War I, the history-altering catastrophe that began 100 years ago this August 4.

The story has been told many times. The government of Great Britain wanted to disrupt the Ottoman Empire's ability to help Germany and the Austro-Hungarian empire in the Great War. So the British dispatched personnel, most famously T.E. Lawrence (Lawrence of Arabia), to persuade the Arab leaders to revolt against the Turks, in return for which they would gain their qualified independence in (roughly) the Levant (what today is Israel/Palestine, Jordan, Syria), Mesopotamia (Iraq), and the Arabian Peninsula. The Arab leadership agreed and proceeded to obstruct the Turks' war efforts.

In the 1915–16 correspondence between the British High Commissioner in Cairo, Sir Henry McMahon, and Arab leader Hussein bin Ali, McMahon acknowledged Hussein's demand for independence in most of the Levant (Palestine included) and the Arabian Peninsula:

> Subject to the above modifications, Great Britain is prepared to recognize and support the independence of the Arabs in all the regions within the limits demanded by the Sherif of Mecca [Hussein].

McMahon did not give a blanket guarantee; he excluded western parts of the Levant (Lebanon) in favor of French interests and declared that

> With regard to . . . Bagdad [sic] and Basra [in Iraq], the Arabs will
> recognize that the established position and interests of Great Britain
> necessitate special administrative arrangements in order to secure these
> territories from foreign aggression, to promote the welfare of the local
> populations and to safeguard our mutual economic interests.

Nevertheless, the British led the Arabs to believe — and the Arabs indeed did believe — that they would gain independence in most of their lands not only from the Turks but also from Britain and France as well if the Allied powers prevailed.

The British officials, however, never intended to honor this promise to let the Arabs go their own way at the war's end. The British (and French) cynically used the Arabs for their own advantage while secretly planning for a postwar Middle East dominated by Europe's leading powers.

In 1916, after McMahon's correspondence with Hussein, Sir Mark Sykes, a Middle East adviser to the British cabinet, and French diplomat François Georges Picot negotiated the famous secret agreement that bears their names. (It was also signed by tsarist Russia's representative.) The Sykes-Picot Agreement presumed to divide up the Middle East among the imperial Allied Powers, even before it had been wrested from the Turks.

Generally, the better developed parts of the Arab lands — Iraq and Greater Syria (including Lebanon) — would be controlled by Britain and France, while the undeveloped peninsula — today's Saudi Arabia and Yemen — would be independent, though divided into British and French spheres of influence. (Its oil potential was yet unknown.) Part of what is today's Turkey would be in Russian hands.

More specifically Britain would control southern Mesopotamia (Iraq), two Mediterranean port cities, and what would become Jordan. France would get Greater Syria, including today's Lebanon, and northern Mesopotamia. Palestine (minus Jordan) would be under international supervision. This is not exactly how things ended up, but it set the stage for the final division of Arab territory between Britain and France after the war.

Obviously, the agreement had to be kept secret or else the Arabs would not have cooperated with the British. Moreover, the Allied powers hoped that President Woodrow Wilson would bring the United States into the war — and Wilson said he opposed territorial gains by the belligerents.

The agreement might have remained secret through the war except that after the Russian Revolution in the fall of 1917, the Bolsheviks discovered it in the files and made it public in order to embarrass the French and British governments.

This did not deter them from going ahead with their plan, in apparent disregard for Wilson's Fourteen Points, issued in January 1918, 10 months before the end of the war. While Wilson is known for insisting on the principle of self-determination, in opposition to colonialism, the closest his Fourteen Points came to endorsing that principle is this:

> A free, open-minded, and absolutely impartial adjustment of all colonial claims, based upon a strict observance of the principle that in determining all such questions of sovereignty the interests of the populations concerned must have equal weight with the equitable claims of the government whose title is to be determined.

Note that the interests of subjugated people are to receive only "equal" consideration with the claims of governments. That hardly sounds like self-determination. At any rate, Wilson, who took sick when the Paris Peace Conference convened, was unable to stop the British and French from carrying out their imperial plans. In the end, his administration acquiesced in return for oil concessions for American companies.

As noted, the actual division of the Middle East did not follow Sykes-Picot precisely because modifications were made in light of subsequent agreements, conferences (such as the 1920 San Remo conference), and events (such as the Russian Revolution). The language of 19th-century colonialism was dropped in favor of the "mandate" system, which (in theory) authorized Britain and France to oversee newly created Arab states until the Arabs were ready for self-government. The British created the states of Iraq and Transjordan (later Jordan). What was left of Palestine (it had different boundaries at different times) would not be designated a state but would be administered by Britain. France took Syria, out of which it created a separate Lebanon.

The arbitrarily drawn "national" boundaries cut through sectarian, ethnic, and tribal lines, planting the seeds of future conflicts that continue to this day. (The imperialists had done the same thing in Africa.)

Regarding Palestine, in the November 2, 1917, Balfour Declaration the British government expressed its approval of "the establishment . . . of a national home for the Jewish people" and pledged to "use their best endeavors to facilitate the achievement of this object." The declaration also stated that "nothing shall be done which may prejudice the civil and religious rights of existing non-Jewish communities in Palestine, or the rights and political status enjoyed by Jews in any other country." These provisos were little more than boilerplate.

Note that the declaration was issued before the British army conquered Palestine. The government was making promises about land it did not yet control — and this promise to the Zionist movement conflicted with the promises made earlier to the Arabs, again setting the stage for later conflict.

The Balfour Declaration, which created anxiety among Arabs and most Jews of course paved the way for the creation of the State of Israel some

30 years later.

It is important to understand that throughout this process, the Arabs, Kurds, and other indigenous people were never consulted about the imperialists' disposition of their lands. No wonder: what they wanted — independence from foreign powers — conflicted with the objectives of British and French politicians. But by what authority did they decide the future of the people in the Middle East?

Here's another heartbreaking aspect to this story, When the Paris Peace Conference convened, Arab leaders looked to the United States to frustrate the imperialists' designs because they associated Wilson with the principle of self-determination. Their hopes, however, were dashed. (For details see Ussama Makdisi's *Faith Misplaced: The Broken Promise of U.S.-Arab Relations, 1820–2001*.) Anyone who protested the callous treatment of the Arabs and others was dismissed or ignored as naïve.

Let that sink in: the Arabs — Muslim, Christian, and secular — looked to the United States as a beacon of liberty and independence. (Whether American history justified that attitude is another matter.) They were let down and have suffered as a result ever since.

America may be despised by many people in the Middle East today — but it did not have to be that way.

The French and British proceeded to create states and governments in their new possessions. In the early 1920s, whenever Arabs tried to resist foreign rule, they were brutally suppressed — by the British in Iraq and the French in Syria. (This was reminiscent of the American suppression of the Filipinos, 1899–1902.) The Arab resistance was no match for the Europeans' bombers, artillery, and mechanized vehicles.

Let's now take a step back from the trees and view the forest.

This is a story about arrogant Western imperialists who thought enlightened, civilized Europeans should govern the Arabs (and Kurds) rather than let them determine their own destiny. Often the British and French described their rule in paternalistic terms. The barely disguised colonial system would be for the Arabs' own good, it was said. When they achieved the elevated condition of their overlords, they will have earned the right to be free.

This view was voiced by men representing countries that had just engaged in over four years of savage trench warfare in the "war to end war," not to mention the previous centuries bloodied by Europe's politico-religious wars. The paternalistic facade of course concealed narrow economic and political interests. (When Britain and France were unable to continue managing the Middle East after World War II, the United States took over.)

What's happening in the Middle East today may be seen as a violent attempt to undo the Sykes-Picot, San Remo, etc., impositions of the last century. ISIS, for example, temporarily erased the artificial boundary between Syria and Iraq. In this light, further Western intervention looks like a recipe for an even greater disaster.

As we look at the violence today in Iraq, Syria, Palestine/Israel, Egypt, and elsewhere in the region, we should remember that it all might have been avoided had the European powers not launched World War I, or if, in the event of war, the British and French had let the Arabs chart their own course.

As Edward Woodward's character, Harry Morant, says in *Breaker Morant* just before being executed by the British army during the Second Boer War, "Well . . . this is what comes of 'empire building.'"

6

Shabbos with Zayde:
Coming to Palestine

The Libertarian Institute, May 18, 2018

Foreword

In March 1989 the estimable magazine *The Washington Report on Middle East Affairs* (WRMEA) published my article "Grandfather Sparks Interest In Debate Over Zionism" in its "Seeing the Light" series. (It was subsequently included in the WRMEA book *Seeing the Light: Personal Encounters With the Middle East and Islam*, edited by Richard H. Curtiss and Janet McMahon.)

The surrealism of this week's contrasting scenes in the Gaza Strip, where Israeli soldiers were murdering dozens and maiming many hundreds of unarmed Palestinians, and Jerusalem, where smarmy representatives of the Trump administration — led by Donald Trump's daughter and son-in-law — flattered Israel's rulers while dedicating the new U.S. embassy, prompted me to post my 29-year-old article, with the gracious permission of the *Washington Report*.

Grandfather Sparks Interest In Debate Over Zionism

I have vivid childhood memories of collecting money to plant trees in Israel. I recall as well the frequent accounts provided by Hebrew-school teachers of Jewish heroism and devotion in the midst of a hostile sea of Arabs. And I'll never forget the day my school mates and I were taken downtown in 1960 to see the eagerly awaited movie *Exodus*.

Mine was a childhood that in large part revolved around Israel. Ben-Gurion, Moshe Dayan, and Golda Meir were heroes. My parents, Conservative Jews, were not Zionists in the strictest sense; moving to Israel, or seeing their children do so, was unthinkable. But they were loyal Israelists, committed to the Jewish state as necessary for the existence of

Judaism and for the victims, present and future, of ubiquitous anti-Semitism.

I have another memory, which stands in sharp relief to these pro-Israel images. It is the memory of my paternal grandfather, Sam Richman [Shlomo Hersh ben Moshe], a joyous, tolerant Orthodox Jew [from Lithuania] and a *shomos* (sexton) at a little synagogue. Every Saturday afternoon, after *Shabbat* [*shabbos*] services, we'd visit Zayde and Bubby at their apartment. The conversation would often turn to the Middle East. I would sit quietly and listen. There, and only there, did I hear criticism of Israel. I think this became particularly pronounced after the Six-Day War in 1967.

"The Jews in Israel are causing all the trouble," he would say repeatedly. "The Arabs want peace."

My father and mother would counter: "How can you say that? Israel wants peace. It is one little slice of land. The Arabs have so much, but they won't sit down and talk." They would suggest that my grandfather visit Israel and see the situation for himself.

Zayde wouldn't budge. "I will never go," he'd say. Each year, as he led our Passover *Seders*, when he was supposed to say, "next year in Jerusalem," he'd improvise with a smile, "next year in Philadelphia." The family always regarded Zayde as the venerable patriarch. But on this issue, he was treated as uninformed and stubborn. It was confusing. Little did I know then that he represented an important position in the original Jewish debate over Zionism. To him Zionism was counterfeit Judaism and the Zionists charlatans. His Orthodox belief held that the re-establishment of Israel was a matter for God in the messianic future. He would have agreed with Yehoshofat Harkabi, a former chief of Israeli military intelligence, who said "The Jews always considered that the land belonged to them, but in fact it belonged to the Arabs. I would go further: I would say the original source of this conflict lies with Israel."

At the time of the 1967 war I was 17 years old. Aside from this one dissenter, I never imagined there was another side to the Israeli-Arab dispute. As I understood it, the Jews had a biblical and legal right to the land and were eager to live peacefully with the Arabs. But the Arabs hated the Jews because they were Jews. So there was no peace. I don't think I'd heard the word Palestinian.

My parents and teachers sincerely believed what they taught me. They bore no ill will toward the Arabs. But like many of us, they were too busy with their lives to research the question themselves, so they relied on the people they trusted, namely, the Jewish and Israeli leaders, who were Zionists.

In the early 1970s I had stirrings of dissatisfaction with what I had been taught. I began to wonder how European Jews came to own land in

Palestine when an indigenous population lived there. My teachers said the Jews bought the land. That satisfied me at first. Meanwhile, I made two trips to Israel, during the 1973 war and a year later. By this time I was a journalist looking for adventure. I put my reservations on hold.

In 1978 I began hearing the land question discussed, and for the first time I came across the argument that most of the land bought by the Zionists was sold by absentee feudal landlords, whose "tenants" were then run off by the purchasers. In my view of property this was illegitimate. The real owners were the people actually working the land: the homesteaders, the Palestinians.

Since my libertarianism puts me on the side of the victims of the state, I began to understand that the Palestinians were the latest in a long line of groups oppressed by political power. Jews, of course, have been similarly oppressed in many places; now some Jews, the Zionists, were in the role of oppressor. My childhood view of Israel was unraveling.

I belatedly began investigating the real story of the founding of Israel. I read Elmer Berger's *Memoirs of an Anti-Zionist Jew* and the writings of Alfred Lilienthal, Noam Chomsky, Edward Said, and others. I revised my views on the relationship between Judaism and Zionism, on the Arab-Israeli wars, and on the Zionist agenda for Eretz Yisroel. I "discovered" the Palestinians. I became satisfied that what my parents and teachers told me was mistaken and that what Zayde had said was right.

He died in 1974. I'm painfully sorry I didn't know then what I know now. He was a wise man, a prophet unsung in his own land.

Afterword

I omitted some steps in my odyssey, which I will rectify now. The first person from whom I heard substantive arguments about who legitimately owned the land in Palestine was Roy A. Childs Jr., the long-time editorial director at Laissez Faire Books and an inspiration to so many libertarians of my generation. In a lecture at the first of the old Cato Summer Seminars (1978), I heard Roy talk about absentee feudal landlordism and the illegitimate sale of property out from under the true Lockean owners, namely, the actual tillers of the soil. I followed up with conversations with Roy, and I have vivid memories of being at the Laissez Faire office feverishly photocopying chapters of David Hirst's *The Gun and the Olive Branch: The Roots of Violence in the Middle East*, the first book on the subject that Roy recommended. (I also recommend it.)

I learned the fine details of the land story from an article by my friend Stephen P. Halbrook in the old *Journal of Libertarian Studies* (Fall 1981), edited by Murray Rothbard. In "Alienation of a Homeland," Halbrook presents the hard data on the ownership and conveyance of land in Palestine. It is an eye-opening article that more people need to read. I could no longer believe that Israel was the result of the legitimate acquisition of property. It could not pass libertarian muster.

Finally, in 1980, while attending a libertarian conference in Maine, I met Imad-ad-Dean Ahmad, an American libertarian and Muslim, who is the son of Palestinians. Dean became a good friend and colleague, especially during my active years in the Libertarian Party (1977–1983). He went on to create the Minaret of Freedom Foundation, whose mission statement I highly commend. It was Dean who taught me about the bloody campaign of the Zionist militias to drive the Palestinians out of Palestine. It was in a heart-rending song that Dean had written and performed at the conference that I first heard the words *Deir Yassin*, the village in which the Irgun paramilitary force, under the command of future Israeli Prime Minister Menachem Begin, slaughtered 354 men, women, and children on April 9, 1948. It was just one piece of the crusade to rid the land of Arabs in order to make way for the future Jewish citizens of the state of Israel.

I have other memories as well. I recall the days after the 1967 war, when American Jews (myself included; I was 17) celebrated Israel's military victory (in what was not a war of defense, as the state's political and military leaders well understood). I recall being at a rally of United Synagogue Youth, of which I was a member in those days, when the exuberant crowd sang the song "*David Melech Yisroel*" ("David, the King of Israel, lives and endures"). At the end of the song, the rally leader began shouting the names of cities in Israel, with the crowd responding each time, "Yisroel!":

"Yerushalayim [Jerusalem]!"

"Yisroel!"

"Tel Aviv!"

"Yisroel!"

"Jaffa!"

"Yisroel!"

Then things became more eerily revealing.

"Amman!"

"Yisroel!"

"Damascus!"

"Yisroel!"

"Baghdad!"

"Yisroel!"

"Cairo!"

"Yisroel!"

I'll never forget it. Maybe that is why I can't remain silent.

Yes, my zaide (who like his Belorussian wife, my bubby, Katie, lost close family in Hitler's Holocaust; they had come to America before World War I) insisted the Arabs wanted peace and did not hate Jews qua Jews. He was not speaking from ignorance, as my later research showed. (See also my "Arab Attempts to Negotiate with Israel," *American-Arab Affairs*, Summer 1991, Chapter 7 of this book.) Arab rulers made repeated offers of a general peace, only to be rebuffed by Israeli governments. (Nothing will be allowed to get in the way of an expansion into all of Palestine and the creation of Greater Israel.)

My article mentions the early Orthodox Jewish objection to Zionism (some Orthodox Jews still vehemently oppose Zionism), but Reform Judaism — on principle — also opposed the movement, which was founded and run by atheists who cared nothing for the Jewish religion but only for an invented "Jewish People." One can reasonably say that the Zionist pioneers were the first self-hating Jews. A huge volume of work on the Reform Jewish case against Zionism, that is, Jewish nationalism, exists thanks to American Council for Judaism founder Rabbi Elmer Berger (who later founded American Jewish Alternatives to Zionism), Alfred Lilienthal, Allan Brownfeld, Israel Shahak (all of whom I've had the great honor of knowing), Moshe Menuhin (author and the father of famed violinist Yedui Menuhin), and many others. (See the excellent historical accounts, *Jews Against Zionism: The American Council for Judaism, 1942–1948* by Thomas Kolsky and *Rabbi Outcast: Elmer Berger and American Jewish Anti-Zionism* by Jack Ross.) I could name books all day.

Reform Judaism opposed any Jewish State for two reasons: first, Judaism, in this view, is a religion comprising a worldwide faith community made up of many different peoples; it is not "a people." Declaring that Jews were a single people with their "own state" would distort a religion that was held as embodying universal values and compromise the Jewish citizens of other countries through the suspicion of dual loyalty.

Second, Palestine was already inhabited largely by Arab Muslims and Christians — the Palestinians. Palestine was not, contrary to myth, a "land without a people." Full stop. Hence, the creation of a Jewish State in Palestine, which was unlawful by any standard, would mean Jewish oppression of non-Jews.

The very thought of such consequences revolted the prophetic Reform Jewish leaders.

No one was more vehement than these lions of the Reform movement in their opposition to Zionism, which they regarded as a form of anti-Semitism and even idolatry because God was pushed aside literally by blood and soil. The only British cabinet opponent of the 1917 Balfour Declaration was also the only Jew, Edwin Montagu, who accused his colleagues of veiled anti-Semitism. (My loose translation of the implicit message of the declaration: "Hey, Jews, here's an idea: why don't you all leave Britain and move to the Middle East. We'll help you pack!")

The Zionist leaders were not clueless about what they were doing. Israel's first prime minister, David Ben-Gurion, said what many of his colleagues were thinking: "Why should the Arabs make peace? If I was an Arab leader, I would never make terms with Israel. That is natural: we have taken their country. . . . We have come here and stolen their country. Why should they accept that?"

To be Socratic for a moment, we are left with this: either Israel is the Jewish State, that is, embodies Jewish values (as its most fervent advocates insist), or it is/does not. If it is/does (which I do not believe), then considering what Israelis do every day to the non-Jews of Palestine, what does that say about Judaism? And if it is/does not, then why are American Jews (and everyone else committed to justice) so attached to it? (Of course, in America, this attachment is diminishing dramatically.)

Nearly two million Palestinians are confined in the open-air prison called the Gaza Strip. What the Israeli government is doing there, and on the West Bank, is unconscionable. These crimes date back 70 years and more and cannot be ignored merely because some Palestinians have committed unjustifiable acts against innocent Israelis. Those who think the relatively small-scale violence perpetrated by desperately long-oppressed individual Palestinians can possibly mitigate the monstrously systematic state brutality committed routinely by the powerful (and nuclear-armed) state of Israel, fortified by the U.S. government, have become enablers of the cruelty and dehumanization visited daily on the Palestinians not only in Gaza and the West Bank but in Israel itself.

I can only hope that future generations will look back on all this with puzzlement and shame.

7

Is Instability the Goal of
U.S. Mideast Policy?

Free Association, October 21, 2015

Donald Trump's indictment of the Bush II administration for failing to prevent the 9/11 attacks presents an opportunity for more of a bird's eye view of American foreign policy in the Middle East, a policy that has killed many hundreds of thousands, maimed countless more, and laid waste to entire societies.

As Peter Beinart reminds us, when George W. Bush took office in January 2001, he and his closest national-security staff showed little interest in al Qaeda and Osama bin Laden, despite alarms set off by the CIA and National Security Council counterterrorism "czar" Richard Clarke. Al Qaeda, of course, had attacked U.S. government assets in the decade before Bush became president.[1]

"But both Clarke and [CIA boss George] Tenet grew deeply frustrated by the way top Bush officials responded," Beinart writes. "Clarke recounts that when he briefed [national security adviser Condoleezza] Rice about al Qaeda, 'her facial expression gave me the impression that she had never heard the term before.'"

Repeated attempts to get Bush's attention were frustrated despite accelerating indications that "Bin Laden [was] Determined to Strike in U.S." Even the prospect of aircraft hijackings was raised.

But Bush and his top national-security aides were interested in other things. What things? Ballistic-missile defense, which Bush had promised in his campaign, and Saddam Hussein, the dictator of Iraq. Let's remember that the overthrow of Saddam, euphemistically dubbed "regime change," was a U.S. goal at least since 1990. In 1991 Bush's father, President George H. W. Bush, sent forces to expel the Iraqi army from Kuwait, but he didn't go in for the kill and send the military to Baghdad to topple Saddam's government. Instead Bush imposed a trade embargo on the Iraqi people, subjecting them to unspeakable hardship, a policy maintained by his

---

[1] Also see "The Deafness Before the Storm," by Kurt Eichenwald in the *New York Times*.

successor, Bill Clinton. The deaths of half a million children — the result, among other things, of U.S. destruction of the sanitation and water infrastructure — constituted the price for regime change that Clinton's UN ambassador, Madeleine Albright, infamously and coldly found "worth it." (Clinton rewarded Albright by naming her secretary of state — something an enterprising reporter might want to ask Hillary Clinton about.) Bill Clinton also conducted regular bombing raids on Iraq in the name of maintaining no-fly zones. When will Clinton get his share of the responsibility for 9/11? (Another question for Hillary Clinton.)

So the Bush II administration had Iraq on its collective mind in the first eight months of its tenure not withstanding repeated warnings from its terrorism specialists that al Qaeda was the likely immediate threat.

Beinart writes:

> When that April [cabinet-level] meeting [demanded by Clarke] finally occurred, according to Clarke's book, *Against All Enemies*, Deputy Defense Secretary Paul Wolfowitz objected that "I just don't understand why we are beginning by talking about this one man, bin Laden." Clarke responded that, "We are talking about a network of terrorist organizations called al Qaeda, that happens to be led by bin Laden, and we are talking about that network because it and it alone poses an immediate and serious threat to the United States." To which Wolfowitz replied, "Well, there are others that do as well, at least as much. Iraqi terrorism for example."

As soon as the 9/11 attacks occurred, the Bush administration's eyes were on Iraq, and the intelligence agencies were ordered to get the proof. Detainees were even tortured to force them to implicate Saddam Hussein, and false stories about contact between al Qaeda and Saddam's regime were floated.

Can we make any sense of this fixation on Iraq? I think we can.

It begins to make sense when we realize that American neoconservatives, who include Wolfowitz and a host of people in the Bush's Pentagon and State Department, have for years acted as a brain trust for the right-wing of Israel's ruling elite (Likud). In that capacity they issued papers, under the auspices of the Israeli Institute for Advanced Strategic and Political Studies, expressing favor toward policies to destabilize the secular regimes in Iraq and Syria, as well as the governments in Lebanon (home of Hezbollah) and, ultimately, Iran — the Shia Crescent. (Hence the general demonization of Iran and the touting of the nonexistent nuclear threat.) These proposed policies would embody a change in strategy for Israel, from seeking a "comprehensive peace" with its neighbors to managing a balance of power. Those signing on to these papers, which were issued in the mid-1990s just as Benjamin Netanyahu was about to become Israel's prime minister, were aware that, at least in the short run, radical Sunnis would profit from the destabilization and fill the vacuums created in Iraq and Syria.[2]

As the first of these papers stated, "Israel can shape its strategic environment, in cooperation with Turkey and Jordan, by weakening, containing, and even rolling back Syria. This effort can focus on removing Saddam Hussein from power in Iraq — an important Israeli strategic objective in its own right — as a means of foiling Syria's regional ambitions." The paper envisioned, bizarrely, King Hussein of Jordan extending his rule over Iraq, a move that the neocon brain trust expected to unite Iraq's Sunnis and Shi'ites and cut Iran out of the picture. Note how well that worked out.

The second paper, in speaking of Syria but with Iraq in mind, stated, "The issue here is whether the West and Israel can construct a strategy for limiting and *expediting the chaotic collapse* that will ensue in order to move on to the task of creating a better circumstance." [Emphasis added.] Observe the hubris in assuming that chaos can be limited, that is, managed.[3]

If this is not enough to make sense of an otherwise seemingly senseless U.S. policy in the Middle East, we may also mention an earlier paper, written in the early 1980s by Oded Yinon, a journalist who had been in Israel's foreign ministry. This paper saw the Arab world as a "house of cards" ripe for "dissolution" by Israel and the United States:

> Lebanon's total dissolution into five provinces serves as a precedent for the entire Arab world including Egypt, Syria, Iraq and the Arabian peninsula and is already following that track. The dissolution of Syria and Iraq later on into ethnically or religiously unqiue [sic] areas such as in Lebanon, is Israel's primary target on the Eastern front in the long run, while the dissolution of the military power of those states serves as the primary short-term target. Syria will fall apart, in accordance with its ethnic and religious structure, into several states such as in present day Lebanon, so that there will be a Shi'ite Alawi state along its coast, a Sunni state in the Aleppo area, another Sunni state in Damascus hostile to its northern neighbor, and the Druzes [sic] who will set up a state, maybe even in our Golan, and certainly in the Hauran and in northern Jordan. This state of affairs will be the

---

[2] The papers are "A Clean Break: A New Strategy for Securing the Realm" and "Coping With Crumbling States: A Western and Israeli Balance of Power Strategy for the Levant." The author is David Wurmser, who later worked in the Bush II administration for both Vice President Dick Cheney and John Bolton in the State Department. The "study group leader" who oversaw the preparation of the papers was Richard Perle, a leading neoconservative intellectual.

[3] For more on these papers see Dan Sanchez's Antiwar.com articles, "From Clean Break to Dirty Wars" https://original.antiwar.com/dan_sanchez/2015/06/29/clean-break-to-dirty-wars/ and "Seize the Chaos." https://original.antiwar.com/dan_sanchez/2015/10/05/seize-the-chaos/

guarantee for peace and security in the area in the long run, and that aim is already within our reach today. . . .

Every kind of inter-Arab confrontation will assist us in the short run and will shorten the way to the more important aim of breaking up Iraq into denominations as in Syria and in Lebanon. In Iraq, a division into provinces along ethnic/religious lines as in Syria during Ottoman times is possible. So, three (or more) states will exist around the three major cities: Basra, Baghdad and Mosul, and Shi'ite areas in the south will separate from the Sunni and Kurdish north. It is possible that the present Iranian-Iraqi confrontation will deepen this polarization.

Inter-Arab confrontation promoted by the United States and Israel — let's recall here Israel's medical care for Syrian al Qaeda fighters — would suit expansionist Israelis who have no wish to deal justly with the Palestinians and the occupied territories. The more dangerous the Middle East appears, the more Israeli leaders can count on the United States not to push for a fair settlement with the Palestinians. The American people, moreover, are likely to be more lenient toward Israel's brutality if chaos prevails in the neighboring states. Chaos would also undercut Hezbollah, which repelled Israel's last invasion of Lebanon, and Hamas, which refuses to disappear despite savage Israeli attacks on the Gaza Strip.

The success of radical Islamists in the wake of the destabilization of Iraq, Libya (home of Benghazi, a source of arms thanks to the CIA), and Syria came as no surprise to people in the know. Indeed, a 2012 Defense Information Agency report, widely circulated through the upper echelons of the U.S. government, noted that U.S. policies to "isolate the Syrian regime" — such as funneling arms indiscriminately to rebels — were enabling the emergence of a "Salafist principality" (i.e., an Islamic state), a development (the report said) that would be viewed favorably by the West and its regional allies. Since that time, U.S. policy in Syria, and Yemen (i.e., the backing of Saudi Arabia's brutal war and starvation blockade), have worked to the advantage of al Qaeda affiliates. Not coincidentally, in both cases the targets are interests that get support (in widely varying degrees) from Iran. This helps us understand why the Obama administration condemned Russian President Vladimir Putin for directing airstrikes against Islamists seeking to overthrow Syrian President Bashar al-Assad.

As a recent Israeli ambassador to the United States, Michael Oren, put it, "The initial message about the Syrian issue was that *we always wanted Bashar Assad to go, we always preferred the bad guys who weren't backed by Iran to the bad guys who were backed by Iran.*" [Emphasis added.] Hence the suggestions, most notably from retired general and former CIA chief David Petraeus, that the U.S. government side with al Qaeda's Nusra Front in Syria — its "moderate" elements of course — against the Islamic

State. (Nusra also opposes the Assad government.)

This is not to say that the neoconservative-Likud alliance is the only force driving U.S. policy. It is well known that Saudi Arabia and the other Gulf states (which are no threat to Israel) wish to throttle Iran, perhaps fearful that a U.S.-Iran detente could be in the offing. Regime change in Syria would suit the Saudis' anti-Iran, anti-Shi'ite agenda, which is another reason why arms, money, and fighters have flowed so freely to the Sunni rebels in Syria. (If bona fide moderates there be among the rebels, their chief role has been as arms conduits to the jihadis.) The U.S. government, it hardly needs saying, does not wish to alienate its Arab allies, as long as their interests do not conflict with Israel's.

Thus, we need not puzzle over a lethal and self-defeating U.S. policy that appears more aimed at Iran and its allies rather than at the radical jihadi network that perpetrated the 9/11 attacks. The U.S. government should not be intervening in the Middle East at all, but working with Israel and corrupt Arab states in order to create an instability that serves Islamist interests is simply crazy.

8

The Trump-Kushner
Delusion on Palestine

The Libertarian Institute, July 6, 2018

Here's a shocker: Donald Trump and his Palestine-Israel fixers think they can buy a peaceful and permanent settlement of the 70-year conflict by getting Arab governments to pressure the Palestinians into forgetting the "politicians' talking points" — you know, superficial things like independence from the routine abuses and indignities of colonial oppression (that's right; the same trifles Americans celebrated on July 4) — and focusing instead on what really matters: roads, jobs, and money.

In Trumpworld, everyone and everything — including the longing for justice — has a price.

According to many indications, including chief envoy/Trump son-in-law Jared Kushner's own interview with the Palestinian newspaper *Al Quds*, the Trump plan is to have Saudi Arabia, the United Arab Emirates, and Egypt gang up on the Palestinians in order to compel them to accept money for economic development in return for dropping their demands for a sovereign and independent state free of Israeli domination, that is, a state consisting of (most of) the West Bank and Gaza Strip with its capital in East Jerusalem.

Instead of insisting that Israel withdraw from the lands conquered in and occupied since the 1967 war, dismantle its illegal settlements, and tear down its wall (which runs not along the 1967 border but through the West Bank), the Palestinians are expected to accept promises of outside investment in infrastructure and jobs. Their "state" would consist of a few disconnected villages, presumably isolated Gaza, and a capital in a Jerusalem suburb.

How bad can one (or in this case four) misjudge a situation?

One might reasonably suspect the plan is being designed precisely to be rejected by the Palestinians in order to brand them, yet again, as anti-peace and to justify continued Israeli atrocities. Further, we have every reason to expect that Israel itself would not accept the plan because even this paper Palestinian state would be unacceptable to nearly every Israeli.

As the song says, "This land is mine. God gave this land to me." Not that Israel's government would reject the plan outright; rather, it will equivocate, letting the Palestinians bear the "rejectionist" label alone.

The plan is being formulated by — *sarcasm alert* — three accomplished diplomats with long records of thoughtful, objective consideration of the events that have brought Palestine and Israel to where they are today: Kushner, a debt-ridden real-estate developer with a history of connections to the illegal Israeli settlements in the West Bank; Jason Greenblatt, the Trump Organization's former lawyer who once was a guard at one of those illegal West Bank settlements and who seems proud to be able to say, "Mr. Trump does not view the settlements as being an obstacle for peace"; and David Friedman, former Trump bankruptcy lawyer and ambassador to Israel, who supports Israeli annexation of some of the West Bank and who ran an organization that raised millions of dollars for the illegal settlements. We might add that Kushner, 37, has known Israeli Prime Minister Benjamin Netanyahu since he was a teenager; they appear to have a godfather-godson relationship.

It would be an understatement to say that this trio, like its boss, is entirely in Israel's corner and have no time whatever for the pesky Palestinians. This is nothing new for the U.S., but Trump has gone to great lengths not to obscure that fact.

The Kushner mission — which seems dedicated in part to enabling Trump to brag that he pulled off the "Deal of the Century" — got off to a rousing start with the president's recognition of Jerusalem as Israel's capital and his moving of the U.S. embassy there from Tel Aviv — on one of the days that Israel was gunning down peaceful protesters in the Gaza open-air prison. The status of Jerusalem has long been regarded as one of those thorny issues to be resolved by the Israelis and Palestinians at the end of the negotiation process, but nevertheless the Israeli position is that Jerusalem is Israel's "eternal and undivided capital." Trump agrees.

So much for Trump's short-lived talking point during a presidential debate that he had to *appear* fair (not actually *be* fair, mind you) if he was to bring peace to the troubled region.

Before looking at what we know about the emerging Kushner plan, a little context would help. Americans who rely on the establishment news media for information would not know that the Palestine-Israel story has been carefully crafted to make the Israelis look good and the Palestinians bad. In tone and particulars, Israel is portrayed as the unambiguously righteous and wronged party, while the Palestinians are portrayed as anything but righteous and wronged. Virtually every commentary assumes it is the Palestinians who must prove they are worthy of peace, security, and (some highly limited measure of) self-governance. The burden of proof is entirely theirs. The Israelis have nothing to prove.

This is surreal, considering that it's the pre-Israel Zionists who, in first Israeli Prime Minister David Ben-Gurion's words, "have come here and stolen [the Palestinians'] country." In 1948, what would become the Israeli army massacred hundreds and drove three-quarters of a million Palestinians out of their homeland and internally displaced many more, creating the refugee problem that exists to this day. This was the *Nakba*, the catastrophe, which Israeli historians call "ethnic cleansing." Then in 1967, Israel conquered what it didn't take in 1948, creating hundreds of thousands more internal refugees.

So why must the Palestinians prove themselves worthy of civil treatment? Because they resisted dispossession and occupation? Because they are inconsequential Arabs, while the ruling Israelis are mostly white European Jews?

According to conventional thinking, it is the Palestinians, not the Israelis, who must make concessions. Every apparent concession by Israel is hailed as amazingly generous; every Palestinian objection is condemned as proof of their unworthiness; and every actual concession by them is shoved down the memory hole. In fact, Israeli "concessions" are mere modifications of Israel's bottom-line demands; it has made no concessions regarding its obligations under international law.

How many people realize that the Palestinians have moved from their initial call for one liberal secular state for Muslims, Christians, and Jews (Yasser Arafat UN speech, 1974); to acceptance of two states along the pre-1967 borders, with the Palestinians thereby conceding 78 percent of Palestine to Israel; to acceptance of 60 percent of the illegal Israeli settlements on 2 percent of the West Bank, with an equivalent land swap nearby? When have those advances toward a resolution ever been called generous by America's political and pundit classes?

What the Palestinians won't accept — the object of their so-called "rejectionism" — is a "state" that is little more than a few uncontiguous villages separated by a wall, a "state" over which Israel asserts ultimate control in the name of security. But even that is too much for most Israelis. They have no objection to the Palestinian Authority exerting authoritarian control over the Palestinians — that's all the Oslo Accords accomplished, relieving Israelis of the bad-PR dirty work — but they will not accept Palestinians in charge of their own security against Israel, which means not only the Israeli military but also the fanatical settlers, many of them Americans, who think nothing of killing, bashing, and humiliating the *goyische* Palestinians with impunity. (See army vets' testimony about gratuitous violence at Breaking the Silence.) A pacification program similar to Oslo seems planned for Gaza.

That's the historical context. The present context bodes equally ill for Trump's "Deal of the Century."

Kusher says Palestinian Authority President Mahmoud Abbas boycotted the American delegation's recent visit because he fears the plan being formulated will be acceptable to the Palestinians. In fact, Abbas boycotted because of the Jerusalem move, but he is indeed out of sync with the Palestinians, so unpopular he would lose an election today. He's disliked because his security forces imprison, torture, and harass Palestinians who resist the Israeli occupation, which moral intuition and the International Court of Justice condemn as illegal, and he has added to the hardship of the Gazans. Moreover, Abbas's presidential term expired in 2009, but he has yet to hold an election.

Even so, the Trump administration deludes itself if it thinks the Palestinians dislike Abbas because he has been *unwilling* to compromise. On the contrary, they think their side has made all the concessions and has received nothing in return. For example, since Oslo 20 years ago, the number of Israeli settlers has more than doubled and Israel has taken more and more Palestinian land. Peaceful protesters in the occupied territories are detained indefinitely without charge and tortured when they are not shot. Homes are demolished as a form of collective punishment and deterrence.

So Kushner's alleged good intentions notwithstanding, the Palestinians won't care what his friend Saudi Crown Prince Mohammed bin Salman wants. They will be unimpressed that Arab rulers are willing to sacrifice them for an alliance with America and Israel against Iran. They will therefore refuse to be "delivered."

Israel's position on what the ICJ calls the Occupied Palestinian Territories has been accurately likened to a guy who eats a pizza while claiming he's ready to discuss how to divide it with his dinner companion. And that's okay with Trump and Kushner.

As I write, more pizza is being consumed in Khan al-Ahmar and Abu Nuwar, two Bedouin villages east of Jerusalem. The Jahalin tribe used to live in the Negev Desert in what became southern Israel in 1948. In 1952 the Israeli government expelled it so a Jewish town could be built and deposited them in the West Bank, which until 1967 was held by Jordan (having colluded with Israel in 1948 to deprive the Palestinians of their own state). The Jahalin "found a niche in the Judean Desert between Jerusalem and Jericho where they could continue their lives as nomadic herders," writes Jeff Halper, co-founder of Israeli Committee Against House Demolitions. As Israel executed its plan to make the illegally acquired West Bank a permanent part of Israel, it "steadily pushed [the Bedouin] into ever more remote and constricted areas." Halper continues:

> In 1976 Israel established Ma'aleh Adumim, today the third largest settlement in the Occupied Territory with more than 40,000 (Jewish)

inhabitants, in the center of Jahalin life. Since 1997 the Civil Administration has been forcing the Jahalin off their land entirely, relocating them by force onto a barren hilltop literally on the Jerusalem municipal garbage dump. Trucks full of garbage pass through their crowded shanty town on the way to dumping the garbage below, and the stench is overpowering. . . .

The declared intent of the Civil Administration is to remove all the Bedouin from Area C, part of a process of removal that affects the Palestinian population as a whole. Area C represents 62% of the West Bank, and it is where the Israeli settlements are located. Two and a half million Palestinians of the West Bank — 84% of the population — are locked into some 70 tiny, isolated and impoverished enclaves called Areas A and B on the other 38%. . . .

Khan al-Ahmar, situated ironically at the biblical site of the Inn of the Good Samaritan, is home to 173 people, 92 of them children. The school, built by Italian volunteers in 2009, the first school the Jahalin ever had, serves 150 kids.

In June the Israeli Supreme Court gave its blessing to the destruction of Khan al-Ahmar. The court said the homes were built illegally, which in a way is true because Israel won't let Palestinians build homes legally — but, then, the Israeli occupation itself is illegal by any civilized moral and legal standard.

Allison Deger updates the story at Mondoweiss:

Israel forces arrived this morning [July 4] to two Palestinian-Bedouin villages and began razing buildings in preparation for taking over the land, alarming human rights groups who say such a move would effectively cut the West Bank into two.

The villages Khan al-Ahmar, and Abu Nuwar are home to just around 2,000 Bedouins, but the impact of their removal would be lasting, making a Palestinian state no longer possible, advocates of the two-state solution warned.

Much could be said about this horrible event: imagine being kicked out of the home you built and seeing it bulldozed. But what occurs to me most forcefully is how much the scene resembles what the Russian tsar used to do when he expelled the Jews from their *shtetls*. The big difference is that now it is Jews working through the Jewish State who are doing the evicting.

And all of this is just fine with the virtuous Trump, Kushner, Greenblatt, and Friedman.

9

Trump Turns to Gaza as Middle East Deal of the Century Collapses

The Libertarian Institute, July 13, 2018

The Trump administration's "Deal of the Century" for Palestine-Israel has, predictably, gone over like a lead balloon. So it's shifting gears. The *Washington Post* reports, "With President Trump's promised Middle East peace plan stalled, administration officials are focusing on improving conditions in the impoverished Gaza Strip — a move that could put political pressure on Palestinian leaders to come to the negotiating table."

Don't hold your breath.

The "Deal of the Century" was dead on arrival because it was based on the idea that Saudi Arabia and Egypt would "deliver the Palestinians" on the cheap in return for a more formal Saudi-Egyptian-Israeli-U.S. alliance against Iran. The Palestinians were expected to be satisfied with economic-development aid while their aspirations for their own state were essentially tabled, that is, confined to the rubbish bin.

Unsurprisingly, as elements of the deal got around, the demoralized Palestinians were underwhelmed. They already had lost confidence in President Mahmoud Abbas and his Palestinian Authority, which under the Oslo Accords had become Israel's subcontractor for suppressing the occupation resistance. Nor had the Palestinians forgotten how Abbas and his negotiators tried, *unsuccessfully*, to compromise to an extent that would have destroyed any prospect of a viable independent Palestinian state. This was revealed by the leak of the Palestine Papers, more than 1,600 secret documents, memos, transcripts, and maps from private Palestine-Israel-U.S. talks held over a decade (1999–2010). The release by Al Jazeera TV and the *Guardian* in 2011 demonstrated the Palestinian officials' willingness to give Israelis stunning concessions on virtually every major issue while asking little in return, including accepting illegal West Bank and East Jerusalem settlements (with minor land swaps), ceding sovereignty over a vast swath of East Jerusalem, forgoing control of the Muslim holy site Haram al-Sharif to a multiparty committee, and relinquishing the right of return for all but a token few of the millions of refugees created by Israel's officially unacknowledged ethnic cleansing of Palestinians in 1948 and

1967. The Palestinian delegation also said the refugees would not be allowed to vote on the eventual settlement proposal, and it made no objection to Israel's description of their country as the Jewish State, despite the fact that 20 percent of the population is Arab Muslim and Christian.

The Israeli side found the offers politically unacceptable in part because two large Israeli West Bank settlements were not included. Moreover, Israel insisted on its own land swaps: Jewish settlement blocs in the West Bank in exchange for Palestinian villages that straddle the pre-1967 border, or Green Line. This would take Israeli citizenship from Palestinians on the Israeli side of the line without their individual consent and make Israel a purer Jewish state. (Under the status quo, Israel directly controls over 60 percent of the West Bank, so-called Area C. What's left to the Palestinians is an archipelago of towns separated by Israel-controlled territory. See Adam Entous's "The Maps of Israeli Settlements that Shocked Barack Obama.")

Since the world to that point had not been told about this Palestinian generosity (many Palestinians preferred the term *sell-out*) or Israel's rejectionism (Israel is never portrayed as recalcitrant), the revelations came as a shock, especially to the long-suffering victims of Zionism and Palestinian "leadership." The eagerness to compromise also gave the lie, as Jonathan Cook points out, to Israel's chronic complaint that it has "no Palestinian partner for peace." It could hardly have dreamed of a more obsequious partner.

So in light of this record and with the Trump initiative "stalled," a new strategy is shaping up, focused on the humanitarian crisis in Gaza. It's an act of misdirection. Gaza's desperate situation could be addressed as part of an overall resolution, but that's not to be the case.

For one thing, the administration views Gaza with blinders on. Gaza is inhabited by, among others, Palestinians driven from their villages as Israeli military forces cleared the land of Arabs for the newly proclaimed Jewish state in 1948. (Since the removal of Palestinians was started and halfway accomplished *before* the Jewish state of Israel declared its own existence in May 1948, it's appropriate to say the removal was begun by Jewish or Zionist terrorist gangs. What has been aptly called ethnic cleansing was not just physical; it was cultural and historical as well. Some 400 Palestinian villages were eliminated, wiped from the map, and replaced by Jewish towns with new names.)

When the dust settled from the war that followed Israel's declaration of independence in 1948, Egypt held the Gaza Strip (without annexing it) and Jordan held the West Bank (after colluding with the Israelis to prevent an independent Palestinian state from coming into being). The war, which the mostly disorganized, outnumbered, ill-trained, and poorly equipped

Arab armies barely fought, enabled Israel to expand its territory from the 56 percent of Palestine recommended by the UN General Assembly to 78 percent. Israel would not declare its borders, preferring to leave that matter for future determination. Then, in its 1967 attack against Egypt, Syria, and Jordan, Israel fulfilled its aspiration to acquire both the West Bank and Gaza Strip. It occupied them militarily and built settlements exclusively for Jews — conduct expressly forbidden by international law, as the International Court of Justice affirmed in 2004.

In 2005 Israel dismantled the settlements in the Gaza Strip and relocated the army outside the fence along the two borders. (The southern border is with Egypt, which is an ally of Israel, and the Mediterranean Sea is to the west.) Thus Israel still controlled Gaza despite the heralded "withdrawal." In 2005 the Palestinians, fed up with corrupt Palestinian Authority (PA) rule, voted Hamas into power in a free election urged by the Bush administration, which was shocked by the results. (For a discussion of Hamas, see Chapter 1.) After an unsuccessful U.S.-backed PA coup against Hamas, the U.S., Israel, and the European Union proceeded to punish the Gazans. In 2007 Israel imposed a full-on blockade, controlling who and what may enter and exit the small territory with nearly two million residents. The point of the blockade is to keep the Palestinians destitute and demoralized. On top of this, Israel has several times waged full-scale air and ground war against the essentially defenseless Gazans, leaving death, injury, homelessness, polluted drinking water, and shocking destruction in its wake. Because the blockade keeps out materials and other goods, needed repairs cannot be made. Gaza is projected to become unlivable in under two years.

Most recently the Israeli military has killed more than a hundred Gazans and injured thousands during mostly nonviolent demonstrations near the fence. Israel claims that it uses force against the Gazans in self-defense, but this rings hollow considering that Gaza is an open-air prison completely controlled by Israel. Inhabitants of occupied territories have the right to resist under international law. (What would we make of Nazi complaints that Jews in concentration camps were flying fire kites over German farmland?)

This is the humanitarian crisis that the Trump administration and the major U.S. media refer to. It is not the result of a natural disaster or mysterious illness. It is the result of Israeli policy. Yet you would never know this by most of the discussion by politicians and pundits.

Take this *Washington Post* article written by Anne Gearan, a respected reporter who surely knows that she misleads her readers. For example, she writes:

The larger [Trump] peace proposal has been stymied by the Palestinian Authority, which would negotiate any settlement but remains incensed at Trump's decision last year to recognize Jerusalem as the capital of Israel.

No clue here that Trump's decision on Jerusalem was a pre-negotiation slap in the Palestinians' face because it fully embraced the position of Israeli Prime Minister Benjamin Netanyahu, who is unwilling to make any real concession to the Palestinians. For all his faults, Abbas wasn't being petulant: the people he claims to represent do not accept Israel's claim to an undivided Jerusalem. (And neither do Trump's Gulf state friends.)

Gearan notes that "unemployment in Gaza is about 40 percent, and residents have only about four hours of electricity per day." Whose fault is that? She notes that the UN "says conditions there are dire and growing worse, and it predicts that without *intervention*, the seaside territory bordering Israel and Egypt will be 'unlivable' by 2020." [Emphasis added.] Without intervention? It's *Israeli intervention* that has brought Gaza to its condition. The Gazans shouldn't have to choose between liberation and economic development; liberation would bring development.

The *Post* reporter writes that "protests on the Gaza-Israel border in April and May *led to the deaths of* scores of Palestinians." [Emphasis added.] But the protests, which were overwhelmingly peaceful, did not lead to the deaths. Those Palestinians were murdered by Israel snipers standing safely outside the prison fence. Gearan acknowledges the agency of the soldiers, but only when pointing out that "the Trump administration has backed Israel against international criticism that its soldiers used disproportionate force by shooting civilians rushing the border fences during protests." Picking off imprisoned protesters who get too close to a fortified fence will sound disproportionate to any reasonable observer.

Gearan goes on:

> A Gaza-focused approach could have at least short-term political benefits for Israel, if a truce on the hostile border replaced images of deadly clashes.

> "We do want to support them," the senior Israeli official said of the U.S. team, adding that it remains unclear whether Hamas would agree to the truce and a prisoner exchange that Israel would demand at the outset of any proposal.

She withholds from her readers the fact that Hamas has honored truces in the past, only to have them broken by Israel when it needed to flex its muscle to the Arab world.

She further points out that "Palestinians also seek redress for Arabs who left homes in what is now Israel when the state of Israel was established." Those Palestinians did not merely leave their homes, as if voluntarily, which contrary to the evidence is what Israeli propaganda has always asserted. They were consciously driven out by a campaign of murder and mayhem. This ethnic cleansing was fully documented by government archives examined by Israeli historians 30 years ago. "Ethnic cleansing" is the historians' term, and even the Israeli military used the term "cleansing" and "purity" in their documents.

Of course Gearan reports — as though it were a fact — that "Israel withdrew from Gaza in 2005." I showed that to be a falsehood above.

Finally, Gearan discusses the Palestinian concern that Trump's turn to Gaza may signal a move calculated to separate that group of Palestinians from their brethren in the West Bank:

> Abbas said last month that he rejected a U.S.-organized economic package for Gaza as an attempt by the Trump administration to divide Palestinians and reduce a political conflict with Israel to a purely humanitarian emergency. A statement from his spokesman warned regional countries against backing a project that would further separate Gaza from the West Bank and require concessions on the status of Jerusalem. . . .

But:

> The U.S. official dismissed suggestions that the focus on Gaza is a prelude to a U.S.-driven plan to create a Palestinian state in Gaza, cutting the recalcitrant Palestinian Authority out of the deal.

We have reason to wonder if that is indeed the U.S.-Israeli plan. Jonathan Cook writes:

> According to reports, Trump hopes soon to unveil a package — associated with his "deal of the century" peace-making — that will commit to the construction of a solar-power grid, desalination plant, seaport and airport in Sinai, as well as a free trade zone with five industrial areas. Most of the financing will come from the oil-rich Gulf states.

> Egyptian diplomatic sources appear to have confirmed the reports. . . .

> It has been left unclear whether Palestinians from Gaza would be encouraged to live close to the Sinai projects in migrant workers' towns. Israel will doubtless hope that Palestinian workers would gradually make Sinai their permanent home. . . .

> It is worth noting that for more than a year an Israeli cabinet minister has been proposing similar infrastructure projects for Gaza located on

an artificial island to be established in Palestinian territorial waters. Israeli Prime Minister Benjamin Netanyahu has repeatedly baulked at the proposal.

Locating the scheme instead in Egypt, under Cairo's control, will tie Egyptian security concerns about Gaza to Israel's, and serve to kill the Palestinian national cause of statehood.

Cook sees why this plan would be attractive to the U.S. and Israel. (He notes that Israeli Gen. Yoav Mordechai, who coordinates strategy in the occupied territories, has proposed "a free trade zone and infrastructure projects in Sinai.") Among other benefits, it would "make permanent the territorial division between Gaza and the West Bank, and the ideological split between the rival factions of Fatah and Hamas"; "downgrade Gaza from a diplomatic issue to a humanitarian one"; "encourage the eventual settlement of potentially millions of Palestinian refugees in Egyptian territory, stripping them of their right in international law to return to their homes, now in Israel"; "weaken the claims of Abbas and his Palestinian Authority, located in the West Bank, to represent the Palestinian cause and undermine their moves to win recognition of statehood at the United Nations"; "and lift opprobrium from Israel by shifting responsibility for repressing Gaza's Palestinians to Egypt and the wider Arab world." Why would Egypt take the deal? Because, Cook says, of "Egypt's susceptibility to financial inducements."

Thus the Trump-Kushner strategy may be to destroy, in the name of humanitarianism, any prospect of genuine Palestinian liberation. The effect could be to dump the Gazans in Egypt, effectively if not physically, while Israel continued to gobble up the West Bank.

Bye-bye, two-state solution. Hello, one-state apartheid.

10

Trump's Middle East Delusions Persist

The Libertarian Institute, October 12, 2018

Jason Greenblatt, Donald Trump's No. 2 special envoy to the Middle East behind son-in-law Jared Kushner, assures us that his boss's plan to settle the Palestine-Israel "conflict" once and for all is still in the works and is going to be great. (It's a conflict in the same way that a confrontation between a car owner and a car thief is a conflict.)

In an interview with the *Times of Israel*, Greenblatt said the plan "will include a resolution to all of the core issues, including the refugee issue, and will also focus on Israel's security concerns." It will, he continued as if the reporter didn't hear him the first time, "be heavily focused on Israeli security needs," adding, "But we also want to be fair to the Palestinians. We have tried hard to find a good balance. Each side will find things in this plan that they don't like. There are no perfect solutions."

Greenblatt went on:

> Previous peace proposals were brief and vague, and no one really understood what exactly was meant by some of the terms used. We will present something that will give both the Israeli and the Palestinian people a concrete idea of what a peace deal could look like.

> It'll be very specific so that they [the Palestinians] can tell their leaders what they think about it. In the end, we want people to think about whether our plan can make their lives better and is worth the compromises.

It's obvious that the many reasonable criticisms leveled at earlier disclosures about the touted "Deal of the Century" have had no effect on Team Trump. Let's have a closer look at what Greenblatt says.

"[The proposal] will include a resolution to all of the core issues, including the refugee issue." Bear in mind that Team Trump uses the word *resolution* differently from how the rest of us would use it in such a context. Team Trump means it will dictate an outcome, using all possible leverage to get the parties to take it and shut up. However, I don't mean to imply that Team Trump is treating the Israelis and Palestinians as equals — far from it, but more on that below.

How do I know what Team Trump means? I've been paying attention; that's how. Trump has already claimed to have resolved the refugee and Jerusalem issues simply through unilateral moves, moves that pleased the Israelis and pissed off the Palestinians, who are expected to relinquish any right of return for the dispossessed and to give up any hope for an East Jerusalem capital of any future state. (For details, see Chapter 11.) And Team Trump has cut all aid to the Palestinians, refugees or not, intending to redirect the money elsewhere (but not to the taxpayers) — unless they play ball.

"[It] will also focus on Israel's security concerns . . . [and] be heavily focused on Israeli security needs." This is the only thing that Greenblatt says will be focused on. Everything else seems like an afterthought. Strange isn't it? Who's been in graver danger in Palestine since the Zionist project got underway a century and a quarter ago, Jews or Palestinians? The question answers itself. The suffering of the Jews/Israelis in Palestine has been minuscule compared to that of the Palestinians, who, truth be told, have not only been the vast majority of Palestine's inhabitants for more than a thousand years but are most likely the descendants not only of the original Israelites but of the pre-Palestine Canaanites. (See Shlomo Sand's *The Invention of the Jewish People* and *The Invention of the Land of Israel*.) A proposal that focuses on *Israel's* security means that any resulting Palestinian state would be a sham since it will be denied the basic means of protecting itself against its U.S.-armed neighboring hegemon, which has nuclear weapons in its vast arsenal. Israel has always insisted that any Palestinian state be demilitarized and have its borders controlled by you know who. You see, Israel and its U.S. enabler begin with the presumption that it is the Palestinians, the ones who were invaded and have been occupied, who must prove that *they* deserve to be free and independent. The Israelis have no burden of proof whatsoever.

This unalloyed tilt — a mild word for what's going on — is not mitigated by Greenblatt's follow-up: "We have tried hard to find a good balance." What exactly is being balanced here? The claims of the beneficiaries of grand theft land and those of the victims thereof. How can those claims really be balanced?

"Each side will find things in this plan that they don't like." I can imagine. The Israelis won't like that they won't get every square inch of historic Palestine and therefore a 100 percent Palestinian-free Israel (in the short run, at least), and the Palestinians won't like that they will be pressured to accept far less than even the 22 percent of the land that their so-called leaders long ago agreed to settle for. And what's more, they won't really get to govern the rump state consisting of isolated towns and villages as a proper country.

"There are no perfect solutions." This is true. Past injustices can never be fully rectified. But "solutions" can be closer to or further from perfection, and we know which Team Trump's solution will be.

"Previous peace proposals were brief and vague. . . . [Ours will] be very specific." Indeed they will be. Team Trump approaches the "conflict" as though the Americans were parents settling an argument between two immature children fighting over Halloween candy of indeterminate ownership — except that in this case, only one side — the Palestinian — is presumed to be a stubborn, immature child who is unwilling to compromise.

"In the end, we want people to think about whether our plan can make their lives better and is worth the compromises." This is no doubt a veiled reference to Team Trump's objective to get the Palestinians' minds off the injustices they've suffered — mass expulsion from their homes in 1947–1948 (the *Nakba*), third-class citizenship for those who avoided expulsion, "apartheid" and oppression in the West Bank, detention and deprivation in the Gaza Ghetto — by offering them jobs. This is part of Trump's grand strategy to isolate the Palestinians while aligning with those paragons of liberalism Saudi Arabia, Egypt, and Israel against Iran. (For details on this grand strategy, see Ted Snider's "Outside In: The Trump Administration's Plan to Remake the Middle East." I've put *apartheid* in quotes because, per Gilad Atzmon, while the South African whites wanted to exploit the blacks, the Israelis want to drive the Palestinians out.)

Clearly, Team Trump has abandoned even the pretense that the U.S. is merely an "honest broker" in the conflict. It sees itself instead as the unabashed pro-Israel dictator of terms. In this context, optimism comes tough to those who care about justice, freedom, and dignity.

11

Trump, Spinoza, and
the Palestinian Refugees

The Libertarian Institute, September 7, 2018

As though we had any ground for doubt heretofore, we can now clearly see — in light of his end to $350 million in annual humanitarian assistance to five million Palestinian refugees — Donald Trump's cruel and spiteful nature.

It was not enough to stack the so-called peace process against the Palestinians in every possible way, not least by appointing unabashed Israeli partisans as his envoys. It was not enough to give Israel a pass when it murdered noncombatants in Gaza and practiced apartheid in the West Bank. It was not enough to rub the Palestinians' noses in their powerlessness by mocking their dream of East Jerusalem as the capital of a future Palestine.

No, he also had to deny the hapless and homeless refugees — victims of the *Nakba*, Israel's systematic ethnic cleansing and expulsion of the Palestinians from their ancestral home in 1948 and again in 1967 — food, medicine, and, for their children, education through the UN Relief and Works Agency for Palestine Refugees in the Near East, UNRWA. (This is a reversal of Trump's position of last year.) Just before that he cut $200 million in other Palestinian aid, including to the Israeli-besieged Gaza Strip prison, where half the population is younger than 18.

Indeed, Trump went still further by seeking to have most refugees declared *non*refugees (and therefore ineligible for a right of return to Palestine), defining them out of existence with the wave of a hand. He's attempted, as Geoffrey Aronson put it, to "remove Palestinians from the diplomatic and humanitarian equation." Of course, if he were to accomplish this end, it would relieve Israel's rulers and military, as well as its pre-independence leaders and militias, of culpability for their crimes.

Some blame victims; others — like Trump and his ilk — pretend the victims don't exist. Anyone who attempted something like this with respect to, say, Jews would properly have been denounced by all decent people.

Donald Trump is many things. What he is not is a *mensch*. But we knew that. This is the same guy who seizes children from parents (who lack government papers), seeks to kick people out of the country who were brought here "illegally" many years ago as children, and strives to deport even Americans *with* papers whom his administration eyes with suspicion.

A *mensch* does not act as though millions of people disappear merely because he chooses to ignore them. But Trump acts just that way, just as he acts as though the issue of East Jerusalem could be expected to go away simply by his moving the American embassy to Jerusalem and decreeing it the unified and eternal capital of the State of the Jewish People (anywhere and everywhere), that is, by taking Jerusalem, as he says, "off the table" — as though *he* had the power to do that. ("So let it be written. So let it be done.")

Bear in mind that Trump's move is a spending *redirection*, not a spending *cut*. Moreover, I plead no case for UNRWA. Again, as Aronson writes, "Palestinians are of two minds about the organization. No one can deny the health and educational benefits it provides, but the price paid for being wards of the international community is considerable, indeed for many unbearable." He paraphrases what a woman in Gaza told him: "UNRWA was an abomination . . . responsible for breeding complacency and fatalism among Palestinians and offering an excuse and a means for powers great and small to let the Palestinian problem fester."

But UNRWA's many failings cannot be used to justify Trump's action. He's not punishing UNRWA's personnel; he's punishing *the Palestinians*. He's not looking for a better way to ease their dire situation. He's looking to erase them in order to help Israel, although of course the resistance his actions will surely provoke will not be viewed favorably by *all* Israelis. But, yes, I'm implying that some Israelis, Israeli Prime Minister Benjamin Netanyahu among many, *will* welcome the resistance because they will use it to justify past and future brutality, oppression, and apartheid.

Axios reports that Netanyahu asked Trump to end U.S. funding of UNRWA. Netanyahu has thus also changed his position from the one that had the backing of Israel's security apparatus, which favored a gradual reduction in funding but no cuts for Gaza out of security concerns. The thinking until now has been that succor for the refugees would keep them quiescent and take their minds off their right of return, even if that is revised to mean homes in the now-occupied Palestinian territories (the future Palestine) or cash compensation.

Unsurprisingly, *Israel Hayom* reports, "Israeli officials [i.e., politicians] welcomed reports Sunday indicating that U.S. President Donald Trump plans to act to end the Palestinian demand for a right of return and to cut hundreds of millions of dollars in funding for the UN agency for Palestinian refugees, a move they say is in line with Israeli policy." The publication added, "A diplomatic official dismissed the criticism of a defense official who had been quoted as saying the U.S. decision 'could set the area, which is already on the verge of a conflict, on fire.'" Jerusalem Affairs Minister Zeev Elkin praised Trump's move, saying it "finally speaks the truth to the Arab lie that has been marketed all over the world for decades."

What lie is that? That the Palestinians were terrorized by Zionist militias and then the Israeli army into fleeing their homes in 1948 and 1967? No serious person has doubted this since Israel's New Historians scoured the government archives in the 1980s and documented the *Nakba*, the catastrophe. Long before that, however, scholars had debunked the lie that the Palestinians left voluntarily only when neighboring Arab rulers requested them to do so as a temporary wartime necessity. (But of course, even under that scenario Palestinian property owners would have a right to return to their homes.)

Let's be clear: Trump has no intention of actually addressing the refugee situation, and Israel has no intention of treating any Palestinian justly. The criticism of UNRWA is simply a ruse for once again sticking it to the Palestinians. Why? Because Trump, like the rest of America's ruling elite, favors Israel for geopolitical, domestic political, and cultural and ethnic reasons having nothing to do with justice, and he's miffed that the Palestinians have rejected his "Deal of the Century," which proposes to bribe them with Saudi economic aid to drop their grievances against Israel and abandon their longing for independence from the self-styled Jewish State. (See Chapter 8.)

Trump's die-hard supporters like to say his extreme measures and tweets are merely opening moves in his art of deal-making. So let's go with that: he's holding five million desperate people hostage in order to convince the corrupt Palestinian Authority to take his deal. That's reassuring.

The "peace process" is and long has been a sham, and the United States has never been an "honest broker." An authentic and promising peace-*through-justice* process would begin, quite literally, with an Israeli apology to all the victims who once lived in Palestine. Then all concerned may go about the business of establishing the terms for coexistence.

To bring this back to Trump (and Netanyahu, among others, I venture to say) and to end on a philosophical note, lately I have been reading Benedict Spinoza and some of his modern commentators. The 17th-century Portuguese-Dutch radical liberal rationalist wrote in the *Ethics* that persons for whom reason is not fully in the driver's seat are to some extent passively driven by feelings and are therefore slaves rather than masters of themselves: "Human infirmity in moderating and checking the emotions I name bondage: for, when a man is prey to his emotions, he is not his own master, but lies at the mercy of fortune." (Douglas Den Uyl, in his *God,*

Man, & Well-Being: Spinoza's Modern Humanism, points out that this statement does not fully capture Spinoza's position because in his view, to the extent a person is guided by reason, he has no *self-sabotaging* emotions that need checking; rather, his emotions propel him in a virtuously rewarding direction. Perfection, of course, is never achieved, but only striven for.)

Reason and understanding thus constitute a person's path to freedom:

> We shall readily see the difference between the man who is guided only by emotion or belief and the man who is guided by reason. The former, whether he will or not, performs actions of which he is completely ignorant. The latter does no one's will but his own, and does only what he knows to be of greatest importance in life, which he therefore desires above all. So I call the former a slave and the latter a free man.

Spinoza further observed of the rational person,

> His prime endeavor is to conceive things as they are in themselves and to remove obstacles to true knowledge [and hence to freedom, virtue, and "blessedness"], such as hatred, anger, envy, derision, pride, and similar emotions. . . .

> Therefore he who aims solely from love of freedom to control his emotions and appetites will strive his best to familiarize himself with virtues and their causes and to fill his mind with the joy that arises from the true knowledge of them, while refraining from dwelling on men's faults and abusing mankind and deriving pleasure from a false show of freedom.

Completely ignorant . . . hatred . . . anger . . . envy . . . derision . . . pride . . . dwelling on men's faults . . . abusing mankind . . . deriving pleasure from a false show of freedom.

Remind you of anyone?

Douglas Den Uyl writes, "The spiteful, the envious, the small-minded, and the jealous are particularly grievous under Spinoza's philosophy. These negative emotions or patterns of conduct retard both the individual as well as the society around her."

Have we a better description of Donald Trump? Indeed, the man who occupies the White House is the personification of Spinoza's passive, weak, and hence self-enslaved man.

12

Defining Anti-Semitism, Threatening Free Speech

The Libertarian Institute, August 24, 2018

In May the benign-sounding Anti-Semitism Awareness Act appeared before the U.S. Congress "to provide for consideration a definition of anti-Semitism for the enforcement of Federal antidiscrimination laws concerning education programs or activities."

No big deal? Let us see.

S. 2940 is sponsored by Republican Sen. Tim Scott and has four co-sponsors: Republican Lindsey Graham and Democrats Ron Wyden, Robert Casey, and Michael Bennet. The House sponsor of H.R. 5924 is Republican Rep. Peter Roskam, with 41 co-sponsors, 30 Republicans and 11 Democrats. Both bills remain in committee. (The Senate unanimously passed a similar bill two years ago, but it never reached the House floor.)

Right off the bat, the legislation seems odd: under what Republican Party theory of limited government does Congress propose definitions of words simply *for consideration* for educational purposes? And I thought Republicans don't like federal involvement in education. We'll see that the answer is steeped in irony: the stated purpose is to help education agencies to combat racial discrimination.

While the act is directed at education, the resulting law would reach beyond that realm because it would officially stigmatize as anti-Semitic any speech and activity, public and private, said to fall within the definition. Since this would at least chill the open marketplace of ideas, advocates of free speech should be concerned about the content of the definition and its revealing support material. We must not assume that merely because the definition is said to brand something anti-Semitic that it is actually anti-Semitic.

The act states that Title VI of the 1964 Civil Rights Act "prohibits discrimination on the basis of race, color, or national origin" (not, mind you, religion) but that "both the Department of Justice and the Department of Education have properly concluded that title VI prohibits discrimination against Jews, Muslims, Sikhs, and members of other religious groups when the discrimination is based on the group's *actual or perceived shared ancestry or ethnic characteristics* or when the discrimination is based on actual or perceived citizenship or residence in a country whose residents share a dominant religion or a distinct religious identity." [Emphasis added.] Hence, those departments have managed to shoehorn religion into a statute that does not mention religion.

The proposed definition directly comes from a 2010 State Department Fact Sheet, which in turn comes, with some modification, from the International Holocaust Remembrance Alliance (IHRA) "working definition of Anti-Semitism." The IHRA has 31 member countries, including the United States and Israel.

Anti-Semitism, according to the IHRA "working definition," is "a certain perception of Jews, which may be expressed as hatred toward Jews. Rhetorical and physical manifestations of antisemitism are directed toward Jewish or non-Jewish individuals and/or their property, toward Jewish community institutions and religious facilities."

This may seem less than helpful — history professor David Feldman, director of the Pears Institute for the Study of Antisemitism at London's Birkbeck University, calls it "bewilderingly imprecise" — so the IHRA furnished examples (couched in conditional terms such as *could* and *might* and to be interpreted by "taking into account the overall context"). And here the problems continue. Writing in the *Guardian*, Feldman, says of the 11 examples: "Seven deal with criticism of Israel. Some of the points are sensible, some are not. Crucially, there is a danger that the *overall effect will place the onus on Israel's critics to demonstrate they are not antisemitic.*" [Emphasis added.] That should be of concern.

Among the *possible* examples of anti-Semitism quoted from the IHRA document in the State Department Fact Sheet, but with some modification, are:

- Accusing Jews as a people of being responsible for real or imagined wrongdoing committed by a single Jewish person or group, *the state of Israel*, or even for acts committed by non-Jews. [Emphasis added.]
- Accusing Jewish citizens of being more loyal to Israel, or to the alleged priorities of Jews worldwide, than to the interest of their own nations.
- Drawing comparisons of contemporary Israeli policy to that of the Nazis.
- Applying double standards by requiring of it [Israel] a behavior not expected or demanded of any other democratic nation.
- Denying the Jewish people their right to self-determination, and denying Israel the right to exist.

Two things are worth pointing out here. The phrase "the state of

Israel" in the first example above does not appear in the IHRA list; that version says only, "Accusing Jews as a people of being responsible for real or imagined wrongdoing committed by a single Jewish person or group, or even for acts committed by non-Jews." The IHRA goes on to say later that "manifestations *might* include the targeting of the state of Israel, conceived as a Jewish collectivity" but immediately cautions that criticism of Israel similar to that leveled against any other country cannot be regarded as "anti-Semitic." [Emphasis added.] The Fact Sheet, which, again, the legislation incorporates, adds, almost as an afterthought, *"However, criticism of Israel similar to that leveled against any other country cannot be regarded as anti-Semitic."* [Italics in original.]

Second, the last example differs from the similar IHRA example, which reads, "Denying the Jewish people their right to self-determination, e.g., by claiming that *the existence of a State of Israel is a racist endeavor."* [Emphasis added.] I am unaware of any criticism of the Fact Sheet or legislation for this key modification. A similar modification has landed the UK's Labor Party leadership in hot water. (More below.)

As we'll see, the inclusion of criticism of Israel in the examples is where much of the danger of this legislation lies. Indeed, Antony Lerman, former director of the Institute for Jewish Policy Research in Britain, who traces the origin and promotion of the IHRA document to the American Jewish Committee and the Simon Wiesenthal Center, both of which routinely conflate criticism of Israel with anti-Semitism, says it was designed to "equate criticisms of Israel with hatred of Jews." Of course it was; today, being a good *anti*-anti-Semite, like being a good Jew, means little more than being unswervingly pro-Israel and pro-Israeli repression of Palestinians.

By way of additional background and contrast, the legislation cites a 2010 U.S. Department of Education "Dear Colleague" letter on religious bigotry to state and local educational agencies stating that they "must take prompt and effective steps reasonably calculated to end the harassment, eliminate any hostile environment, and its effects, and prevent the harassment from recurring." However, the legislation states that letter "did not provide guidance on current manifestations of anti-Semitism, including discriminatory anti-Semitic conduct *that is couched as anti-Israel or anti-Zionist."* [Emphasis added.] That's right: the Education Department did not mention Israel or Zionism in its letter about combating anti-Semitism. So the authors of the legislation seek to "correct" that "shortcoming."

The legislation goes to state that "anti-Semitism, and harassment on the basis of actual or perceived shared ancestry or ethnic characteristics with a religious group, remains a persistent, disturbing problem in elementary and secondary schools and on college campuses."

Is that so? It doesn't ring true. The Pew Research Center "finds that when it comes to religion, Americans generally express more positive feelings toward various religious groups [including Jews] today than they did just a few years ago. Asked to rate a variety of groups on a 'feeling thermometer' ranging from 0 to 100, U.S. adults give nearly all groups warmer ratings than they did in a June 2014 Pew Research Center survey." For all age groups, atheists and Muslims rank far below Jews. (In another survey, Muslims ranked below atheists.) For Americans 30 years and up, Jews rank at or near the top, and the score has risen since 2014. For Americans 18–29, Jews rank just below top-ranking Buddhists, Catholics, and Hindus. No religious group scored more than 69 "degrees" except for, among people 65 and older, Mainline Protestants, Jews, and Catholics, who scored in the 70s. Where's the widespread anti-Semitism?

And where's the evidence of growing anti-Semitism on college campuses? The legislation "finds" that "students from a range of diverse backgrounds, including Jewish, Arab Muslim, and Sikh students, are being threatened, harassed, or intimidated in their schools," but it would be interesting to see the groups broken out. One suspects the atmosphere on campus is more hostile to Arab and Muslim professors and students than to Jews. (See "Fracas Erupts Over Book on Mideast by a Barnard Professor Seeking Tenure" by Karen W. Arenson in the *New York Times* and "Abdulhadi Has Been Subjected to a Smear Campaign to Censure Her Support of Palestinian Human Rights" at Mondoweiss.) And we cannot discount the likelihood that criticism of Israel is simply interpreted as criticism of Jews qua Jews. Indeed, the lead author of the IHRA definition, Kenneth Stern, said last year in congressional testimony that it is untrue that "antisemitism on campus is an epidemic. Far from it. There are thousands of campuses in the United States, and in very few is antisemitism — or anti-Israel animus — an issue."

Anti-Semitism exists, of course, but it's clearly confined to the fringes of American society. It is so disreputable that people have shied away from criticizing Israel for fear of being accused of Jew-hatred, which can destroy careers and friendships. The legislation seems designed to reinforce that fear, which fortunately has been fading in recent years, especially among younger people, in light of Israel's periodic military assaults on the essentially defenseless people of Gaza. Every so often the word goes out that anti-Semitism is on the rise, but it's hard not to notice that those alarms follow the broad international criticism of Israeli systematic brutality against Palestinians resisting the 51-year occupation of their property. As Norman Finkelstein, who monitors this phenomenon closely, writes, "Whenever Israel commits another atrocity, its propagandists stage a revival of the 'New Anti-Semitism' extravaganza to deflect or squelch global condemnation." (See Finkelstein's book *Beyond Chutzpah: On the Misuse of Anti-Semitism and the Abuse of History*.)

I won't try to define *anti-Semitism*, let's just go with Stephen Sedley's definition: "Shorn of philosophical and political refinements, anti-Semitism is hostility towards Jews as Jews." I'll only add that it has something to do with seeing all Jews as members of a malignant and world-controlling racial or ethnic entity, with each member being responsible for any wrongdoing, real or imagined, by any other Jew. This is rank collectivism that no liberal individualist will accept. We must note the irony, however, that many Jews themselves believe that all Jews without exception constitute a genetic entity, though this is patently absurd. Jews are of many races, ethnicities, nationalities, and cultures and until a couple of hundred years into the Common Era, Judaism was a proselytizing religion with many successes at converting whole kingdoms, nations, and tribes. In other words, many Jews today are descendants of people who converted to Judaism, sometimes unwillingly, and who never were in the Land of Israel.

Note further the irony of the legislation's condemnation of those who conflate all Jews with the state of Israel. Israel's recently passed Nation-State Law declares that the "land of Israel is the historical homeland of the Jewish people." That includes *all* Jews no matter where they were born, where they live now, or whether they ever set foot in Israel. In other words, the government of Israel claims to speak for all Jews, which is an affront to any Jew who does not wish to be spoken for by a foreign government or who no longer regards himself as a Jew. (If the Jewish people are not a racial or ethnic entity but a diverse religious group, one can, like Spinoza, stop being a Jew.) It would be wrong for anyone to presume that Prime Minister Benjamin Netanyahu speaks for or acts on behalf of American, British, French, and other non-Israeli Jews, but that is what Israel's Basic Law claims. (Former *Meet the Press* host David Gregory once addressed Netanyahu on the air as the "leader of the Jewish people.")

And this claim, which predates the Nation-State Law, is what has given rise to the (dual) loyalty suspicion. So we have yet another irony in the Anti-Semitism Awareness Act's condemnation of statements "accusing Jewish citizens of being more loyal to Israel, or to the alleged priorities of Jews worldwide, than to the interest of their own nations." A great way to dispose of the loyalty issue would be for Israel and its supporters to stop pretending it represents all Jews (and former Jews) everywhere. (By the way, the act's language implies that accusing Jews of being just as loyal to Israel as they are to the U.S. is not anti-Semitic. Wouldn't that be dual loyalty?)

As noted, the legislation says that "denying the Jewish people their right to self-determination, and denying Israel the right to exist" is anti-Semitic. But what about denying the Jewish people the right to self-determination *on land taken from its rightful owners*, as Jewish and non-Jewish anti-Zionists have long denied? And when will Congress get around to condemning those who deny the right of Palestinians to self-determination? The Nation-State Law says that the "right to exercise national self-determination in the State of Israel is unique to the Jewish people." So Palestinians are lesser people than Jews? What's the word for that attitude?

The condemnation of people who "apply double standards by requiring of it [Israel] a behavior not expected or demanded of any other democratic nation" is also filled with problems. The first is that Israel's unconditional defenders themselves are guilty of applying a double standard. If any national group treated another group the way the Zionists and Israelis have treated the Palestinians, they would have been condemned by liberal-minded Jewish Americans along with most other Americans. Second, where is the double standard in the criticism of Israel? Name another country that occupies other people's land, recognizes no rights in the occupied population, systematically discriminates against 25 percent of its "citizens," gets billions of dollars in military aid every year from American taxpayers, has a highly influential lobby ready to smear any critic, claims to be the most moral military in the world, and insists it's the only democracy in its region? When we have another country like that we'll see if Israel's critics apply a double standard.

The example of anti-Semitism allegedly found in "drawing comparisons of contemporary Israeli policy to that of the Nazis" is also worth examination. Is it really the case that Israel's rulers are incapable of acting like Nazis, even when it seizes Palestinians, including children, in the dark of night; holds them indefinitely without charge; tortures them; shoots them or breaks their bones when they protest their oppression peacefully; requires internal travel permits; maintains military checkpoints; bars them from much of the land and Jewish-only roads; and destroys homes as collective punishment or to clear land for use by Jews only? What's the theory underlying that claim? Do the oppressed never become oppressors?

And here's another question: are *Jews* who make that comparison also anti-Semites? The fact is that Jews have repeatedly made that comparison, for example, the late Hajo Meyer, a Holocaust survivor, and Yair Golan, the former deputy chief of the general staff of the Israel Defense Force. Indeed, in 1948 Albert Einstein, Hannah Arendt, and other Jews sent a letter to the *New York Times* expressing concern over the emergence of the Israeli "'Freedom Party' (Tnuat Haherut), a political party closely akin in its organization, methods, political philosophy and social appeal to the Nazi and Fascist parties. It was formed out of the membership and following of the former Irgun Zvai Leumi, a terrorist, right-wing, chauvinist organization in Palestine." That party and the Irgun were led by Menachem Begin, who became prime minister of Israel in the 1970s. The party merged with Netanyahu's Likud party in 1988.

Yet one more question: if neither Jews nor non-Jews may liken Israeli policies against the Palestinians to some Nazi policies, why are Israelis and their supporters allowed to claim that any and all perceived adversaries (Nasser, Saddam Hussein, Qaddafi, and Ahmadinejad and the Iranian ayatollahs, for example) are reincarnations of Adolf Hitler?

Since Jews as well as non-Jews often commit the "offenses" specified by the IHRA, maybe the congressional legislation should have been called the Anti-Semitism and *Jewish Self-Hatred* Awareness Act. Or perhaps only men and women with Jewish mothers are to be permitted to do what is forbidden to others. That would be an odd view indeed.

No, the Israeli regime does not operate death camps, but it does things that resemble what the Nazi and other totalitarian regimes did to Jews and other groups. Gaza, where the more-than-decade-old Israeli blockade causes two million Palestinians, half of them children, to be undernourished and forced to drink polluted water, has been called by Jews a concentration camp and a ghetto.

Real anti-Semitism is ugly and execrable. And that's why diluting the concept with extraneous elements is what's really dangerous. Sure, some of Israel's critics could be anti-Semites, but some of Israel's biggest fans might be too. I would be suspicious of anyone who was eager to pack my bags and shuffle me off to Tel Aviv. There simply are no reasonable grounds for a presumption of anti-Semitism about opponents of Israel, certainly not in people of good faith. Conflating anti-Semitism even with foundational criticism of Israel makes anti-Semitism seem not so bad in some people's eyes. As Antony Lerman wrote, "Rather than make it easier to identify antisemitism, the promotion of the 'working definition' and the entrenchment of the concept of the 'new antisemitism' have so extended the range of expressions of what can be regarded as antisemitic that the word antisemitism has come close to losing all meaning."

Why would anyone want to encourage that outcome? Lerman also points out that "if . . . only 'antisemities' would dissociate themselves from the 'working definition,' this places a significant number of highly respected Jewish and non-Jewish academics working in the field of antisemitism research in the dock."

Those who continue to lobby for this conflation are unwittingly pursuing an evil course even on their own terms — unless they intend such an outcome. (Real or imagined anti-Semitism can be useful in deterring Jewish assimilation and disillusionment with Israel.) Moreover, they are encouraging organizations that harass students and teachers sympathetic to the Palestinians' plight. Free speech and inquiry must be protected. As the ACLU said about the legislation:

The overbroad definition of anti-Semitism in this bill risks incorrectly equating constitutionally protected criticism of Israel with anti-Semitism, making it likely that free speech will be chilled on campuses. The examples incorporated into the bill's definition of anti-Semitism include actions and statements critical of Israel, including many constitutionally protected statements. As a result, the proposed legislation is likely to chill the speech of students, faculty, and other members campus communities around the country, and is unnecessary to enforce federal prohibitions on harassment in education as such protections already exist under federal law.

As the ACLU letter opposing the legislation notes, even the lead author of the definition, Kenneth Stern, a self-described Zionist, "has himself opposed application of this definition to campus speech." In a 2016 op-ed opposing South Carolina's adoption of the definition, Stern wrote,

> It is really an attempt to create a speech code about Israel. It is an unnecessary law which will hurt Jewish students and the academy. . . . It was never intended as a vehicle to monitor or suppress speech on campus. But that's what some right-wing Jewish groups and individuals behind this legislation seek. . . .

> [The legislation advocates'] intent is clear: to have the state define a line where political speech about Israel is classified as anti-Semitic, and chilled if not suppressed. . . .

> If the definition becomes law, campus administrators will fear lawsuits when outside groups complain about anti-Israel expression, and the leadership of the university doesn't punish, stop or denounce it. . . .

> [I]f the anti-Semitism definition is enshrined into law, what professor will want to walk into this minefield, fearful that the selection of certain texts or the expression of certain opinions will put his or her university's funding in jeopardy?

> Indeed, if certain expressions about Israel are officially defined as anti-Semitic, pro-Israel Jewish students will be further marginalized, having gained the reputation for suppressing, rather than answering, speech they don't like.

In 2017 testimony before the House Judiciary Committee, Stern elaborated:

> The proponents of the legislation have made a business model of seeking out speech they believe transgresses the Department of State Definition. They will hunt for such instances and then press administrators to either suppress or condemn such statements, threatening Title VI cases if they don't act, with the added weight of a

Congressionally endorsed, campus-focused definition behind them. . . . Armed with a congressional determination that effectively says campus anti-Zionism is antisemitism, . . . professors will correctly see themselves at risk when they ask their students to read and digest materials deemed anti-Zionist, whether the writings of leading 20th century Jewish thinkers who were skeptical of Zionism, such as Hannah Arendt and Martin Buber, or of contemporary Palestinians. Professors do not get combat pay. It will be safer and wiser for them to teach about Jews in the *shtetl* than Jews in modern Israel, and Zionism as a concept from the late 19th century, rather than how it plays out today. . . . My fear is, if we . . . enshrine this definition into law, outside groups will try and suppress — rather than answer — political speech they don't like. The academy, Jewish students, and faculty teaching about Jewish issues, will all suffer.

The definition has also been faulted, as Lerman put it, for its "go-it-alone exceptionalism as the way of managing heightened fears of antisemitism, rather than pursuing open-hearted collaboration with other minority groups to fight the resurgent racism that blights society."

If the Anti-Semitism Awareness Act passes and is signed into law, it would threaten free speech in the academy and beyond, notwithstanding it obligatory "Nothing in this Act shall be construed to diminish or infringe upon any right protected under the First Amendment to the Constitution of the United States."

Moreover, it will make political campaigns even less meaningful than they are now. As it is, American politicians are afraid to defend the Palestinians against Israel or to question the huge annual military appropriation that enables the brutality; candidates have much to lose both in campaign contributions and reputation. Those who slip, like Bernie Sanders, Cory Booker, and Alexandria Ocasio-Cortez, will have hell to pay and will likely be more careful in the future. (Sanders has had his ups as well as downs.) The UK Labor Party and its leader, the lifelong anti-racist Jeremy Corbyn, are learning the same lesson.

We must hope that things do not get as bad in the U.S. as they are in the UK, where a hysterical smear campaign against Israel's critics has conjured up the term "political anti-Semitism targeting Israel" (in contrast to "racial antisemitism targeting Jews") and alarm in some quarters about the alleged "existential threat to Jewish life in this country [Great Britain] that would be posed by a Jeremy Corbyn-led government." The Labor Party's National Executive Committee has been accused of Jew-hatred because its new code of conduct on anti-Semitism allegedly failed to incorporate the entire IHRA definition of anti-Semitism — hence, its apparent cowardly retreat. Jonathan Freedland of the *Guardian* tweeted, "So Labour have rejected a definition of antisemitism accepted by UK, Scottish and Welsh govts, 124 local authorities, gov'ts around the world and most Jews."

Note the authority Freedland, like others, vests in the now-holy IHRA definition — as though it were an amendment to the tablets allegedly handed down at Mount Sinai.

But Lerman shows that Freedland's charge is utter rubbish; the executive committee's code explicitly incorporates and quotes the *definition*, but the authors modified some of the IHRA's *examples* and (like the State Department's Fact Sheet) removed from another the phrase "claiming that the existence of a State of Israel is a racist endeavor."

But can it be anti-Semitic to call Israel a racist endeavor when leading Israeli intellectuals such as historian Benny Morris acknowledge that ridding Palestine of the indigenous Palestinians — that is, ethnic cleansing — was intrinsic to Zionism?

Lerman also shows, as already noted, that by its own word choices, the IHRA suggests that its illustrations may *or may not* qualify as examples of anti-Semitism depending on the context. Lerman notes that defenders of the definition make opposing claims — that the examples both are and are not part of the definition — depending on which position is convenient at the time.

Clearly, the Labor Party leadership stands accused of anti-Semitism purely for adopting a code of conduct that distinguishes anti-Semitism from criticism of Israel.

Is this sort of smear campaign that is in store for members of Congress who vote against the Anti-Semitism Awareness Act?

13

Anti-Israelism and Anti-Semitism: The Invidious Conflation

The Libertarian Institute, August 31, 2018

I and others have warned that enactment of the Anti-Semitism Awareness Act now before Congress would threaten free speech and free inquiry on America's college campuses and beyond. As I've explained, this bill incorporates a conception — a "definition" plus *potential* examples — of anti-Semitism that conflates criticism of Israel's founding and continuing abuse of the Palestinians with anti-Semitism for the purpose inoculating Israel from such criticism. Anti-Zionist Jews and others have objected to this conflation for over 70 years.

What makes us so confident in predicting a threat to free speech?

We are confident in part because Donald Trump's assistant secretary of education for civil rights, who would enforce the legislation, is Kenneth L. Marcus, whose record makes him the poster boy for the invidious conflation.

Dima Khalidi, founder and director of Palestine Legal, writes in *The Nation*:

> If this definition [of anti-Semitism] were adopted and implemented as Marcus would like, the DOE would be empowered to conclude that universities nurture hostile, anti-Semitic environments by allowing the screening of a documentary critical of Israel's 50-year military occupation of Palestinian lands such as *Occupation 101*, a talk critical of Israeli policy by a Holocaust survivor, a mock checkpoint enacted by students to show their peers what Palestinian life under a military occupation is like, a talk on BDS [boycott-divestment-sanctions] campaigns for Palestinian rights, or student resolutions to divest from companies complicit in Israel's human-rights abuses.

> These aren't hypotheticals. These speech activities were the subject of real legal complaints, filed or promoted by Marcus and his Brandeis Center against Brooklyn College (2013), University of California Berkeley (2012), and University of California Santa Cruz (2009). The

complaints were filed to the same DOE office which Marcus has been nominated to head [and to which he has since been confirmed].

Crucially, all of these complaints were dismissed. Both a federal court and the DOE made clear that the activities at issue were not harassment against a protected group but constituted speech on matters of public concern, and therefore were protected by the First Amendment.

Marcus founded and ran the Louis D. Brandeis Center for Human Rights Under Law (not affiliated with Brandeis University), which declares on its website, "In the Twenty-first Century [sic], the leading civil and human rights challenge facing North American Jewry is the resurgent problem of anti-Semitism and *anti-Israelism* on university campuses. This social problem requires an immediate, effective, and coordinated legal response." [Emphasis added.]

Note the conflation. How could anti-Israelism on campus or anywhere else pose a "civil and human rights challenge to North American Jewry"? If Judaism values universal justice, which the great prophets admonished the ancient Hebrews to honor, attention to the systematic injustice that Israel inflicts on the Palestinians qua non-Jews should be welcomed rather than feared by all, including Jews. As I've argued, there is no reason to view even foundational criticism of Israel through a presumption of anti-Semitism. Indeed, the Center itself claims that "the civil and human rights of the Jewish people are inextricably bound to the pursuit of justice for all peoples." Unfortunately, that sentiment turns out to be mere lip service; it is not reflected in its actions — unless Palestinians are to be regarded as nonpeople. Alas, that seems to be the case.

The Center is not alone in this belief or activity. Similar programs are carried out by the Canary Mission (an until recently anonymous website[1]), which "documents people and groups that promote hatred of the U.S.A., Israel and Jews on North American college campuses," and the David Horowitz Freedom Center, the self-identified "school of political warfare," which through its Israel Security Center headed by Caroline Glick stigmatizes criticism of Israel as the "mainstreaming of anti-Semitism" and smears professors who are Palestinian or who express sympathy for the Palestinians' plight. An assortment of other individuals, such as former student activist Bari Weiss, now a *New York Times* writer and editor feted for her courageous advocacy of free speech on campus, have also made it their mission to smear Palestinian sympathizers as Jew-haters.

---

[1] See "Censored Film Names Adam Milstein as Canary Mission Funder," by Asa Winstanley and Ali Abunimah at the Electronic Intifada and "Canary Mission's Veil of Anonymity Pierced" at PalestineLegal.org.

Marcus previously worked in the George W. Bush administration's Education Department, Office of Civil Rights (OCR), and the U.S. Civil Rights Commission.

As assistant secretary of education, he would have the power to move against colleges and universities that in his view failed to discipline pro-Palestinian student activists and professors on grounds that their statements and activities create a hostile climate for Jewish students and thereby violate their rights under Title VI of the 1964 Civil Rights Act.

However, even the lead author of the notion of anti-Semitism embodied in the Anti-Semitism Awareness Act has bridled at its use to police debate on campus. Kenneth Stern has written articles and given testimony in Congress warning against such use. As Stern wrote to the House Judiciary Committee in 2016, when a similar bill was under consideration and was eventually killed because of First Amendment concerns:

> I write as the lead author of the . . . "Working Definition on Antisemitism," to encourage you not to move "The Anti-Semitism Awareness Act of 2016," which essentially incorporates that definition into law for a purpose that is both unconstitutional and unwise. If the definition is so enshrined, it will actually harm Jewish students and have a toxic effect on the academy. . . .
>
> Antisemitism — like all forms of bigotry — has an impact on some campuses. The worst way to address it is to create a de facto hate speech code, which is what this bill proposes to do.
>
> In years past various Title VI cases were brought asserting that a hostile environment was created in substantial part by anti-Israel speech. All of them lost. . . .
>
> Students should not be harassed and intimidated and threatened. But a campus must be a place where students are challenged by difficult — and yes, disturbing and even hateful — ideas.

In testimony before the committee, Stern said it is not true that "antisemitism on campus is an epidemic. Far from it. There are thousands of campuses in the United States, and in very few is antisemitism — or anti-Israel animus — an issue."

At the Mondoweiss website, civil rights advocates Abed A. Ayoub, Phillip Agnew, and Harper Jean Tobin write that, while at the Brandeis Center, Marcus "abused the OCR complaint process by pushing frivolous protests that only serve to harass and stifle the speech of students he disagrees with."

Losing cases did not deter him, however. As he wrote in the *Jerusalem Post* in 2013, "These cases — even when rejected — expose administrators to bad publicity."

Harassment is a nice word for that kind of behavior. Why aren't such activities called racism? (Marcus suggests that his complaints were exclusively against assault, physical intimidation, and the like, but the OCR dismissals say otherwise.)

Marcus continued, "Just last week, I heard from a university chancellor who is eager to work with the Schusterman Center for Israel Studies at Brandeis University to avert the possibility of a civil rights complaint." In light of the threat from the Brandeis Center, I doubt the chancellor was likely to err on the side of free speech and free inquiry. What one perceives as a hostile environment is highly subjective, but some believe that the mere perception of something as anti-Semitic is sufficient to *make* it anti-Semitic. Intentions and truth are irrelevant.

"As Assistant Secretary," Ayoub, Agnew, and Tobin write, Marcus will "be able to wield the threat of bad publicity in an attempt to force universities to restrict the rights of groups such as Students for Justice in Palestine."

That's a good reason to favor defeat of the Anti-Semitism Awareness Act: it would enable Marcus, in Khalidi's words, to "try to do from the inside of the DOE what he has failed to do from the outside."

14

The Art of the Smear —
The Israel Lobby Busted

The Libertarian Institute, November 16, 2018

In 2016 and 2017 Al Jazeera produced a program that unmistakably documents the Israel government and U.S.-Israel lobby's all-out effort to spy on, smear, and disrupt American students and other activists who are working to build an understanding of the Palestinians' plight. *The Lobby — USA*, however, has never been broadcast by Al Jazeera. Reporting indicates that it was suppressed after pressure from the lobby on the government of Qatar, which funds Al Jazeera. Nevertheless, it is now available at the Electronic Intifada and on YouTube. What the program presents is shocking.

The Lobby — USA, which features an undercover journalist who won the trust of key pro-Israel operatives and who videoed revealing meetings, demonstrates beyond question the lengths to which the Israelis and their supporters in the United States will go to prevent a change in American thinking about the beleaguered Palestinians. The effort aims to smear Palestinian students in the United States and pro-Palestinian American activists and political candidates who criticize Israeli policy as anti-Semites and enablers of terrorism. The paid pro-Israel operatives, guided by Israeli government officials and embassy staff, have used social media and other channels in an attempt to destroy the career potential of student activists who work to raise Americans' consciousness about the Palestinians. Establishment news operations, such as the *Washington Post*, are also implicated. Major targets are activists in the Boycott, Divestment, Sanctions (BDS) Movement and Students for Justice in Palestine.

Al Jazeera produced a similar program about Israeli interference in British politics, which led to resignations of a key Israeli embassy official and other reactions that confirmed Al Jazeera's damaging charges.

I could not do justice to the program even in a long article. Instead, I will urge readers to watch it in its entirety — and think carefully about what it means.

As one critic of Israel asks on the program, if Russia or Iran or China were doing what Israel and its American friends are doing, most people would be outraged. This is hardly the first time that Israel and friends have been caught covertly and overtly trying to influence discourse and even elections here through smear campaigns against activists, writers, and political candidates, but this is certainly among the most flagrant and elaborate examples.

Let's step back from the poisonous trees for a moment to view the forest. In 1948 the leaders of a European and nominally Jewish movement, Zionism, *unilaterally* declared the existence of the State of Israel, which they proclaimed the nation-state of *all Jews everywhere*, a status recently reaffirmed by the Israeli Knesset. (The UN General Assembly *recommended* partitioning Palestine into a larger Jewish state and a smaller Palestinian state, but it had no power to actually create the state of Israel.)

It so happened this state was built on land taken by force from the long-standing majority indigenous Palestinian population, most of which was Muslim and Christian. Hundreds were massacred, three-quarters of a million were driven from their homes, and the remainder were subjected to martial law for two decades, before being given third-class citizenship with no power to improve their legal status. (Arab nations half-heartedly tried to assist the overwhelmed Palestinians, although the king of Jordan worked with Israel to divide the spoils.) Almost 20 years later, the rest of Palestine was taken through warfare, producing what are known as the occupied territories in the West Bank, with its apartheid-like regime, and the Gaza Strip, which is nothing more than an open-air prison under a cruel Israeli blockade.

Why? Because a "Jewish State" could not be realized if it were populated by non-Jews. And if some non-Jews remained, the state could not be a liberal democratic state, with equality under the law, for obvious reasons. All this was aided from the start by European Christians who, apparently guilt-ridden over how the Jews of Europe had been tyrannized, culminating in the Nazi genocide, opted to assuage their guilt with the land, blood, and liberty of the innocent people of Palestine, long the plaything of colonial powers.

Since that time, Israel has repressed the Palestinians in a variety of ways, depending on whether they are in the state as it existed in 1949; the West Bank, which was seized during the June 1967 war; or the Gaza Strip (also called the Gaza Ghetto), also seized in that war. Meanwhile, millions of refugees — people (and descendants of people) driven from their homes by Zionism's terrorist militias, have been confined to refugee camps, stateless, rightless, and destitute. At various times, Israel, with America's backing, has cut deals with Arab states and Palestinian quislings for the purpose of keeping the Palestinians from winning their rights either in a single secular democratic state or through a two-state plan. Western political and media establishments have overwhelmingly sympathized with the Israelis and demonized the Palestinians (and Arabs and Muslims generally). It didn't take long for the public to be propagandized, *against all evidence*, into believing that the Palestinians are the aggressors and the Israelis the victims. Apparently, a person is anti-Semitic if he objects to having his property stolen by someone who claims that property in the name of the Jewish People.

But after so many decades of Israeli wars, massacres, repression, and routine brutal dehumanization, the tide has started to turn. Israel pulverized Gaza and its people one too many times; it shot and broke the bones of too many children before too many video cameras. And so public opinion, especially among younger Americans — and particularly among younger Jewish Americans — has been turning against Israel. Then the BDS Movement arose to accomplish what a similar movement helped to accomplish against apartheid South Africa: bringing world attention to an intolerable situation and taking concrete steps to change it.

All of this has been too much for Israel's ruling elite and its supporters in the United States, Great Britain, and elsewhere, and they are fighting back. They know they can't win on the merits. Well-documented historical studies and basic morality have seen to that. So they smear their opponents as Jew-haters and supporters of terrorism. As one Israel lobby operator puts it in the Al Jazeera program, you discredit the message by discrediting the messenger — which is what The Israel Project, Foundation for Defense of Democracies, Israel on Campus Coalition, Canary Mission, Emergency Committee on Israel, Israeli Embassy in Washington, Israeli Ministry of Strategic Affairs, and the other co-conspirators have set out to do. Their goal, as their leaders themselves acknowledge, is to identify criticism of Israel with anti-Semitism. (Also see Chapter 12.)

But it goes beyond that. The Israel lobby realizes that the anti-Semitism charge no longer sticks so tenaciously to people who merely indict Israel for its obvious mistreatment of the Palestinians. So the lobby has resorted to a broader brush: it says that those who support BDS and the Palestinians are anti-American, anti-democracy, and anti-all blessed things. BDS and Students for Justice in Palestine, the lobby contends, are hate groups. This of course is patently absurd, but Israel's side observes no limits it what it is willing to say and perhaps do to destroy the reputations anyone who realizes that the Israeli emperor has no clothes.

Al Jazeera, the Electronic Intifada, The Gray Zone Project, and others have performed a much-needed service on behalf of freedom, justice, and decency. I urge you to watch this program and spread the word.

15

How an Anti-Semitic American Law Created the State of Israel and a Whole Lot of Trouble

The Libertarian Institute, June 1, 2018

Shlomo Sand, a remarkable scholar who studies how "peoples," including the Jewish people, have been invented through myths propagated by court historians and politicians, makes a startling yet obvious connection in his book *The Invention of the Land of Israel* (2014):

> In fact, it was the United States' refusal, between the anti-immigration legislation of 1924 and the year 1948, to accept the victims of European Judeophobic persecution that enabled decision makers to channel somewhat more significant numbers of Jews toward the Middle East. Absent this stern anti-immigration policy, *it is doubtful whether the State of Israel could have been established.* [Emphasis added.]

In the same book, Sand writes:

> It is fair to say that the [British] Balfourian legislation of 1905 regarding foreigners, along with a similar law enacted two decades later in the United States that further toughened the terms of immigration (the Immigration Act of 1924, also known as the Johnson-Reed Act), contributed to the establishment of the State of Israel no less than the Balfour Declaration of 1917, and perhaps even more. These two anti-immigrant laws — along with Balfour's letter to Rothschild regarding the United Kingdom's willingness to view favorably "the establishment in Palestine of a national home for the Jewish people" — lay down the historical conditions under which Jews would *be channeled* to the Middle East. [Emphasis added.]

According to the U.S. Office of the Historian, "The Immigration Act of 1924 [Johnson-Reed] limited the number of immigrants allowed entry into the United States through a national origins quota. The quota provided immigration visas to two percent of the total number of people of each nationality in the United States as of the 1890 national census. It completely excluded immigrants from Asia. . . . In all of its parts, the most basic purpose of the 1924 Immigration Act was to preserve the ideal of U.S. homogeneity." (The act was revised in 1952.)

In its intention and effect, the law, which passed the houses of Congress with overwhelming majorities, blocked people from Southern and Eastern Europe, Catholics, Arabs, and Jews. A. James Rudin writes:

> The bill's co-sponsor, U.S. Rep. Albert Johnson, R-Wash., said the law would block "a stream of alien blood, with all its inherited misconceptions" from entering America. Sen. David Reed, R-Pa., the other co-sponsor, represented "those of us who are interested in keeping American stock up to the highest standard — that is, the people who were born here." Southern and Eastern Europeans (many of them Catholics and Jews), he believed, "arrive sick and starving and therefore less capable of contributing to the American economy, and unable to adapt to American culture."

Unsurprisingly, Hitler praised the act as model legislation for keeping a population racially pure.

For supporting material, see "Foundations of Holocaust: 1924, Congress Decides No More Jews" in the *Jerusalem Post* and "Trump's Move to End DACA and Echoes of the Immigration Act of 1924" in the *New Yorker*. From the latter:

> The policy was so defiantly and arrogantly racist that, as James Q. Whitman, a professor at Yale Law School, writes in *Hitler's American Model*, it earned praise from Adolf Hitler. "The American Union categorically refuses immigration of unhealthy elements, and simply excludes the immigration of certain races," Hitler wrote in *Mein Kampf* [1925]. This, he said, made the country a leader in preserving racial purity through immigration policy.

All very well and good, you say, but how did the 1924 law — which is so relevant today — create, or help to create, the State of Israel? To answer this question, it must be recalled (if not learned) that in 1924 very few Jews had any interest in Palestine. The Orthodox Jews, believing that God had expelled the Jews from the Holy Land (the Babylonian exile), thought it the height of impertinence for any mere mortal to decide when the Jews should return. That was up to God. They certainly were not going to take their lead from atheist so-called Jews from Eastern Europe, such as David Ben-Gurion. True, some old Orthodox men went to the Holy Land to die (planning on resurrection later) or to await *mashiach* (messiah). But they did not seek the creation of a political entity — a Jewish State. That was the furthest thing from their minds. In Sand's words, it was a Holy Land, not a homeland. "Next year in Jerusalem" was not a statement from a political program. It was a messianic hope.

On the other hand, Reform Judaism was organized in opposition to the then-small Zionist movement, which in the Reform view was counterfeit, idolatrous "Judaism" in which (purported) blood and soil replaced God, Torah, and the universalism of the great prophets. Reform Jews explicitly rejected that they were part of a Diaspora. They believed that Judaism in fact represented a worldwide *religious* community comprising many different citizens of many different countries of many different cultures — not a distinct racial or ethnic entity. ("Jewish blood" was of interest only to anti-Semites.) Indeed, earlier Reform Jews would have opposed the formation of the State of Israel even had Palestine been a "land without a people" — which of course it was not.

As the Reform founders put in the Pittsburgh Platform (1885):

> We consider ourselves no longer a nation, but a religious community, and therefore expect neither a return to Palestine, nor a sacrificial worship under the sons of Aaron, nor the restoration of any of the laws concerning the Jewish state.

Despite this deep opposition, the Zionist movement picked up steam, after World War II, ostensibly as a humanitarian project to resettle the displaced Jews of Europe. But this was merely a public relations move, albeit a most effective one even for many Reform Jews. One must realize that Zionism was *never* a refugee project. Its intention was to "ingather" the whole of the Diaspora, especially those "Jews [in other lands who] are absorbed in sinful self-satisfaction," to Palestine, the only place (so the Zionists preached) where Jews could be a "normal people." (In portraying the Jew as an alien anywhere else — as an authentic Jew *only* in Israel — Zionism parroted the vilest views of the anti-Semites. Indeed, its leaders feared — ironically? — that without anti-Semitism and anti-assimilationism, there would *be* no Jews after a short while.)

Sand's point is that Jews from Eastern Europe and other parts of Christendom — unlike most of their more-fortunate coreligionists in Islamic countries like Iraq — longed to move to America or, if not America, elsewhere in the West. Like his creator, the writer Sholom Aleichem, Tevye the dairyman in *Fiddler on the Roof*, takes his family not to Palestine but to "New York, America," when the awful tsar expels the Jews from Anatevka, their *shtetl* in the Pale of Settlement in the Russian empire. (Tevye's brother had previously moved to America.) His neighbor and almost-son-in-law, the butcher Lazar Wolf, is excited that they will be neighbors, for he is going to "Chicago, America."

(For the record, in Aleichem's story "Tevye Leaves for the Land of Israel," Tevye agrees to go to Palestine to see the religious sites when his youngest daughter's *nouveau riche* social-climber husband bribes him to leave because his low station is an embarrassment. The aging Tevye, a loving father, not a Zionist, expects he will die there — but in fact he never gets to the Holy Land. Just before boarding a ship, he receives word that another son-in-law has died, so he returns home to comfort his widowed daughter and her children.)

This attitude was and remained typical. For most Jews who left their homes (for whatever reason), Israel was the last "choice" and only when all other routes were blocked (including, for example, with the Soviet Jews, by Israel itself) or tax subsidies were offered to the poor. After the 1956 Suez Crisis, most Jews who left Egypt moved to the United States, Argentina, France, or Switzerland. Why is that? We know why.

If between the world wars, Sand is saying, the Jews of Christendom had been free to go to America, the Zionist movement would have had far too few people with which to fulfill its dubious dream.

But we can push this further. Could the Holocaust have occurred if Jews had been free to move to America in the interwar period? Remember that the Roosevelt administration turned away the German ship M.S. *St. Louis*, filled with nearly a thousand German Jews fleeing the Nazis, from Miami in 1939 under the strict immigration quotas signed into law 15 years earlier by Republican President Calvin Coolidge, beloved by a few libertarians for his putative devotion to limited government. "America must remain American," Coolidge said when signing the bill.

Had the surviving Jews of Central and Eastern Europe not become displaced by the Nazis because they had been living safely in America since the 1920s, the campaign for a Jewish State in Palestine would have certainly flopped. Think about it: No UN General Assembly recommendation for partition. No *Nakba*. No Palestinian refugees. No policy- and politics-distorting "Israel lobby." Perhaps no 9/11. It's mind-blowing!

Not to put too fine a point on it, but we could blame someone else besides Coolidge: Woodrow Wilson. It was he who took the United States into World War I, setting the stage for the punitive "peace" treaty declaring Germany uniquely guilty for the war, the emergence of Hitler and his regime bent on vengeance for the indignity visited on the proud German nation, World War II, and the Holocaust.

Not a bad day's work in the Oval Office. Let it sink in: without Wilson's war, no Versailles Treaty; without the Versailles Treaty, no Hitler; without Hitler, no Holocaust; without the Holocaust, no State of Israel; without the State of Israel, well, you get the idea. I'm not saying everything today would be sweetness and light in the Middle East, of course. The Great Powers would have still wanted to control the oil, but the major source of strife and war in that region — not to mention immeasurable domestic political corruption — would not have materialized.

Blame aside, we may confidently say that the 20th century and beyond would have looked very different had America welcomed rather than scorned immigrants. What say you, Donald Trump?

16

America Must Reject
Netanyahu's War Cry on Iran

The Freedom of Freedom Foundation, March 4, 2015

Israeli Prime Minister Benjamin Netanyahu came to Washington this week to prepare the American people for war against Iran. Backed by American neoconservatives, the Israel lobby, and assorted other war hawks, Netanyahu insists that Iran intends to build a nuclear weapon and thus is an "existential threat" to Israel. He has no confidence that President Obama will negotiate an agreement that once and for all will end Iran's alleged nuclear ambitions.

Thus the prime minister's objective is nothing less than to wreck the current negotiations and push America into a regime-changing war against Iran.

Netanyahu's narrative is a fabric of lies and omissions.

To begin, Iran has not sought a nuclear weapon, and the country's leader declares such weapons contrary to Islam. (For details, see Gareth Porter's well-documented *Manufactured Crisis: The Untold Story of the Iran Nuclear Scare*.) For a quarter-century, Netanyahu has warned that an Iranian bomb is imminent. But U.S. and Israeli intel say he's wrong.

Iran nevertheless wants to reassure the world so that crushing economic sanctions will be lifted. Hence, the current negotiations. (Iran made similar overtures before.)

Iran's government is a signatory to the nuclear Non-Proliferation Treaty (NPT), subjecting it to inspections by the International Atomic Energy Agency, which can account for every atom of uranium.

Members of the NPT are free to have a civilian nuclear-power program, including the ability to enrich uranium, and Iran insists that it be treated as other members are. Nevertheless, for decades the U.S. government has exerted pressure to stop Iran from having a civilian nuclear industry. When Iran a few years ago agreed to forgo enrichment and obtain enriched uranium from abroad, the U.S. government blocked the deal. Netanyahu and his American allies oppose Iran's having any enrichment capability.

Moreover — and this ignored fact seems rather important — *Israel is the nuclear monopolist of the Mideast.* That hardly anyone talks about this is at once remarkable and unsurprising. But think about it: Israel has hundreds of nuclear warheads — some of them on invulnerable submarines capable of surviving a first strike. Even if Iran built one warhead, it would be useless — except as a deterrent against Israel — and the country's rulers know it. Israel has not signed the NPT and does not submit to IAEA inspections. It is a nuclear rogue state.

As Gideon Rose, editor of *Foreign Affairs* magazine (published by the establishment Council on Foreign Relations), said on CNN recently, Israel could "destroy Iran this afternoon." If there is an existential threat, Israel is the source and Iran is the target.

How does Netanyahu's alarmist narrative look now?

It is erroneously believed that Iran has threatened to attack Israel. In fact, Israel and the United States have been waging war — economic, covert, proxy, and cyber — against Iran for decades. Starting about 10 years after the repressive U.S.-backed Iranian regime of Shah Mohammad Reza Pahlavi, a close friend of Israel, was overthrown in 1979, Israel's leaders have openly rattled sabers at the Islamic Republic. American presidents have repeatedly declared that "all military options are on the table" — which would include nuclear weapons. The United States helped Iraqi dictator Saddam Hussein fight a war of aggression against Iran in the 1980s, providing him with components for chemical weapons and satellite intelligence. Why wouldn't Iran feel threatened by the United States and its close ally Israel? Even so, Iran has not threatened to attack Israel or America.

Netanyahu would have us believe the Iranian regime wants to exterminate all Jews. But that's hard to square with the continuous presence of a Jewish community in Iran — today the largest in the Muslim Middle East — for two thousand years. Iran's steadfast opposition to Israel's institutionalized injustice against the Palestinians is not anti-Semitism.

So why is Netanyahu pushing war? Among several reasons, demonizing Iran reduces pressure on Israel to negotiate *seriously* with the Palestinians. Most Israelis prefer building Jewish settlements on Palestinians' land instead. Moreover, Israel's rulers oppose any development — such as an Iranian-U.S. detente — that could diminish Israel's U.S.-financed hegemony in the region.

War with Iran would be a catastrophe all around. Netanyahu and his hawkish American allies — the same people who gave us the disastrous Iraq war and ISIS — must be repudiated.

17

Arab Attempts to Negotiate with Israel

American-Arab Affairs, June 30, 1991

In the rich mythology of the Middle East, no myth has more malign effects on current affairs than the one which says that for 40 years Israel has stood ready to negotiate peace but, until Egypt's Anwar Sadat came along, could find no responsible Arab interlocutor. Rather, so goes this myth, the Arab leadership has been committed (and remains committed) to Israel's destruction.

Countless examples could be provided. A. M. Rosenthal of the *New York Times* has written that "Israel has been saying yes to peace talks with Arabs decade after decade — as Anwar el-Sadat proved, to Egypt's everlasting gain. Second reality: For all those decades every other Arab nation refused to make peace, refused to talk."

More recently, Martin Indyk of the pro-Likud Washington Institute for Near East Policy, wrote that Iraqi President Saddam Hussein tried to return to the "pre-Sadat method of settling the Arab-Israeli conflict . . . threatening to destroy Israel." What I wish to draw attention to is not what Indyk says about Hussein, but what he characterizes as the "pre-Sadat method." For Rosenthal, Indyk, and others, Sadat is unique: neither before nor after him has an Arab leader been willing to talk peace with Israel.

This sort of thing is written rather often, but is it true? The answer is an emphatic no. From before the very founding of the Jewish state, Arab leaders have shown interest in peaceful discussion and coexistence. As the late Israeli historian Simha Flapan wrote in *The Birth of Israel: Myths and Realities,* "There is, however, a good deal of evidence that Arab leaders and governments were ready to negotiate a solution to the conflict before, during and after the War of Independence."

As far back as 1919, Feisal of the prominent Hashemite family and leader of the revolt against the Ottoman Turks, showed a willingness to cooperate with the Jews. He and Chaim Weizmann, a leading Zionist, signed an agreement, which stated in Article IV:

> All' necessary measures shall be taken to encourage and stimulate immigration of Jews into Palestine on a large scale, and as quickly as possible to settle Jewish immigrants upon the land through closer

settlement and intensive cultivation of the soil. In taking such measures the Arab peasants and tenant farmers shall be protected in their rights, and shall be assisted in forwarding the economic development.

That final sentence is reminiscent of the neglected caveat about Arab rights in the Balfour Declaration. Weizmann at this time was telling the Arabs that the Zionist movement would protect their rights. But at the same time he told Western audiences that his goal was to make Palestine as Jewish as England is English. And when he said Palestine, he also meant the territory that had become, by the grace of Winston Churchill, Transjordan. ("Trans-Jordania has from the earliest time been an integral and vital part of Palestine," Weizmann said. This position has never been renounced.) In fact, the Arab peasants were not respected in their rights — which helps explain the change in the Arab attitude from accommodation to opposition.

Feisal submitted a memorandum during the Paris Peace Conference which revealed that he saw a distinction between Jews and Zionists. As recalled by U.S. aide Stephen Bonsal, Feisal wrote:

> If the views of the radical Zionists, as presented to the [Peace Conference] should prevail, the result will be a ferment, chronic unrest, and sooner or later civil war in Palestine. But I hope I will not be misunderstood. I assert that we Arabs have none of the racial or religious animosity against the Jews which unfortunately prevail in many other regions in the world. I assert that with the Jews who have been seated for some generations in Palestine our relations are excellent. But the new arrivals exhibit very different qualities from those "old settlers" as we call them, with whom we have been able to live and even cooperate on friendly terms. For want of a better word I must say that new colonists almost without exception have come in an imperialist spirit. They say that too long we have been in control of their homeland taken from them by brute force in the dark ages, but that now under the new world order we must clear out: and if we are wise, we should do so peaceably without making any resistance to what is the *fiat* of the civilized world.

Of course, Great Britain backed the Zionists and ignored the rights of the region's inhabitants, to the dismay of Feisal and the Arab people. As British Foreign Minister Arthur Balfour wrote in August 1919:

> For in Palestine we do not propose even to go through the form of consulting the wishes of the present inhabitants of the country. . . . The four great powers are committed to Zionism and Zionism, be it right or wrong, good or bad, is rooted in age-long tradition, in present needs, in future hopes, of far profounder import than the desires of

700,000 Arabs who now inhabit that ancient land. . . . In fact, so far as Palestine is concerned, the power has made no statement of fact that is not admittedly wrong, and no declaration of a policy which, at least in the letter, they have not always intended to violate.

It would be an understatement to say that the combined efforts of the British and the Zionists have left a bitter taste in the mouths of the Arabs. So it is remarkable that Arab leaders still sought accommodation with the Zionist movement and, after May 1948, the new state of Israel.

There is much documentation now in the public record regarding Emir (later King) Abdullah's secret accord with Israel. Abdullah, Feisal's brother, was made ruler of Transjordan by the British after World War I. In recent books by Avi Shlaim and Mary C. Wilson, we learn that Abdullah and Zionist leader David Ben-Gurion had a common interest in preventing a Palestinian state from coming into existence. As the idea of partition of Palestine into Jewish and Arab states won favor after World War II, Abdullah, who aspired to be king of the Arab world, backed the idea, but with a twist: part of Palestine would be a Jewish state and the rest would be annexed by Transjordan. He found an eager partner in the Zionist leadership and met with Golda Meir (then a Zionist official) more than once. Abdullah kept his plan from other Arab leaders, but when they, and especially Haji Amin al-Husayni, *mufti* of Jerusalem, suspected he was being duplicitous, they feared his ambition. Other Arab leaders also wanted at least a piece of Palestine. This is significant, because it shows that the Arabs were not united in all things and that Palestinian self-determination was not everyone's objective.

The United Nations General Assembly recommended an independent Palestinian state beside the Jewish state. What Abdullah and the Zionists could not get from the General Assembly, they would get from war. The war of 1948 is usually portrayed as a united Arab attempt to destroy Israel. It apparently was not. There was little coordination among the Arab states, which at any rate did not decide to fight until the last minute, after Israeli forces massacred Palestinians and drove thousands of others from their homes.

Jordan's British-trained Arab Legion was the most powerful of the Arab armies. But "contrary to the old historiography," wrote Israeli historian Benny Morris, "Abdullah's invasion of eastern Palestine was clearly designed to conquer territory for his kingdom — at the expense of the Palestinian Arabs — rather than to destroy the Jewish state. Indeed, the Arab Legion stuck meticulously, throughout the war, to its non-aggressive stance *vis-à-vis* the *Yishuv* [the Jewish community] and the Jewish state's territory." Morris points out that it was the Israeli forces that violated the understanding with Abdullah and "repeatedly assaulted the Arab Legion in areas earmarked by the partition resolution for Arab sovereignty." As Morris sums up, "Certainly Abdullah was far more troubled by the prospects of the emergence of a Palestinian Arab state and of an expanded Syria and an expanded Egypt on his frontiers than by the emergence of a small Jewish state."

Shlaim notes that the main concern of the other Arab states was not Israel but rather Abdullah's expansionism. They fought only half-heartedly against Israel, never committing their full strength.

The lack of a desire to conquer or destroy Israel during the war became a desire to find a *modus vivendi* after it. Each of the Arab governments sought to make peace with Ben-Gurion's government; some even offered to accept Palestinian refugees. The Israelis stonewalled and rebuffed the offers. Israel and Egypt, Lebanon, Transjordan, and Syria eventually signed armistice agreements, but no final peace treaties, with the exception of the 1979 treaty with Egypt, were ever concluded.

Secret negotiations between Abdullah and Israel continued when the war ended, with the emir ceding, essentially at gunpoint, a strip of West Bank territory containing 15 Arab villages. The 15,000 Palestinian residents were not consulted about that change in their destiny. This territorial gain was ratified in the UN-sponsored armistice negotiations.

Egypt was interested in a full settlement after the 1948 war. Its position at the postwar armistice talks tacitly accepted the recommended UN partition of Palestine and the creation of Israel, according to *Document on the Foreign Policy of Israel, vol. 3, Armistice Negotiations with the Arab States, December 1948–July 1949* and its "Companion Volume," edited by Yemima Rosenthal. Rosenthal refers to Egypt's "willingness to negotiate" and, in contrast, quotes the Israeli government's decision, in its own words, "not to agree to withdrawal from any outpost which is held by the Israeli army." Rosenthal added, "The delegation was directed not to deviate from the above-mentioned framework nor to make any concessions."

The Israeli negotiators themselves recognized Egypt's congeniality. In a January 19, 1949, note to Foreign Minister Moshe Sharett, chief negotiator Walter Eytan wrote, "Whenever we have made a suggestion sufficiently well-founded to convince [UN mediator Ralph] Bunche . . . of its reasonableness, the Egyptians have accepted it without a murmur. The Egyptians on their part have so far not put forward any suggestion which we have found it impossible to accept."

The Israeli attitude, by Eytan's own description, was far different. In a January 22, 1949, dispatch to Sharett, he wrote that, "the talks may have to go on for another four of five days. It is simply a matter of wearing the Egyptians down. The process is rather callous and extremely tiring, but we think it worthwhile making the extra effort over the next few days in view of the great political possibilities which success would open for us."

Israeli journalist Yossi Melman and Rabbi Elmer Berger have pointed out that recently declassified American and Israeli documents show that in 1949, then-President Hosni Zaim of Syria offered Israel peace for concessions on land near the sea of Galilee which was to be part of the Jewish state. Zaim, who had recently taken power, also offered to resettle up to 300,000 refugees. Prime Minister David Ben-Gurion refused to surrender "areas of strategic importance to our security."

The negotiations with Syria differed from the others since Syria was the only Arab state to have occupied Israeli territory in the war. Whereas Israel demanded in the other negotiations that the final battle lines, not international borders, be accepted, in Syria's case Israel took the opposite position. It wanted Syrian forces to move back to the international border. (Before the negotiations began, Israel had moved troops across the Syrian border.) As a result of prolonged armistice negotiations in which both sides engaged in questionable conduct, Syria withdrew from the small area it occupied during the war and a demilitarized zone was declared. (Israel's later encroachment on the zone and Syria's artillery response from the Golan Heights eventually led to the outbreak of the Six-Day War in 1967.)

The respective Israeli and Arab attitudes toward negotiation are also apparent from the proceedings of the UN's Conciliation Commission at Lausanne, Switzerland, in 1949. Historian Tom Segev has written that "the Arab states agreed to negotiate with Israel on the basis of the UN Partition Resolution of 1947." But Israel demanded that Egypt leave the Gaza Strip and Jordan the West Bank; both territories were to have been part of the Palestinian state. Israel no longer felt bound by the partition resolution, claiming that its survival required "certain vital areas not comprised originally in the share of the Jewish state."

The Arab leaders raised the refugee problem, but Israel replied that any solution would have to be part of a comprehensive peace agreement. At a private meeting between the Israeli and Egyptian delegates, Segev writes, it was clear to the Israeli members that the "Arabs 'recognized' Israel and were ready to discuss peace." But Israel did not accept the conditions. Egypt proposed that in exchange for a peace treaty, the Negev and the West Bank would become an independent Arab state where refugees could resettle as well as a buffer between Egypt and Israel. The Israelis objected on the grounds that the United Nations had allocated the Negev to the Jews. The Egyptians replied that Israel was occupying western Galilee, which had been assigned to the Palestinians, but was refusing to relinquish it. The Israelis stood firm in their determination to give up neither the Negev nor western Galilee. There was no basis for further discussions.

The Israeli officials themselves admitted that they were in no rush to reach a permanent settlement with their Arab neighbors. Foreign Minister Moshe Sharett, writes Segev, warned that "some very creative people" wanted Israel "to stop reiterating declarations about our desire for peace, since the Arab world interprets them as a sign of weakness and as an indication of our willingness to surrender. We should say the opposite," Sharett reported. "We do not need peace. We are satisfied with the present agreement. Perhaps the Arabs need peace." Segev writes that Ben-Gurion also could wait for peace; Ben-Gurion told the *London Times*, "Though I would get up in the middle of the night to sign a peace treaty, I am in no rush. I can wait ten years. We are under no pressure."

The post-armistice period saw a continuation of what had gone before. For various reasons, Arab leaders showed interest in normalization. After Gamal Abdel Nasser became leader of Egypt in 1954, his government engaged in informal discussions about peace with Sharett, who became prime minister when Ben-Gurion temporarily retired. But Sharett was repeatedly undercut by hardline officials loyal to Ben-Gurion. Nasser persisted in his efforts, despite the infamous 1954 Lavon affair, in which Israeli and Egyptian-Jewish terrorists blew up American installations in Cairo and Alexandria in an attempt to disrupt U.S.-Egyptian relations, and Israeli military attacks in the Gaza Strip in 1955. Nasser's peace initiative, involving American Quaker Elmore Jackson as a go-between, is described in *Middle East Mission: The Story of a Major Bid for Peace in the Time of Nasser and Ben-Gurion* (1983). In his book, Jackson quotes Ben-Gurion saying, "Nasser is a decent fellow who has the interest of his people genuinely at heart." And according to Jackson, Nasser said, "Egypt has no aggressive intentions toward Israel. . . . No Arab is saying now that we must destroy Israel." He was, however, concerned about Israel's offensive military power and wished to buy arms for deterrence. When the Eisenhower administration refused to sell them, Nasser turned to his only alternative, the Soviet Union (through Czechoslovakia). Rigid Cold-War thinking led U.S. officials to dismiss Nasser now as a tool of the communists, which was not true. The chance for a peace treaty was lost. About a year later, Israel, France, and Great Britain attacked Egypt in the Suez crisis. Israel captured the Sinai and Gaza Strip and did not withdraw until Washington applied immense public pressure.

Nasser did not give up on peace. Although the 1967 Six-Day War was a humiliating defeat, in February 1970 he again expressed interest in a settlement. "It would be possible," he said, "to institute a durable peace between Israel and the Arab state, not excluding economic and diplomatic relations, if Israel evacuates the occupied territories and accepts a settlement of the problem of the Palestinian refugees." Israel and its patron, the United States, were not interested. President Nixon's national security adviser, Henry Kissinger, wanted to stall any progress in the Middle East so as not to, as he saw it, reward radicals.

In November 1967 and again in 1971, King Hussein of Jordan offered recognition of, and security guarantees for, Israel in return for its withdrawal from the occupied territories. Israel rejected the offers. After the 1973 war, Henry Kissinger writes in his memoirs, the Israeli government refused to negotiate even a disengagement of forces with King Hussein, in deference to a coalition partner (the National Religious Party) that opposed the ruling Labor Party's Allon plan. That plan called for return of the West Bank to Jordan.

Anwar Sadat himself made a significant offer of peace in 1971, involving security guarantees, a return to 1967 borders and reopening of the Suez Canal, which had been closed since the 1967 war. (He and King Hussein also accepted Secretary of State William Rogers's land-for-peace plan.) It was only after Israel and the Nixon-Kissinger administration rejected Sadat's overture that he turned to war — not to destroy Israel but to regain the Sinai and be taken seriously.

According to former Secretary of State Kissinger, after the 1973 war, Syrian President Hafez al-Assad's actions "bespoke a desire for accommodation," but Israel's determination to hold the Golan Heights precluded progress toward peace. Also at this time, Yasser Arafat, chairman of the Palestine Liberation Organization, communicated his willingness to enter the peace process, but Kissinger barred his participation. Nevertheless, Palestinian interest in a two-state settlement grew. In January 1976, the UN Security Council considered a resolution, supported by the Arab states and formulated by the PLO, that called for such a settlement based on the pre-1967 borders, including "appropriate arrangements . . . to guarantee . . . the sovereignty, territorial integrity and political independence of all states in the area and their right to live in peace within secure and recognized borders" — in other words, recognition of Israel. Israel opposed the resolution, and the United States vetoed it.

At the end of 1976, Egypt submitted a resolution to the General Assembly to reconvene the Geneva Middle East conference with all parties participating. Israel and the United States opposed it. Israel feared that inclusion of the Palestinians would lead to a Palestinian state. This was consistent with an Israeli cabinet action the year before when it formally refused to accept negotiations even with Palestinians who recognized Israel and renounced terrorism. Is it true that the PLO declared that a two-state solution was a first step toward the *peaceful* establishment of a secular, democratic Palestine. But it should be understood that Israel still claimed the right to an exclusivist Jewish state in all of Mandate Palestine, including Jordan. That claim was reaffirmed by the Israeli Knesset in 1972, and to this day it has not been renounced.

This only scratches the surface, but it is sufficient to demonstrate a definite pattern, one at odds with the standard picture given in the news media. Repeated Arab offers of a negotiated peace have been turned aside by Israel. Israel's advocates may say that the offers were not sincere, but that will not do. Any one of them could have been tested with little risk. None was. (What made Sadat's offer worth testing?) At any rate, there is no basis for claiming that the Israelis have been ready to talk but have been unable to find an Arab to talk to. In a narrow sense, Israel can claim that it has "always" been ready to talk peace. But it must be realized that its willingness has always been laden with preconditions related to territory, refugees, and the denial of Palestinian self-determination. Thus today's reports about Israeli willingness to attend a U.S.-Soviet-sponsored peace conference — as long as it approves of the Palestinian delegates and no territorial concessions are required — sound like old news.

18

Who Wanted Peace? Who Wanted War? History Refutes Israel's US Image

Washington Report on Middle East Affairs, October 1991

"These are the myths and lies that Americans hear and read day after day," wrote *New York Times* columnist A. M. Rosenthal in June. "Israel blocks peace. Israel will not negotiate with the Arabs or give an inch to Palestinians." Those myths, Rosenthal wrote, distort several realities of Arab-Israeli relations:

> One is that Israel has been saying yes to peace talks with Arabs decade after decade — as Anwar El-Sadat proved, to Egypt's everlasting gain. Second reality: for all those decades every other Arab nation refused to make peace, refused to talk.

In fact, it takes an enormous evasion of reality to believe this. Arab leaders have repeatedly tried to make peace. Even Egyptian President Sadat's famous effort in late 1977 was not his first. He made a significant peace overture in 1971 and was rebuffed. But neither was Sadat's earlier offer the first from Egypt. His predecessor, Gamal Abdel Nasser, made "a major effort for a settlement with Israel" in the spring of 1955. The words are those of Elmore Jackson, a Quaker representative to the United Nations, and the go-between in Nasser's initiative.

Jackson wrote about what could have been a historic breakthrough in his 1983 book, *Middle East Mission: The Story of a Major Bid for Peace in the Time of Nasser and Ben-Gurion*. That little book alone refutes Rosenthal and anyone else who blindly chants, as though it were a mantra, that the Arabs have always wanted to destroy Israel.

In April 1955, the Egyptian ambassador to Washington and a friend of President Nasser's, Dr. Ahmed Hussein, asked the Quakers to inquire whether grounds for a settlement with Israel could be found. Jackson met with Egyptian officials first, then with Israelis, including then Prime Minister Moshe Sharett.

The Egyptians' terms included some repatriation of Palestinian refugees, compensation for those unwilling or unable to return, and boundary adjustments to link the Arab communities. Sharett's response was generally favorable, and each side regarded the other as serious. "Our meeting closed with his saying he would go anywhere to talk to President Nasser — even to Cairo," Jackson wrote. "He [Sharett] said, 'Nasser is a decent fellow who has the interest of his people genuinely at heart.'" In conversations with Nasser, Jackson learned that Egyptian leaders had conducted informal discussions with the Israeli government after Prime Minister David Ben-Gurion retired and Sharett succeeded him in 1953. But the discussions broke off when Ben-Gurion returned to the cabinet as defense minister and Israel resumed attacks against Palestinian guerrillas and Egyptian soldiers in the Gaza Strip. (Palestinian refugees would infiltrate Israel to retrieve crops and property as well as to exact vengeance for their dispossession.)

The biggest Israeli attack occurred Feb. 28, 1955, at the town of Gaza, ostensibly in retaliation for Egypt's hanging of two saboteurs in the 1954 Lavon affair, in which Israeli agents tried to sabotage Egyptian American relations by planting firebombs in U.S. diplomatic installations in Cairo and Alexandria. (Israel denounced the Egyptian charges as fabrications, only to come clean six years later. The surviving agents, released from Egyptian prisons, were welcomed as heroes in Israel.)

Nasser's confidence in the possibility of a settlement was shaken by the Israeli escalation of violence. Back in Israel, Sharett and Ben-Gurion told Jackson that, because of the guerrilla attacks, they had ordered a massive strike against the southern Gaza town of Khan Yunis. The order was canceled when Jackson warned that the attack would probably end the short-lived negotiations. Egypt accepted a ceasefire proposed by the UN Truce Supervision Organization, but Israel equivocated. A short time later, Ariel Sharon's Unit 101 went ahead with the attack on Khan Yunis. It struck an Egyptian police station and also terrorized a village. Thirty-six people were killed, including civilians.

The following day, Sharett asked Jackson to fly to Cairo to tell Nasser that, although Israel had to retaliate for the guerrilla attack, it wanted to end the reciprocal violence. Ben-Gurion said he was willing to meet Nasser. Jackson returned to Cairo and was able to head off the mobilization Nasser had been contemplating in response to the attack.

Nasser said he would try to restrain the guerrillas, but that it was not always possible because of their decentralized command. (Documents later captured by Israel confirmed his attempts to quiet the border.) Jackson shuttled between Cairo and Jerusalem trying to arrange a prisoner exchange and promote a meeting between Ben-Gurion and Nasser. Ben-Gurion was interested, but Nasser, though not dismissive, feared he could be embarrassed by an Israeli attack during the negotiations. The prospects for success faded in September 1955, when Nasser arranged to buy Soviet arms from Czechoslovakia.

According to Jackson, Nasser felt increasingly vulnerable to Israeli military might (warplanes routinely violated Egyptian airspace). He could not accept the conditions the Eisenhower administration insisted on attaching to an arms sale. At a press conference after the Czech deal, Nasser said:

> Egypt has no aggressive intentions toward Israel. War is not an easy decision for anybody, especially for me.
>
> No Arab is saying now that we must destroy Israel. The Arabs are asking only that refugees receive their natural right to life and their lost property, which was promised to them by United Nations resolutions seven years ago.
>
> No, we are not aggressive. The threat is from the other side. I have said many times that I want to build up my country. Now I am obliged to give defense priority over development.
>
> It was the other way around before Ben-Gurion's vicious attack on Gaza February 28. . . . There was an arms race going on, but it was one-sided. Israel was running and we were standing still.

Nasser's feeling of vulnerability was no fantasy. A year later, in 1956, Israel, Britain and France attacked Egypt. When the war broke out, Sharett, who by then was out of the cabinet, wrote in his diary, "We are the aggressors," Israel conquered the Sinai for the first time, but later gave it back under U.S. pressure. Israel would conquer it again in 1967.

Nasser's successor, Sadat, would make his own bid for peace in 1971, only to have it rejected by Israel and the Nixon-Kissinger administration. It took another war to force Israel to take Sadat's bid for peace seriously.

19

The Road Not Taken

Middle East Policy, Vol. 1, No. 4, November 1992

Book Review: *The Road Not Taken: Early Arab-Israeli Negotiations*, by Itamar Rabinovich. New York: Oxford University Press, 1991.

Itamar Rabinovich, a scholar who is currently Israel's chief negotiator with Syria, wrote *The Road Not Taken* in response to revisionist historians whose work has at least implicitly indicated that Israel's first leaders missed opportunities for peace with the Arabs in the years after the 1948 war. (Those revisionists include Simha Flapan, Benny Morris, and Avi Shlaim.) He faults the revisionists mostly for their method and interpretation but also for the materials they draw on.

As he writes in the final chapter:

> The revisionist school focused its research on the following questions: Were opportunities missed for making peace? Who is to blame for the failure to make peace? What are the myths and accepted truths that can and should be debated? The revisionist school, however, was hampered by several flaws — its point of departure was political and moralistic rather than academic; it relied almost exclusively on Israeli and Western rather than Arab sources, thereby presenting an unbalanced picture; and it introduced emotional issues that were not always the most important ones.

Those criticisms will strike some readers as hollow. The criticism of the revisionists' reliance on Israeli and Western sources is curious since Rabinovich relies mainly on the same sources: official Israeli, American, and other documents made public in the 1980s and participants' diaries and memoirs. Rabinovich perhaps used Arab newspapers and memoirs more than other writers. No account has been able to use Arab government records because they have apparently not been made public. One might expect that the preponderance of Israeli materials would redound to Israel's benefit, but Rabinovich somehow believes it prejudices Israel. One could easily imagine a critic of Israel being chided for relying too heavily on Arab sources.

Rabinovich does credit the revisionists with revealing "significant weaknesses in the traditional historiography and orthodox version of Arab-Israeli relations that were dominant in Israel. All arguments made by revisionist historians," Rabinovich adds, "need not be accepted in order to recognize the need to correct and refine the orthodox version." The opening of diplomatic archives has "exposed a political reality far more complex than that portrayed by traditional scholarship." One of the "weaknesses" of the orthodox version that falls to Rabinovich's study is the notion that Israel faced a monolithic, implacably hostile and anti-Jewish Arab world that refused to engage in any civil relations with the Jewish state.

Rabinovich writes that he does not seek to apportion blame or to "focus on the ever-intriguing issue of 'missed opportunities.'" Nevertheless, he suggests that despite the willingness of pragmatic Arab leaders to negotiate, we cannot be certain that Israel's conduct was responsible for the failure of the peace talks. Rabinovich examines the start-and-stop negotiations between Israel and Syria, Transjordan, and Egypt and concludes that Israel sincerely tried to reach agreements. The obstacles, he writes, were on the Arab side. "The three sets of negotiations we have considered in this book reveal the extent to which the conflict with Israel had already been internalized in the Arab consciousness by the end of the 1948 war." Rabinovich understands that each nation's government had its advocates of negotiation. But he concludes that they faced constraints that kept them from consummating a peace.

Rabinovich presents the reader with a glut of details (despite the brevity of the book), but with all those trees to contemplate, it is hard to keep the forest in view. The details are often enlightening, even to the point of working against the book's theme that the Arab regimes were unreliable peace partners. For example, in 1949 Husni Zaim staged a coup in Syria (with the blessing of the United States) and attempted to negotiate peace with Israel. His proposal included the resettlement of 300,000 Palestinian refugees-nearly half. Antirevisionists point to Zaim's own overthrow later that year to show that even if Israel had been more willing to make concessions, the chaos of Syrian politics would have undermined a peace agreement. Rabinovich points out, however, that Zaim's successors did not criticize his overtures to Israel and did not want relations with Israel to worsen. Rabinovich asks whether Israel missed a historic opportunity with Syria and responds: "The question cannot be answered definitively" but asserts that "Ben-Gurion's refusal to meet Husni Zaim in April-May 1949 did not destroy the prospect of reaching an agreement that would have transformed the Arab-Israeli relations." Others will draw different conclusions.

Rabinovich provides another juicy fact when he notes that in January 1950, Egypt formed a new government, with Mahmud Azmi as liaison with Israel. Who was Azmi? "Azmi was not a professional diplomat but a political figure associated with the Wafd party," writes Rabinovich. "Azmi had a Jewish wife and thus empathy for Israel's concerns." That is hardly the sort of appointment that would be made by an implacably hostile regime. Azmi was no insignificant figure; he was a member of the Egyptian delegation to the United Nations and an influential adviser to Egypt's foreign minister.

In the case of Transjordan, we already know from Avi Shlaim's work that King Abdullah desperately sought a peace agreement with Israel. Rabinovich strives to show that the government was increasingly out of the king's control and that his desire for peace was impotent.

Thus *The Road Not Taken* helps to demolish the Zionist claim that Israel could not find Arab interlocutors with whom to talk peace. The real issue is whether Israel, intentionally or not, let chances for peace slip by. The answer to that question depends on one's premises. If one believes that the creation of Israel entailed no injustice and that its founders were justified in securing all the territory it could, then one will conclude that Israel did nothing wrong in the crucial years beginning in 1948. But if one holds other premises, the answer will be different.

The issues that blocked peace agreements might not have seemed so important had Israel's leaders had a different attitude about their state and its place in the Middle East. An obstacle between Israel and both Egypt and Transjordan was the disposition of the Negev Desert. Most of it was assigned to the Jewish state in the UN partition resolution. Egypt and Transjordan both wished, for strategic and political reasons, to acquire at least some of it. Israel refused to compromise and invoked the UN partition in its defense. Yet for Israel, UN intentions carried no weight when it came to the western edge of the Negev and western Galilee, which was supposed to be part of the new Arab state, but was taken by Israel in the war. This is a recurring theme: for Israel, borders were negotiable only when Israel stood to gain. Again, with Syria an agreement might have been reached, but Israel would not consider the Syrian proposal to move the border westward to the middle of the Lake of Tiberias. Security does not appear to have been the chief Israeli concern in these matters. The other stumbling block was the refugees. Most Israeli leaders were opposed to allowing any of them to return to their homes whether they had lived on land allocated to the Zionists or to the Palestinians. (The Palestinians were permitted no official status in the peace talks.) That refusal had an undeniable dampening effect on the postwar negotiations. But the Israeli attitude was that if those matters precluded formal peace treaties, then the Jewish state could get along well enough with the armistice agreements. Nothing in Rabinovich's study contradicts Israeli diplomat Eliyahu Sasson's 1949 observation that "the Jews believe it is possible to obtain peace without either a minimal or a maximal price."

What Rabinovich's study is most assailable for, then, is context-dropping. He takes for granted the justice of Israel's demands and implies that Arab response was obstructionist. There is much to criticize in the position of the Arab governments. They often put their own ambitions ahead of concern regarding the developing Palestinian tragedy. But regardless of the conduct of the Arab nations, the crafting of the Israeli nation was an imposition on the Palestinians and the step that initiated the cycle of violence. Since 1917 Great Britain, the League of Nations, and the United Nations were bent on giving away land that was not theirs to give and thereby denying Palestinian individuals the right to determine their own destinies. In 1947 Jews made up only one-third of the population of Palestine and owned less than 7 percent of the land. Yet the United Nations gerrymandered a partition that gave the Zionist movement more than half the land with a slight majority of the population. Zionist paramilitary forces then launched operations to rid the land of Palestinians both inside and outside their sector. The results included massacres of innocents and hundreds of thousands of refugees. Only then did the Arab states take irresolute, uncoordinated measures to block further Israeli expansion.

Rabinovich is not completely oblivious of the context. He acknowledges that the Arab governments were worried about Israel's territorial aims, and their negotiating positions reflected that worry. Nor were they irrational for having such a concern, considering that Israel relied on the intimidation of superior force and continued to acquire territory through military action after ceasefires had been agreed to and even after an armistice had been signed with Egypt. (Nowhere in Rabinovich is there the suggestion that the Arabs were motivated by anti-Semitism.)

This neglected context gives shape to Rabinovich's often shapeless data. Considering how Israel was created and with whose aid and how the Palestinians were cleared from the land, why wouldn't even the most pragmatic Arab politician be embarrassed to appear too eager to negotiate with Israel? Rabinovich makes clear that Arab leaders believed they needed a significant concession from Israel to make an agreement acceptable to their constituencies. And considering Israel's origins, how appropriate was it for Ben-Gurion et al. to confront the Arab world as if concessions were due them? While no one should have expected Israel's leaders to admit and redress the injustices, less presumptuous leaders might have understood the importance of turning Israel into something resembling a normal Middle East state as rapidly as possible. Such a policy would have required a humility and a sagacity not evident in Ben-Gurion and most of his colleagues. That policy represents the real road that was not taken.

Whether it would have led to lasting peace cannot be known for certain, but I am not nearly as sure as Rabinovich that it would not have.

20

Podhoretz: Revising the History of the Palestinian Dispossession

Washington Report on Middle East Affairs, March 1992, Page 46.

> The plain truth is that the Arab-Israeli conflict has from the beginning been rooted in the refusal of the Arab peoples to accept the existence of a sovereign Jewish state in 'their' part of the world, no matter where its boundaries might be drawn and irrespective of what its policies might or might not be.

So writes Norman Podhoretz in the January issue of his magazine, *Commentary*. In criticizing the Bush administration for what he regards as its irrational preoccupation with the Palestinian problem, Podhoretz denies that that problem is the key to the wider Arab-Israeli conflict.

"The war against the Jewish state was launched by the Arabs long before the existence of a distinct Palestinian nationality was recognized even by the Arab world itself," he writes. "Nor, during the 19 years of Jordanian control over the West Bank, did anyone speak of establishing an independent Palestinian state there." Podhoretz goes on to target "Arab propaganda, which has pulled off the Orwellian trick of transmuting a war by the Arab world against the Jewish state into a war by the Jewish state against the Palestinian people."

A more perfect example of willful blindness could not be found in an American commentator. Here is the prose of one who believes that words determine reality. In his cocksure manner, Podhoretz makes two claims: 1) that Arabs have an ingrained, unprovoked hatred of Jews, and 2) that the Arabs would have opposed a Jewish state in the Middle East regardless of the particular circumstances of its founding. How does he know this? Podhoretz doesn't say.

Yet he ignores what we do know, namely, that the Jewish state was established where people already lived. The early political Zionists too believed — or at least hoped — that words could shape reality.

They said repeatedly that Palestine was a land without a people awaiting a people without a land. Some knew better. When Theodore Herzl's friend Max Nordau went to Palestine in the 19th century, he was surprised to find people — Palestinians — living in this people-less land.

"I didn't know that," he said. "But then we are committing an injustice." When Herzl had a Zionist student leader, Leo Motzkin, tour Palestine, Motzkin reported: "One must admit that the density of the population does not give the visitor much cause for cheer. In whole stretches throughout the land one constantly comes across large Arab villages, and it is an established fact that the most fertile areas of our [sic!] country are occupied by Arabs."

When Herzl himself traveled to Palestine, he failed to mention the Arabs in his notes. These were the same people he elsewhere had said "We shall try to spirit . . . across the border" after denying them employment in their own land.

In fairness, Herzl's biographer, Ernst Pawel, points out that the founder of Zionism was complex. Before the Third Zionist Congress, he wrote in his diary: "My Testament for the Jewish People: Build your state so that the stranger will feel at ease among you."

This was one piece of advice that was not taken by the state's founders. The Palestinian Arabs were not only slighted in early Zionist writings, they also were treated badly.

In 1891, the Jewish writer Ahad Ha'Am described the conduct of the early Zionist settlers: "Serfs they were in the lands of the Diaspora. Now, as they suddenly find themselves enjoying unconstrained freedom, they become despots themselves. They treat the Arabs with hostility and cruelty, deprive them of their rights, offend them without cause, and even boast of these deeds; and nobody among us opposed this despicable inclination."

Some years later, Ahad Ha'Am pointed out that the Zionists "wax angry towards those who remind them that there is still another people in Eretz Israel that has been living here and does not intend at all to leave." In a letter to a settler he wrote, "I can't put up with the idea that our brethren are morally capable of behaving in such a way to . . . another people, and unwittingly the thought comes to mind: If this is so now, what will our relations to the others be like if, at the end of time, we shall really achieve power in Eretz Israel? And if this be the 'Messiah,' I do not wish to see his coming."

There were many other expressions of grief over how the Zionists treated the indigenous population, the boycott of Arab labor and the evictions from the land. For example, in 1907 Dr. Yitzhak Epstein, an early settler, wrote:

> Among the grave questions linked with the concept of our people's renaissance on its own soil, there is one question more weighty than all the others put together. This is the question of our relations with

the Arabs. Our own national aspirations depend upon the correct solution of this problem. . . .

The regrettable fact that our attention could be diverted from such a fundamental question, and after 30 years of settlement activity it is being talked about as if it is a new topic — all this proves that our movement is unreasonable. . . . We forget that the people now living in this land also has a heart and a soul. . . . We shall commit a grave sin against our people and our future if we throw away so lightly our principal weapons: righteousness and sincerity.

These first-hand observations by Jewish Palestinians and others paint a picture quite opposite from the one Podhoretz proffers. It was the political Zionists who refused to accept the existence of the Palestinian Arabs. By in effect making war on them, the Zionists disrupted peaceful relations between Arab and Jew.

Even in the late 1940s, there was no monolithic Arab objection to a Jewish state, as historian Avi Shlaim notes. King Abdullah of Transjordan formed a partnership with the Zionists to quash the proposed Palestinian state and did not challenge Israel. And the prominent Nashashibi family of Palestine, rival of the Mufti Haj Amin Al-Husseini, supported partition and peaceful coexistence. Thus Podhoretz depends upon ignorance of the writings of early Zionists for acceptance of his myth of a congenital Arab hatred of Jews and categorical hostility to a Jewish homeland.

21

Israel's War on Gaza: The Context

Free Association, July 21, 2014

Any discussion of Israel's war on Gaza that does not focus on 1) the Zionist military's and Israel's systematic ethnic cleansing of Palestinians through roughly 1948 (that's how Palestinian refugees ended up in the Gaza Strip); 2) the military conquest of the West Bank and the Gaza Strip in 1967; 3) the Israeli/Egyptian blockade of the Gaza Strip since 2007, following the Israeli withdrawal in 2005 (yes, the occupation ended, but Gaza remains a prison camp — as though guards left a prison but maintained strict control over who and what — food, medicine, infrastructure supplies, etc. — could enter and leave); and 4) the exploitation of the kidnapping and murders of three young Israeli residents of an illegal West Bank settlement (one a 19-year-old soldier) to rout Hamas (which denied responsibility; it normally claims credit for his acts) in the West Bank (Israeli forces rearrested several hundred West Bank Palestinians, including some who had been released in an earlier prisoner exchange; political leaders stirred up revenge fever and one Palestinian youth was burned to death, while another was severely beaten by police) — any discussion that fails to take all these things into account is worse than worthless. It is crudely dishonest. (Compare the reaction to the murder of the three Israelis with the murder by Israeli soldiers of two Palestinian youth on May 15 while peacefully commemorating the 1948 destruction of Palestine, known as the *Nakba*.)

Hamas is wrong to fire rockets at civilians (though few hit their targets), even considering that the villages those civilians live in were once Palestinian villages that Zionist/Israeli forces seized during the 1947–1948 ethnic cleansing. The rocketing, however, is a sign of weakness versus Israel, not strength, and must not permit us to overlook this background of brutality against Palestinians. This year Hamas agreed to join the Palestinian Authority's coalition government (after the Israeli government, again, made a mockery of "peace talks") signaling an endorsement of the PA's agenda — including recognition of Israel. Was this a welcome step for the Israeli government? No. It immediately set out to punish the Palestinians for this new unity — it prefers a divided Palestinian community and a Hamas it can demonize. (Years ago, the Israeli government nurtured the emergence of Hamas precisely because it could serve as a religious rival to the popular secular Fatah.)

Hamas, it is true, maintains a charter that calls for the destruction of Israel, but that has not kept it from issuing statements over the years — joining the coalition is only the most recent — indicating a willingness to accept Israel as part of a two-state solution. It is Israel that has broken truces with Hamas. Its soldiers have often killed and injured Gazans minding their own business on their own side of the fence between the Gaza Strip and Israel, while Hamas leaders have been assassinated by the Israeli government following offers of a truce. It is clear that Israeli leaders do not want a Hamas they can make peace with, just as they don't want an Iran with which they can have normal relations. They need the specter of an "existential threat" to maintain their iron rule. In particular, Prime Minister Benjamin Netanyahu must push this intransigent line especially hard to keep the members of his coalition government who are further to the right than he is (yes, further) on the reservation.

Israeli leaders and spokesmen continually say that their only goal in this war is "peace and quiet" for the people of Israel. Maybe a decent goal would include justice for the long-suffering Palestinians. This is not about Hamas, an organization that endangers the innocent people it claims to champion with futile yet criminal activities like the rocket fire. This does not let the Israelis and their brutal response — underwritten by American taxpayers and supporter by their rulers — off the hook, however. On the contrary, since Israel created and maintains the open-air prison, it is responsible for all the evils that go on inside. Its hardline policies embolden the most extreme elements and undercut the moderate voices. Has the "peace process" even slowed the building of illegal settlements on Palestinian land in the West Bank?

No, it's not about Hamas; it's about the Palestinians, who do not deserve this punishment at the hands of the Israelis.

BBC reporter Jon Donnison says that Israeli police spokesman Micky Rosenfeld told him that the perpetrators of the kidnapping/murders were a Hamas-affiliated cell that did not take orders from the Hamas leadership and that had defied the leadership in the past. According to journalist Max Blumenthal, the Netanyahu government early on had reason to know who the perpetrators were, but used his broad accusation of Hamas as a pretext for cracking down on the organization in the West Bank, arresting hundreds of members in a mass sweep and holding them without charge, a move that could in no way be related to legitimate law-enforcement investigation into the kidnapping-murders.

For further discussion of the larger context, see Ramzy Baroud's "Ravaging Gaza: The War Netanyahu Cannot Possibly Win." Also worthwhile are Nathan Thrall's "How the West Chose War in Gaza," Neve Gordon's "On 'Human Shielding' in Gaza," and Omar Baddar's "Debunking the Myths about Gaza: The Truth Behind Israeli and Palestinian Talking Points."

22

Israel's 1967 Attack Was Aggression; Israel's Current Occupation Is Illegal

Washington Report on Middle East Affairs, July 1991

In the *Wall Street Journal* of April 22, Harry V. Lerner, an attorney in Bethesda, Maryland, issued a challenge to anyone who believes that the Israeli occupation of the West Bank and the Gaza Strip is illegal. In his article "Read the Law: Gaza Is Not Kuwait," Lerner states that the Israeli occupation is in no way parallel to Saddam Hussein's occupation of Kuwait. "Under international law," he wrote, "an occupying power is a state that holds territory taken from its legitimate sovereign in an act of aggression. . . . Iraq in Kuwait was an occupying power in the classic sense of the term. Israel in the West Bank and Gaza is not."

Lerner asserts that UN Security Council Resolution 242, which was passed six months after the Six-Day War of June 1967, did not condemn Israel, or refer to an Israeli invasion, or demand an unconditional withdrawal from the territories.

The dictionary says that something inadmissible is "not to be allowed, accepted, granted, or conceded."

"The reason for these omissions is simple," Lerner writes. "The Security Council concluded in 1967 that Israel had not committed an armed attack or invasion against its neighbors, but was in fact the victim of aggression by the Arab states. Until the Arab states comply with the clause of Resolution 242 that expressed Israel's right to 'live in peace within secure and recognized boundaries free from threats or acts of force,' Israel's status in the West Bank and Gaza was held to be that of a lawful administrator, holding territories taken in a defensive war."

Lerner acknowledges that Israel actually launched the Six-Day War, but argues that it came in response to acts of war by Egypt, after nearly 20 years of "defensive war" against the Arabs. He also acknowledges the use of the term "occupied" in Resolution 242, but explains that it means merely "possessed" or "taken into possession" without a violation of international law.

According to Lerner, Resolution 242 does not require total Israeli withdrawal from the territories, only negotiation between the parties to the conflict. Citing the late U.S. Ambassador to the UN Arthur Goldberg, Lerner wrote that the "territory for peace" formula "is not a principle under 242. It is an option available to Israel." In other words, Israel has no prior obligation to withdraw from the territories. In fact, if Lerner is right, Israel and Jordan could legally sign a treaty establishing Israeli sovereignty over the West Bank.

The first thing to be said about Lerner's position is that it is highly selective. Lerner ignores the preamble to Resolution 242, the second paragraph of which begins, "Emphasizing the inadmissibility of the acquisition of territory by war." The dictionary says that something inadmissible is "not to be allowed, accepted, granted, or conceded." One cannot have a right to the inadmissible. Furthermore, in 1980 the UN Security Council said the Geneva Convention applies to all the occupied territories. So much for Lerner's claim that "under 242 Israel is in possession of the West Bank and Gaza as a matter of right, not as an occupying power."

According to the diplomat who drafted the language of 242, Lord Caradon, the preamble clears up any ambiguity in the resolution's call for "withdrawal of Israel's armed forces from territories occupied in the recent conflict." Israel and its partisans never tire of asserting that the absence of the definite article "the" from before "territories" means that a full withdrawal is not required. Lord Caradon has said, "The text means all and not some of the territories." He has pointed out that in the other four official UN languages (French, Russian, Spanish, and Chinese), the phrase "the territories" is used.

Thus, the resolution does condemn the taking of the land and demands withdrawal. The resolution also affirms "the right [of all states in the area] to live in peace within secure and recognized boundaries." But this implicitly and logically must include the right of the Palestinians to secure and recognized borders, because any alternative would violate the preamble. Lerner's sleight of hand notwithstanding, these principles amount to the familiar "land-for-peace" formula.

This is not to say that Resolution 242 is unflawed. It was a troubling compromise, the most outstanding deficiency of which was the short shrift given to the Palestinians, who were called merely "refugees." But regarding the status of Israel's possession of the territories, the resolution is clear.

To make his thesis fly, Lerner must rely on a twisted interpretation of the Six-Day War. The Israeli attack on Egypt that launched the war was neither a defensive measure nor a response to perceived acts of war. Indeed, President Nasser had asked the United Nations Emergency Force to leave Egyptian territory, placed troops in the Sinai, and announced that the Straits of Tiran were closed to Israeli and Israel-bound ships. But these moves came after overt Israeli threats against Egypt's ally Syria.

Nevertheless, Israel's leaders did not regard Nasser's acts as threatening. As Mordecai Bentov, at the time a member of the Israeli government, said, "The entire story of the danger of extermination was invented in every detail, and exaggerated a posteriori to justify the annexation of new Arab territory."

What Lerner ignores is that Zionist and Israeli leaders have never dropped their dubious claim to the whole of Palestine. As Israel's first prime minister, David Ben-Gurion, said before the state's founding, "No Zionist can forgo the smallest portion of the Land of Israel."

In 1967, Israel seized the hoped-for opportunity to acquire territory it had always aspired to possess. Jordan merely provided a pretext when it responded to the Israeli attack on its treaty partner, Egypt.

Regardless of whether King Hussein was right or wrong in attacking Israel, it is unjust to blame the Palestinians of the West Bank. They did not make Jordanian policy in 1967, just as the Gazans did not make Egyptian policy. In fact, the West Bank Palestinians were under the king's jurisdiction only because his grandfather, King Abdullah, and Israel had conspired in 1948 to deprive them of their own state. Jordan's control of the West Bank was as inadmissible as Israel's.

No advocate of moral and political individualism can justify denying the Palestinians self-determination because of something over which they had no control. Both legally and morally, the occupation is wrong.

23

The Golan Heights:
A History of Israeli Aggression

Washington Report on Middle East Affairs, November 1991

As the prospects of a Middle East peace conference inched toward realization and the "land-for-peace" principle moved to center stage, Israel's apologists in the United States launched an effort to persuade the American public that asking Israel to give up the occupied territories was like asking it to commit suicide. The territories, we are told repeatedly, were taken in self-defense after the Arabs launched an aggressive war in 1967. Therefore, Israel has no obligation to return them, since its very survival is at stake.

This argument is pressed most vigorously in the case of the Golan Heights, which until the Six-Day War of June 1967 were part of Syria. William Safire of the *New York Times* took the standard Israeli line when he wrote in July that the Golan Heights were "so often used as the launching site of attacks on Israel, and won from Syria after its 1967 aggression." Other examples could be given. According to this line, the peaceful farmers of nonthreatening low-lying kibbutzim were continually shelled by bloodthirsty Syrians from the Golan's strategic vantage point. Israel had no choice but to seize the property. Returning it would only invite future repetition of the aggression.

Just as one is apt to get a distorted view of a movie plot if one walks in after the show has started, so one is bound to misconstrue events involving the Golan Heights if one looks no further than the standard version of this story. Yes, there was shelling from the Heights. But an important question is, what preceded the shelling? The answer is: much.

We have to go back to the aftermath of the 1948 war between the new state of Israel and the Arab countries. In that war, fighting occurred between Israel and Syria along their border. Although the Israeli side of the border was part of the land allocated to the Zionists by the 1947 UN partition resolution, it contained fertile farmland and villages long occupied by Palestinians. Syria occupied a small part of this land during the war, but withdrew under an armistice agreement, which also required the demilitarization of the territory by both sides. Under the agreement, the Jewish and Arab villages were to coexist, protected by police forces drawn from their respective communities. The armistice agreement was to be temporary, pending a peace treaty. Syrian President Hosni Zaim offered a full peace agreement in return for concessions on Palestinian land, but Prime Minister David Ben-Gurion turned him down.

Instead of negotiating for peace, Israel declared sovereignty over the demilitarized zone. To carry this out, it violated the prohibitions on having military forces and fortifications in the zone by disguising soldiers as police. It also aggressively developed the area, draining water from Arab farms, leveling Arab villages, driving out residents, building roads and transplanting trees in order to move the frontier eastward to the old Palestine border. Israel refused to let the protests of the UN observers stand in the way. Swedish General Carl von Horn, of the UN peacekeeping forces, observed that "gradually, beneath the glowering eyes of the Syrians, who held the high ground overlooking Zion, the area had become a network of Israeli canals and irrigation channels edging up against and always encroaching on Arab-owned property."

This policy continued well into the 1950s. Most of the 2,000 Arabs living in the zone had been forced out by 1956. Many moved to the sloping land below the Golan Heights. In response to the expulsion of Arabs from the zone, the otherwise helpless Syrian forces on the Heights began firing on Israelis, particularly when, each year, their tractors plowed further into the demilitarized zone. General von Horn was convinced the instances of firing would not have occurred without the specific Israeli provocations.

This finds some concurrence with former Israeli General Matityahu Peled, who said that more than half of the border clashes before the 1967 war "were a result of our security policy of maximum settlement in the demilitarized area." Israel retaliated for the shelling. In April 1967, after an incident that began with an Israeli tractor incursion, Israel launched a big air attack that cost Syria six planes, one of them shot down over Damascus. One hundred Syrians were killed. This was the direct prelude to the Six-Day War. Israel was able to cast itself in the role of victim by pointing to Syria's bellicose rhetoric, its (modest) plan to divert the Jordan River's headwaters, and its support for Palestinian guerrillas. But these were more than offset by Israel's own water-diversion plan, its own bellicosity, and its own expansionist designs.

Israel of course took the Golan Heights in the Six-Day War — in an attack launched more than a day after Syria had agreed to a ceasefire. What the Israeli government did after that is instructive. Contrary to its claim that it needs the Golan as a safety buffer, Israel began settling residents in that territory, which it annexed in 1981. So far 11,500 Israelis have settled in 32 towns, kibbutzim, and agricultural cooperatives in the 500-square-mile territory. Obviously, settled territory cannot be a buffer against a hostile neighbor. As General Peled observed, "The very act of populating the territories is an act which contradicts the concept of secure borders." Had Israel actually been seeking a depth of defense, it would not have moved population up to its new border with Syria.

The history of the dispute involving the Golan Heights belies Israel's argument that it must retain the territory for its security. That is not what the facts demonstrate. Israel's leaders see the Golan Heights as part of Eretz Israel, and thus the property of the Jewish people. Security is not the issue. On the contrary, Israel's security depends on a just settlement with the Palestinians and its neighbors. But that is precisely what is undermined by Israel's expansionist land policy.

24

The 'Jordan Option' Is Based Upon Blatant Falsification of History

Washington Report on Middle East Affairs, February 1992

Benjamin Netanyahu, the Israeli official whom my colleague Leon Hadar calls the "Joe Isuzu of the Middle East," lived up to his billing during his service as spokesman for the Israeli delegation at the December peace talks in Washington. "We think," he said, "that the Palestinian problem should be resolved within the context of Jordan, that is the national aspiration side, which would be solved within that context."

For anyone still tuned in, Netanyahu continued: "We envision an ultimate settlement that has from the desert to the sea two states. A state — an Arab state — that is Jordan of course, that compromises a Palestinian majority and satisfies the national aspirations of the Palestinian Arabs — and a Jewish state."

In other words, there already is a state for the Arabs who call themselves Palestinians: Jordan. The Arabs, he said, "are trying to create an artificial state [in the occupied territories] on the false assumption that there is a separate peoplehood, Palestinian . . . on this small rock, this barren rock, called the West Bank. They're saying that a new people has formed. That's simply not true. No one will tell me that an Arab living in Nablus or an Arab living in Hebron, or an Arab living in Bethlehem, a Palestinian living there, is of a different people than his brother or his cousin or his mother that is living 20 miles away in Amman or in Irbid."

All this recalls Golda Meir's invidious remark: "How can we return the occupied territories? There is nobody to return them to. . . . There was no such thing as Palestinians. It was not as though there was a Palestinian people in Palestine considering itself a Palestinian people, and we came and threw them out and took their country away from them. They did not exist."

Netanyahu's tack is so ridiculously false to the historical reality as to call into question his good faith. The fraudulent history upon which both Meir and Netanyahu draw was elaborated in one of those propaganda pieces by the organization amusingly called Facts and Logic About the Middle East (FLAME). As the ad put it, "All of 'Palestine' — east and west of the Jordan River — was part of the League of Nations mandate. Under the Balfour Declaration all of it was to be the 'national home for the Jewish people.' In violation of this mandate, Great Britain severed the entire area east of the Jordan — about 75 percent of Palestine — and gave it to the Arabs, who created on it the kingdom of Transjordan."

In fact, the British never promised the entire mandate area to the Zionists. The Balfour Declaration said only that the British government approved of the "establishment in Palestine of a national home for the Jewish people." The British had rejected the Zionist draft declaration calling for "recognizing Palestine as the National Home for the Jewish people."

Contrary to FLAME's contention that Britain violated the mandate by severing Transjordan from Palestine, what the British actually did was violate the evolution of the Middle East by severing Transjordan from Syria. During the 400-year rule by the Ottoman Turks, Palestine and Transjordan were part of separate administrative divisions. Palestine was divided between the Wilayet of Beirut and the Sanjak of Jerusalem. Transjordan was part of the Wilayet of Syria.

At the end of World War I, the area that became Transjordan continued to be ruled initially from Damascus and continued to have a character different from that of the area west of the Jordan River. Great Britain had no problem with this arrangement until the French drove the Hashemite scion and British client Feisal from the throne in Damascus. As historian Mary C. Wilson writes: "Britain did not want to see France extend its control southward to the borders of Palestine and closer to the Suez Canal. It suddenly became important to know 'what is the 'Syria' for which the French received a mandate at [the] San Remo [conference]?' and 'does it include Transjordania?' The British foreign secretary, Lord Curzon, decided that it did not, and that Britain henceforth would regard the area as independent, but in the 'closest relation' with Palestine." As a result, Transjordan was created, with Feisal's brother Abdullah, another British client, as ruler.

It must be noted that the League of Nations mandate system had no objective legitimacy. It was merely a form of colonialism devised by the stronger British and French to maintain control over strategic parts of the weaker Arab world. Transjordan was not Britain's to give to the Arabs, who already had it, just as Palestine was not Britain's to give to the Zionists. Thus, Lord Balfour's privately expressed thoughts of drawing the Jewish border east of the Jordan River are of no moral import.

Palestinians have lived on the West Bank with legitimacy for millennia; fathers have handed down property to their children. That is what entitles them to the territory and makes it a proper homeland. (If Palestinians choose to confederate with Jordan, that of course is their business alone and none of Israel's.) Yes, there is a Palestinian majority in Jordan, though it takes inordinate chutzpah for Israel to raise that point. Those Palestinians are the refugees from the 1947–1948 and 1967 exoduses that resulted from the Israeli policy of ridding Eretz Israel of non-Jews.

FLAME asserts that "the so-called 'Palestinians' are no more different from the Arabs in the neighboring countries of Lebanon, Syria and Jordan, than Wisconsinites are from Iowans." It should not take much reflection to see how cruelly collectivist that statement is. Should it comfort the Wisconsinites, were they forcibly relocated to Iowa, to know they are no different from Iowans? What if the Jews of Crown Heights were "transferred" involuntarily to Tel Aviv? Would it be just for the non-Jews who replaced them to say: "No big deal; they're all Jews, right?"

The view that it does not matter whether a particular Arab lives (regardless of his wishes) in Nablus or Amman because both are Arab cities callously ignores the individual's life, aspirations, and freedom. Such an outlook may come naturally to socialist Israel. It is not something that individualist America should be asked to countenance — or subsidize.

25

The Politics of Partition

Middle East Policy, Vol. 1, No. 3, September 1992.

Book Review: *The Politics of Partition: King Abdullah, the Zionists and Palestine, 1921–1951*, by Avi Shlaim. New York: Columbia University Press, 1990.

As the Middle East stands on the threshold of a possible new phase in the peace process, it is perhaps a good time to reconsider how the present situation was reached. As the popular history has it, in 1947 the United Nations partitioned Palestine into Jewish and Arab states. The Zionists, according to this rendition, supported partition: the Arabs universally opposed it: and when Israel declared its statehood on May 15,1948, the Arab nations, egged on by the Arab inhabitants of Palestine, invaded the new nation in an attempt to destroy it. Against all odds, the valiant nascent state withstood the fearsome coordinated attack and built a prosperous society. The Arab parts of Palestine were taken by Jordan and Egypt, which, along with the other Arab states, maintained a state of war with Israel and several more times tried to destroy it. In one of those attempts, the 1967 Six-Day War, Israel defensively seized the remainder of Palestine.

In recent years, a number of Israeli and Jewish historians have taken a fresh look at this account of events and have decided that it is wrong in fundamental ways. One of those historians, Tom Segev, has written that the "founding fathers of Israel were much less idealistic and more cynical than was commonly assumed. The 'good old days' were not so good after all."

Avi Shlaim is firmly in this young-revisionist tradition, which has been called the new historiography. In 1989, Shlaim, who teaches international relations at Oxford University, wrote a 600-page book entitled *Collusion Across the Jordan*. A year later, he revised and abridged his book (removing the scholarly apparatus) for the present paperback volume. The book is a prodigious achievement. Stated in its barest essentials, his theme is that the Palestinian state intended by the United Nations never came into being because Israel and Jordan (then Transjordan) agreed that it should not. In the earlier book Shlaim called this agreement "collusion." In the revision, he seems to back off somewhat. Shlaim's new preface notes that that charged word got him into a certain amount of trouble. "It is clearly a loaded and pejorative term," he writes, noting that his critics pointed out that Israeli Prime Minister David Ben-Gurion and King Abdullah of Transjordan "behaved as any realistic statesmen would have done in seeking to avert a clash through peaceful adjustment and mutual recognition of each other's essential interests."

But, Shlaim adds, Ben-Gurion's and Abdullah's "long-term process of dialogue and coordination," while neither immoral nor fraudulent,

> did involve at least some of the elements of collusion: it was held behind a thick wall of secrecy, its existence was hotly denied by the participants: it was directed against a third party; it involved a modicum of underhand scheming and plotting; and it was consciously and deliberately intended to frustrate the will of the international community, as expressed through the United Nations General Assembly, in favour of creating an independent Arab state in part of Palestine.

It would be a mistake to become distracted by the term "collusion," for Shlaim's book persuasively demonstrates that Israel and Transjordan, while they had important differences, indeed had an essential harmony of interests in 1947-48 and acted in concert and in secret to realize those interests. Moreover, to the extent the parties came into conflict, it was due to Israel's aggressive and expansionist designs. King Abdullah early on decided that an autonomous Jewish presence was favorable, not inimical, to his territorial ambitions in quest of Greater Syria. Beginning in 1937 he saw the Zionist movement as a potential ally in his annexation of the Arab part of Palestine. In this cause he was willing to deal secretly with the Jews against his putative Arab allies. Importantly, Abdullah commanded, at least theoretically, the British-trained Arab Legion, the best-organized Arab fighting force. The British, to whom Abdullah owed his throne, supported his ambitions as well as his intention to leave the Jewish sector of Palestine unmolested.

For its part, the Jewish Agency, and later Israel, regarded the Hashemite monarch as an ally of convenience who would offer a guarantee against Arab unity. The Israelis did not hesitate to play one Arab state off against another. The Arab states made this easy by secretly offering to talk peace separately with Israel. The Israeli officials represented a range of attitudes toward the king, with Ben-Gurion swinging from one side to the other. The other Arab countries, Egypt, Iraq, Lebanon and Syria, were reluctant participants in the conflict, motivated in the end by a fear of Abdullah's territorial ambitions, designs of their own on the Arab parts of Palestine, and concern over the fate of the Palestinian Arabs at the hands of the Israel Defense Force. A desire to extinguish the new state seems to have figured least in their motivation, although they did not approve of the partition. The Palestinian Arabs who harbored the greatest animus toward Israel — those led by the mufti of Jerusalem, Haj Amin al-Husseini — had too small a following and too few resources to cause the Jewish state much harm.

A meeting (not the first) between the Jewish Agency and Abdullah took place at the Zionists' request on November 17, 1947, in Naharayim, south of the Sea of Galilee. This was 12 days before the General Assembly recommended partition. Representing the Agency was Golda Meyerson (later Meir), head of its Political Department, accompanied by top Agency Arabists, Elias Sasson and Ezra Danin. Before the meeting, Danin had briefed Meyerson on Abdullah's belief, as Shlaim puts it, "that Providence had scattered the Jews throughout the Western world in order that they might absorb European culture and bring it back to the Middle East with them, thus contributing to its renaissance." Abdullah enjoyed cordial relations with the Jews in Naharayim who were involved with the Palestine Electric Corporation.

At the meeting, Abdullah proposed "an independent Hebrew Republic in part of Palestine within a Transjordan state that would include both banks of the Jordan, with me at its head, and in which the economy, the army and the legislature will be joint." His idea for Jewish autonomy within an enlarged Transjordan was clearly his preference. But it was unacceptable to the Jewish Agency. Meir replied that the Jewish Agency would view with favor Abdullah's capture of Arab Palestine if it did not impede the creation of the Jewish State and if he said his purpose was to keep order until the United Nations could set up a government there. To this Abdullah responded, "But I want this area to myself, in order to annex it to my kingdom and do not want to create a new Arab state which would upset my plans and enable the Arabs to ride on me. I want to ride, not be ridden."

When the meeting ended, Israel and Transjordan understood that neither would impede the other in its objectives and that their forces would not clash. Abdullah advised the Zionists to hit the forces of his rival, the mufti, hard if they attacked. Publicly, Abdullah did not let on that he was dealing with the Jews. He participated in Arab League planning meetings at which military intervention by its volunteer force, the Arab Liberation Army (to be distinguished from the Arab Legion), was discussed. That led some Jewish leaders to doubt Abdullah's reliability.

The Arab Liberation Army was under the command of Fawzi al-Qawukji, a Syrian with a grudge against the mufti. He was not eager for a fight with the Jews and was reportedly looking for a way to avoid it. When Qawukji and the Haganah intelligence officer Yehoshua Palmon met on April 1, 1948, they agreed to have their forces refrain from attacking each other. Palmon, writes Shlaim, "went away with a clear impression that Qawukji would remain neutral in the event of a Jewish attack on the mufti's forces in Palestine." Qawukji kept his word.

As the end of the British mandate (May 14, 1948) approached, the Arabs were disunited and apparently in no mind to go to war against what seemed inevitable, the founding of the Jewish State. But the Arab League rhetoric was militant, causing the Zionists to fear that the king would break his agreement. At the second meeting with Golda Meir, on May 10, 1948, Abdullah was evasive when asked if their understanding was still in force. He said the involvement of the other Arab nations changed the context. Meir in later years charged Abdullah with reneging on the agreement. But in her contemporary account she portrayed Abdullah's position as midway between renouncing the agreement and fully adhering to it. Shlaim writes that "though lacking in precision, what he said was most consistent with the . . . scenario of limited military intervention to gain control of the Arab part of Palestine."

The key question is, what happened between the first and second meetings? In a word, much. In March 1948, the United States had second thoughts about partition and proposed a UN trusteeship. The Zionists bitterly opposed the idea. On April I, to prevent reversal of the partition, they launched Operation Nachshon to open the road to Jerusalem. (Under the UN partition plan, Jerusalem was to be an international city under neither Jewish nor Arab jurisdiction.) Next, the Haganah (later the Israel Defense Force) blew up the mufti's headquarters in Ramleh. Qawukji's Arab Liberation Army stood by, as promised. The Zionist force then moved to Kastel, where the mufti's cousin and best commander was killed, A Palestinian request for arms from the Liberation Army brought the dishonest reply that there were none. The defeat at Kastel destroyed the mufti's forces.

In the wake of that success, the Haganah proceeded with "Plan D," which was to secure the territory reserved for the Jewish State and Jewish settlements within the Arab territory-as well as corridors from the former to the latter. "The novelty and audacity of the plan lay in the orders to capture Arab villages and cities . . . ," Shlaim writes. *The Jews no longer felt constrained to remain within the narrow and awkward boundaries laid down for them by the UN cartographers."* [Emphasis added.]

The decisive event occurred April 9, 1948. Deir Yassin, a small Arab village west of Jerusalem and outside the Jewish partition, had faithfully observed its nonaggression pact with the Haganah. Nevertheless, on April 9, fighters from the Zionist terrorist groups Irgun (led by Menachem Begin) and the Stem Gang (led by Yitzhak Shamir) fell upon the village with the purported intention of forcing its inhabitants to flee. When the inhabitants offered resistance, the attackers opened fire indiscriminately, and savagely massacred 245 men, women, and children. Some of the villagers were driven in a lorry through the streets of Jerusalem in a "victory parade" before they were taken back to the village and shot against the wall. News of the massacre spread like a whirlwind through the land, striking terror in Arab hearts. More than any other single event, it was responsible for breaking the spirit of the civilian population and setting in motion the mass exodus of Arabs from Palestine.

Abdullah was outraged. He hoped for British help. It was only at this point that he offered the Arab Legion's services to the Arab League to save Palestine. (Egypt accepted; the mufti and Syria, fearing Abdullah's ambitions, did not.) Things continued to worsen. Later in April, Tiberias, Haifa and Jaffa fell to the Zionists and the Arab residents fled, many of them to Transjordan. Only then did the Arab Legion cross the Jordan River into Arab Palestine. On April 29, more than two weeks after Deir Yassin, the Arab nations finally decided, in principle, to use their regular armies to intervene.

Abdullah said the Deir Yassin massacre and the other Zionist attacks made a peaceful solution impossible. Even so, Abdullah talked the Arab League out of its aggressive plan to cripple Israel, and the Arab Legion minimized its contact with the Jewish forces. Except for fighting in Jerusalem (initiated by Israel), which was not part of the Abdullah-Meir agreement, and two minor engagements (which may have been accidents), the Arab Legion did not battle the Jewish forces or fight in areas reserved for the Jewish State. Yet the Haganah did not hesitate to capture land intended for the Arabs, including the western Galilee and parts of the West Bank.

The IDF broke ceasefires to grab some of this territory. When Israel attacked Egyptian forces in the Negev, the Arab Legion stayed neutral. In the end, Israel took control of about 80 percent of Palestine, although only about 55 percent had been recommended by the United Nations. During secret postwar negotiations, the Israelis intimidated, even humiliated, Abdullah with their military might to gain more of the West Bank, including some 15 Arab villages. At least one other village, Baqa el Gharbiya, was divided by the arbitrary armistice line drawn by the Israelis. The IDF expelled the Arabs from the half that would now be in Israel. Despite their agreement with Abdullah, Israel's leaders never recognized Jordan's annexation of the West Bank. In fact, they considered conquering the entire West Bank. Only their concern with Jewish immigration, their courting of world opinion, and their wish to be admitted to the United Nations stayed their hand. (Nineteen years later, during the Six-Day War, they would complete the operation.) Jordan continued to press for a peace agreement and a resolution of all outstanding issues. Israel dragged its feet, seeking only to gain whatever advantage it could for itself. Private peace overtures from Egypt, Lebanon and Syria were received with cynicism. Even Arab offers to take in Palestinian refugees in return for concessions were turned aside. Armistice agreements were eventually signed with Jordan, Egypt, Lebanon and Syria, but no final peace agreements. Jerusalem was divided between Jordan and Israel because both sides preferred that to internationalization. (Abdullah offered to give Israel the Jewish quarter of the Old City, including the Wailing Wall, but Israel would make no serious concession in return.)

The attempts to accommodate Israel had serious repercussions later. King Farouk of Egypt and Husni Zaim of Syria were overthrown. Most dramatic of all, King Abdullah was assassinated in July 1951, in the presence of his grandson, the future King Hussein, at the threshold of al-Aksa Mosque in the Old City. The gunman was a Palestinian associated with the mufti. (Shlaim writes that the king's efforts for peace were not the only reason for his murder.)

Many Arabs celebrated the death of the "dog who sold Palestine to the Zionists." His son Talal did not share his father's desire for a separate peace with Israel. But neither did he want to go to war. Thus, he continued to observe the armistice agreement. Nevertheless, Ben-Gurion feared the worst and began contemplating the conquest not only of the West Bank but also of the Sinai Peninsula. He approached Great Britain for help, but got nowhere — until 1956.

Shortly before his death, Abdullah told an American UN official: "I am an old man. 1 know my power is limited; I know that I am hated by my own son . . . . I also know that my own people distrust me because of my peace efforts. But despite all that, I know that I could get peace settled if I only had some encouragement and could get any reasonable concessions from Israel." To the end, Abdullah — if not many members of his government-hoped for peace and normalization with Israel, Shlaim writes, even if it meant expulsion from the Arab League. But Israel's leaders were preoccupied with their own agenda, on which comity with its neighbors was not a high priority. They never seemed serious about making concessions for peace. That apparent lack of interest in real negotiations made it impossible for Abdullah to win public favor for his accommodating course. Shlaim's gripping account, to say the least, puts the whole of Israel's modem history into a light few people are familiar with. It is obviously an unflattering light. Shlaim writes,

> It was to become an often-repeated charge that the quest for peace
> was frustrated . . . by Arab intransigence and Arab refusal to recognize

Israel's right to exist. . . . [I]n 1949 most Arab leaders were prepared to recognize Israel's right to exist. They were willing to meet face to face to negotiate peace, they had their conditions for making peace with Israel. And Israel rejected those conditions because they were incompatible not with her survival as an independent state but with her determination to keep all the territory she held and to resist the repatriation of the refugees.

But the story is unflattering not just to Israel. The Palestinians are revealed by Shlaim as mere bargaining chips in the hands of the Arab leaders. Virtually all of them were prepared to sell out the Arabs of Palestine, including the hundreds of thousands of refugees, for the right price. They never even asked the Palestinians to conduct guerrilla operations against the Zionists during the war. The only consistent advocate of the Palestinians, the mufti, had too little influence to be of consequence.

This meticulously researched book is indispensable for anyone wishing to understand the tragic history of Palestine.

26

Shimon Peres and 9/11

The Libertarian Institute, October 2, 2016

The death of former Israeli prime minister and president Shimon Peres (age 93), the last major figure of Israel's founding generation, has brought an outpouring of tributes for a man who reputedly had, as President Obama put it in his eulogy, "the capacity to see all people as deserving of dignity and respect."

Unfortunately, the Polish-born Peres's life did not display such a capacity. Many Palestinians and Lebanese suffered and died because of him. Considering his prominent role in the founding of the self-declared State of the Jewish People, this should go without saying. Israel was established largely by Europeans on land from which three-quarters of a million Muslim and Christian Palestinian Arabs were expelled. Others were massacred by Zionist paramilitary forces, one of which Peres worked for. The year before Israel declared independence (1948), largely on Palestinian-owned land, Peres was put in charge of personnel and weapons acquisition for the paramilitary force called Haganah. This systematic ethnic cleansing is known as the *Nakba*, or catastrophe. Hundreds of former Arab villages were destroyed to make room for Jewish villages. Zionist and Israeli leaders were not shy about acknowledging this. In their view Jewish land had to be redeemed and restored to its rightful owner — the Jewish People — and the "exiled" had to be in-gathered, no matter the cost to others. This was the Zionist project.

As a member of the Labor Party, Peres also played important roles in creating Israel's Mideast monopoly nuclear-weapons arsenal (unlike Iran, it has not signed the Non-Proliferation Treaty and does not permit international inspections) and in building illegal Jewish-only settlements in the Israeli-occupied West Bank after the June 1967 war against Egypt, Syria, and Jordan. Before that war, he helped administer military rule over the remaining Palestinian Arabs inside Israel. He also forged Israel's military and nuclear alliance with apartheid South Africa.

In 1995 Peres, who maintained that the Palestinians had victimized themselves, became prime minister after Yitzhak Rabin was assassinated by a Jewish fanatic for entering into the Oslo Accords with the Palestine

Liberation Organization. (Rabin, like some other Israeli leaders, feared a loss of a Jewish majority in Israel and so favored a rump Palestinian state in parts of the West Bank. Rabin, Peres, and Yasser Arafat won the Nobel Peace Prize for this dubious agreement.) In his campaign for prime minister a year later against Benjamin Netanyahu, Peres (who was also defense minister) sought to establish his hawkish credentials by launching a war against Lebanon (which Israel had devastated and occupied for nearly 20 years beginning in 1982). Peres named his war Operation Grapes of Wrath. According to veteran Middle East reporter Robert Fisk:

> The joint Nobel Peace Prize holder used as an excuse the firing of Katyusha rockets over the Lebanese border by the Hezbollah. In fact, their rockets were retaliation for the killing of a small Lebanese boy by a booby-trap bomb they suspected had been left by an Israeli patrol. It mattered not.

> A few days later, Israeli troops inside Lebanon came under attack close to Qana and retaliated by opening fire into the village. Their first shells hit a cemetery used by Hezbollah; the rest flew directly into the UN Fijian army camp where hundreds of civilians were sheltering. Peres announced that "we did not know that several hundred people were concentrated in that camp. It came to us as a bitter surprise."

> It was a lie. The Israelis had occupied Qana for years after their 1982 invasion, they had video film of the camp, they were even flying a drone over the camp during the 1996 massacre — a fact they denied until a UN soldier gave me his video of the drone, frames from which we published in *The Independent*. The UN had repeatedly told Israel that the camp was packed with refugees. This was Peres's contribution to Lebanese peace. He lost the election and probably never thought much more about Qana.

Fisk was an eyewitness to the atrocity. "When I reached the UN gates, blood was pouring through them in torrents. I could smell it. It washed over our shoes and stuck to them like glue. There were legs and arms, babies without heads, old men's heads without bodies. A man's body was hanging in two pieces in a burning tree. What was left of him was on fire." Over 100 civilians were killed. Fisk continued:

> There was a UN inquiry which stated in its bland way that it did not believe the slaughter was an accident. The UN report was accused of being anti-Semitic. Much later, a brave Israeli magazine published an interview with the artillery soldiers who fired at Qana. An officer had referred to the villagers as "just a bunch of Arabs" ("arabushim" in Hebrew). "A few Arabushim die, there is no harm in that," he was quoted as saying. Peres's chief of staff was almost equally carefree: "I

don't know any other rules of the game, either for the [Israeli] army or for civilians."

This atrocious record — hardly the record of a humanitarian — has been cited in critical obituaries of Peres. But much less noted was Peres's role in helping to pave the road to 9/11.

What possible role could Peres have played in the attacks on the World Trade Center and Pentagon? Recall Peres's cynical election-year onslaught against Lebanon and the massacre in Qana. It was his Operation Grapes of Wrath that radicalized key individuals who would plan and carry out those attacks.

As Middle East scholar Juan Cole wrote:

> In 1996, Israeli jets bombed a UN building where civilians had taken refuge at Cana/Qana in south Lebanon, killing 102 persons; in the place where Jesus is said to have made water into wine, Israeli bombs wrought a different sort of transformation. In the distant, picturesque port of Hamburg, a young graduate student studying traditional architecture of Aleppo saw footage [of the destruction]. He was consumed with anguish and the desire for revenge. As soon as Operation Grapes of Wrath had begun the week before, he had written out a martyrdom will, indicating his willingness to die avenging the victims, killed in that operation — with airplanes and bombs that were a free gift from the United States. His name was Muhammad Atta. Five years later he piloted American Airlines 11 into the World Trade Center.

Lawrence Wright, author of *The Looming Tower*, reported:

> On April 11, 1996, when Atta was twenty-seven years old, he signed a standardized will he got from the al-Quds mosque. It was the day Israel attacked Lebanon in Operation Grapes of Wrath. According to one of his friends, Atta was enraged, and by filling out his last testament during the attack he was offering his life in response.

The Egyptian Atta was the leader of the cell in Hamburg and then in the United States without whom the hijacking of airplanes on 9/11 almost certainly could not have happened.

Atta was not the only one moved to action. Investigative reporter James Bamford told Scott Horton that Osama bin Laden "frequently mentioned Qana during those times. It was a very inflaming incident in terms of his own development of his hatred for the United States, and as well for other people throughout the Middle East."

In his 1996 declaration of war against the United States, bin Laden wrote that among other crimes perpetrated against Muslims,

The horrifying pictures of the massacre of Qana, in Lebanon are still fresh in our memory. . . . All of this and the world watch and hear, and not only didn't respond to these atrocities, but also with a clear conspiracy between the U.S.A. and its' [sic] allies and under the cover of the iniquitous United Nations, the dispossessed people were even prevented from obtaining arms to defend themselves. . . . The youths hold you responsible for all of the killings and evictions of the Muslims and the violation of the sanctities, carried out by your Zionist brothers in Lebanon; you openly supplied them with arms and finance.

Lebanon and Qana were not the jihadis' only grievances against the United States, but Peres's war was one more count in a long bill of indictment against the United States, whose government has underwritten the Israeli military to the tune of hundreds of billions of dollars. Peres would have had no way of knowing that five years later his war would produce such a dramatic act of revenge against the American people. But that should not lessen our condemnation of him. His mission in life — Zionism — required the degradation and destruction of the indigenous people who did not fit into his vision. It was inevitable that some kind of vengeful backlash would result. As usual, the victims were innocent bystanders. Perpetrators like Peres get to die of old age.

27

"Who is a Jew" Matters in Israel

Washington Report on Middle East Affairs, March 1990

Most Americans miss the point of the "who is a Jew?" controversy raging again in Israel. This old debate has come alive with two 1989 Israeli Supreme Court decisions. First, contrary to the position of the ruling Orthodox authorities, the court held that Jews converted by Conservative and Reform rabbis are to be recognized as real Jews. Then, late in the year, the court ruled that Messianic Jews, who practice Judaism but also believe in the divinity of Jesus are, despite their profession, Christians and thus do not qualify as Jews in the eyes of the state.

The debate masks a monumental issue that many outside Israel underestimate. After all, in what other country — in what other "democracy" especially — are religious qualifications an official matter?

In Israel, qualifications are an official matter because the country is a Jewish state. Those words, "Jewish state" are usually misinterpreted as a humanitarian issue even by Jews. Until World War II, Jews in the U.S. were largely uninterested in Israel and Zionism. They did not see themselves as exiled from the "Promised Land," and they did not seek a "return," despite a major effort to get them to think that this was their destiny. Things changed in the 1940s with Hitler's "final solution," and American Jews became devout supporters of Israel. But they largely saw it as a safe haven for Europe's uprooted and brutalized Jews, not as a place for American Jews to "return." For them, America was still Zion.

Because the murderous Nazi actions were the source of their support for Israel, most American Jews still see that state as primarily a humanitarian entity, a place where Jewish refugees will always be accepted and kept safe. Israel's founders, however, repeatedly said that Israel is not primarily a haven for refugees, but rather a fulfillment of God's promise to all Jews. The state claims to speak not only for the Jews living in Israel, but for all Jews no matter where they live.

This is the source of the "who is a Jew?" controversy. Israel was established as a Jewish state not in the sense that the laws of the Old Testament or the Talmud constitute the civil law, but in the sense that it is a state of, by, and for the Jewish people (conceived by some Jews as a distinct race, contrary to all evidence). This secular notion of the Jewish state has long been troublesome. At first, anyone who claimed to be a Jew was considered a Jew. This suited most Israeli Jews, who were and are secular. But it dissatisfied the minority of religious Jews. The definition later was changed to include only people whose mothers were Jewish and people who converted to Judaism.

This led to the question of whether conversions performed by Conservative and Reform rabbis would count. To the secular Jews governing the state, it was no problem. But to the Orthodox rabbis it was critical because their authority was at stake. They have long wanted only Orthodox conversions recognized. (The ruling against them was coupled with one that undoubtedly delighted the rabbinate. The court said that only Orthodox rabbis could perform weddings. There is no civil marriage in Israel.)

The debate is not just a matter of obscure religious doctrine. Jews from anywhere in the world can come to Israel and immediately become citizens, entitling them to services provided by a nominally private organization [the Jewish National Fund] that acts as an agent of the state. This right is not available to non-Jews. Obviously, if the Law of Return is to have any meaning, there must be a way to distinguish Jews from non-Jews.

Each Israeli must carry an identity card, which has a line indicating "nationality." One would think that an Israeli citizen would have the word "Israeli" on that line. Not so. The nationality of any Jew is "Jew;" the nationality of an Israeli Arab — even one who has lived for decades in, say, Jaffa — is "Arab." In 1970 a Jewish human rights activist tried to challenge this practice by asking the Interior Ministry to change his registration to Israeli. It refused and the Supreme Court upheld the decision. The court stated that "there is no Israeli nation separate from the Jewish people."

Where does that leave Israelis who are non-Jews or not recognized as Jews by the state? On its face it implies second-class citizenship.

If the Orthodox rabbis get their way, many people now regarded as Jews will be excluded from full civil rights in Israel. That would be bad. But what of the people who never have had the same rights as those extended to Jews, namely, the Palestinians living in Israel?

Israel is a state-socialist country; the government owns much of the economy. Thus, to be a non-Jew has countless practical disadvantages. Over 90 percent of the land is managed by a state authority. Precious water resources and electrical power are controlled by the state. As in any socialist country, politicians ultimately decide who gets what.

Since Israel is a state of, by, and for the Jewish people, the resources primarily benefit Jews. Arabs are taxed like Jews, but they do not have the same access to resources as Jews. The land managed by the state may be sold or leased to Arabs, but only on a limited basis. Less-official restrictions bar Arabs from much of the land. Arab villages and farms do not get the same quality of services — electrical, water, and so on — as Jewish towns and farms. Arab farmers in Israel are not free to sell their produce directly to buyers outside the country. (Only threats of retaliation against Israeli products by the European Community persuaded the authorities to let Arabs in the occupied territories export directly.)

The Arabs of Israel are like serfs in a socialist state run for the benefit of someone else. They can have representatives in the Knesset, but they can't change the system.

It is important to understand the essential relationship between socialism and Israel as it has existed since 1948. Were Israel to adopt free-market liberalism, as some American economists urge, the state's character would change radically. If all land and industry were privately owned, free trade practiced, and the government limited to a neutral referee, the country, by definition, could not discriminate. Equal rights and the rule of law are hallmarks of classical liberalism. There is no second-class citizenship in the free market. This point is more radical than it may appear at first: Israel's "fundamental laws" are incompatible with the distinctive Western political philosophy and tradition known as classical liberalism.

Israel can either maintain the status quo, including the socialism that is sinking its economy into an abyss and causing significant emigration, or give up socialism and adopt liberalism, in which case it would no longer discriminate against non-Jews. Few Israelis want to face this choice. But, like it or not, the need to choose is something about which they have no choice.

28

Zionism Mandates Official Discrimination Against Non-Jews

Washington Report on Middle East Affairs, December/January 1991/1992

By calling on the United Nations General Assembly to rescind the 1975 resolution condemning Zionism as racism, President Bush has reopened discussion of an emotionally explosive issue. Unfortunately, the discussion has taken place at a predictably low level. The commentators praising Bush's initiative have spent most of their words analyzing how Resolution 3379 was passed.

"The campaign on behalf of the resolution occurred when the Arab states routinely received support from numerous Third World nations as well as from the Soviet Union and its former Eastern Bloc allies," wrote Stephen Green of the Copley News Service. Christopher Gacek of the Heritage Foundation pointed out that 1975 was "a time when the United Nations served only as a battleground for Cold War tensions and Third World hostilities." Senator Daniel Patrick Moynihan wrote in the *Washington Post* that the resolution was not even an Arab idea; it was cooked up by the Soviet Union.

These commentators note that, with the Cold War over and the United States the only surviving superpower, it is opportune to ask the General Assembly to erase the resolution from its record.

Conspicuous by its absence in these and other commentaries, however, is any evaluation of the resolution's content.

Instead, it is taken for granted that the charge — that Zionism is a form of racism — is absurd, and thus the only issue is the invidious motive of the sponsors and those who supported it.

Motive, however, is a separate matter from merit. The moral character of a speaker does not necessarily determine the truth of his words. Although it was hypocritical for governments that do not respect the freedom of their own citizens to condemn Israel for discriminating against some of its citizens, that does not absolve Israel of the charge. Righteous indignation is no substitute for rational scrutiny.

The question is whether under Zionism, Israel's guiding ideology, people are being treated differently on the basis of race, or, more precisely,

125

ethnic or national origin. Can there be any serious doubt that they are?

The first law enacted by the Israeli Knesset was the Law of Return, part of the Basic Law, the closest thing Israel has to a constitution. Under the Law of Return, a Diaspora Jew, no matter where he was born or where he lives, may "return" to Israel as a full Israeli national. But an Arab (or other non-Jew) born in Palestine but who fled or was driven out, may not. The criterion is simple: One is a Jew, the other is not.

"National," not citizen, is the operative word in this case. Unlike other countries, Israel distinguishes nationality from citizenship. Non-Jews can be citizens of Israel. But they cannot be nationals. Only Jews can be nationals. And in Israel, many rights proceed from nationality rather than citizenship.

As an Israeli court has declared, "There is no Israeli nation separate from the Jewish people. The Jewish people is composed not only of those residing in Israel, but also of Diaspora Jewry." Writer Roselle Tekiner has commented, "Israel is the only nation in the world to grant privileges to some foreigners that are denied to some native-born citizens."

This matter is not purely academic. It affects the way people are treated day to day in Israel. Since the government dominates the economic life of Israel, the distribution of many goods and services is directly affected by the basic discrimination against non-Jews.

This is most obvious in the case of land. Nearly 93 percent of the surface of pre-1967 Israel is owned by the state or the quasi-governmental Jewish National Fund. In the early 1960s the Knesset adopted the JNF's principles governing the land. Among these are the principles that the land is owned by the Jewish people, that it is inalienable, that it is to be worked only by Jews, and that it is to be leased to Jews only.

Some land has been leased short-term to Arabs; nevertheless Arabs are barred from most of the land and from long-term leases. As Walter Lehn and Uri Davis write, "Thus we are unaware of a single instance of a large tract of land, whether zoned for agriculture or industry, or for housing development, under a long-term lease to a non-Jewish lessee. Such leases are much more likely to be for small tracts and for relatively short periods, sometimes for only one year, or if agricultural land, for one crop season. . . . In short, leases of Israel-land to non-Jews appear to be exceptional in one way or another, not typical, and relatively few in number."

Professor Uzi Ornan of Hebrew University has written that land controlled by the Israel Lands Administration cannot be leased to non-Jews "unless the apartment or plot of land is located in the special 'zone of residence' assigned to non-Jews, and where non-Jews are permitted to apply for an apartment or land." Ornan has compared Israeli treatment of Arabs to South Africa's treatment of blacks.

Unsurprisingly, Jewish lessees are not permitted to sublet land to Arabs or to subject it to other "non-conforming uses." Lehn and Davis write that "a Jewish farmer lost his leased land for having violated this [1967] law by selling his crop of tomatoes in the field to an Arab; this was held by the court to be a non-conforming use of Israel-land." They add that in 1974, a year before the UN resolution, Israel's minister of agriculture "denounced the continuing presence of Arabs on Israel-land as agricultural laborers and share-croppers. In his words, 'The domination of Jewish agriculture by Arab laborers is a cancer on our body.'"

What is true of land is also true of water and other services dominated by the state, for example, electricity and education. Arabs do not have the access to necessities that Jews do. Nor can representation in the Knesset, which is allowed to Arabs, change the fundamental laws that make that discrimination possible.

The ideology that mandates official, governmental discrimination against non-Jews is Zionism. Without it, Israel could not be a Jewish state. Nearly 30 years ago, the United Nations defined racial discrimination to include invidious distinctions based on ethnic or national origin as well as race. If the reconsideration, therefore, is based not on the motives of the original sponsors of the resolution, but simply on whether or not Zionism is a form of racism, UN members, and readers of this article, should have no trouble arriving at the correct answer.

29

Washington's Interventionist Record
in the Middle East

The following is Chapter 9 of *America Entangled: The Persian Gulf Crisis and Its Consequences*, Ted Galen Carpenter, editor, (Washington: Cato Institute, 1991) [[[change to what]]]

Anyone who tries to understand contemporary events in the Middle East without cognizance of the record of American intervention in that region labors under a severe disadvantage. American intervention, particularly since World War II, is the indispensable context for grasping many important events there. The links are not always direct and explicit. But however oblique some of the connections are, they exist, and we ignore them at our peril.

Unfortunately, Americans, and especially their leaders, have no patience for history. When the American hostages were seized by Iranians in 1979, President Jimmy Carter dismissed references to the U.S. record of intervention in Iran as "ancient history." That was tantamount to calling those interventions irrelevant. Knowledge of the past, however, can help us understand deplorable actions, even though it does not excuse them.

Before looking at details, it is worthwhile to back up and view the full forest. America's interest in the Middle East can of course be summed up in one short word: oil (regardless of what President Bush might say on alternate Wednesdays). Oil is what made the Middle East, in the words of a State Department official in 1945, "a stupendous source of strategic power, and one of the greatest material prizes in world history."[1] The United States aspired to control that oil-rich region, however indirectly, because it was seen as the key to world leadership. U.S. policymakers always regarded war as potentially necessary to maintain control of the region: "threats to the continuous flow of oil through the Gulf would so endanger the Western and Japanese economies as to be grounds for general war."[2] The United States had its own oil, to be sure, but during

---

[1] *Foreign Relations of the United States*, vol. 8 (Washington: Government Printing Office, 1945), p. 45.

[2] *U.S. Senate Committee on Energy and Natural Resources, Access to Oil—The United States Relationships with Saudi Arabia and Iran* (Washington: Government Printing Office, 1977).

World War II, it was widely believed to be running out. Thus, America would need to conserve domestic reserves while developing foreign sources. Hardly anyone believed that private enterprise could perform that feat without government assistance. As Republican Senator Henry Cabot Lodge said, "History does not give us confidence that private interest alone would adequately safeguard the national interest."[3] Nor did the oil industry wish to keep the government out of the matter.

More broadly, during World War II, U.S. policymakers envisioned a postwar world in which America was architect and chief executive of a new world order. That order was to be one in which unpredictability was minimized, if not eliminated; in which change was closely controlled; in which American interests were paid their proper respect; and in which those interests were protected by an amenable world economic system — namely, state capitalism (as opposed to free-market capitalism). Those requirements necessitated certain conditions, most particularly, access to natural resources. In light of the postwar breakdown of the old colonial empires, which the United States aspired to succeed in some manner, enlightened American leaders understood that a new form of control would be necessary. Direct rule was rendered impractical by the awakening nationalism in the Middle East, as it was in Africa and the Far East. New forms of influence would have to be improvised. The obvious choice was the maintenance of friendly, even if brutal, regimes and, where necessary, the replacement of insufficiently obeisant regimes. Some of those client-regimes would be suited for extraterritorial duty — that is, helping to keep order beyond their borders. Those appointed gendarmeries would act as bulwarks against rivals to American influence. (The strategy of appointing proxies would be formalized in the Nixon Doctrine.)

While an American consensus was built around the Soviets as the most likely threat to "order" in the Middle East, in fact, indigenous forces, in the form of unruly nationalism, were feared most. As John Foster Dulles put it in 1958, the United States "must regard Arab nationalism as a flood which is running strongly. We cannot successfully oppose it, but we could put sand bags around positions we must protect — the first group being Israel and Lebanon and the second being the oil positions around the Persian Gulf."[4] In service of that goal, Dulles established the principle that neutrality was impossible. Nations were either for or against the United States.

That did not mean that the United States never found nationalism useful. The United States supported nationalists against King Farouk of

---

[3] Daniel Yergin, *The Prize: The Epic Quest for Oil, Money and Power* (New York: Simon & Shuster, 1991), p. 396.

[4] Quoted in Michael B. Bishku, "The 1958 American Intervention in Lebanon: A Historical Assessment," *American-Arab Affairs*, no. 31 (Winter 1989–90): 117.

Egypt in 1952–1953 in order to weaken the position of Britain, still something of a rival at that point.[5] But when Gamal Abdel Nasser, who gained power in the crisis, was seen as a threat to American interests, the U.S. policymakers had no hesitation in trying to undermine him. His elimination was even contemplated. Then in 1956, the United States opposed the Israeli, French, and British assault on Nasser — the "Hitler on the Nile," according to the *New York Times* (how little things change).

I've used the term "American interests," but we should not be lulled into taking that concept too literally. American interests should be interpreted as the interests of the relatively small group that makes policy inside and outside of government, as well as its patrons in the corporate world. They make decisions to further their own good, although, because of various economic fallacies, they may believe the country's interests are also served. The important point is that their policies actually impede the mass of Americans from pursuing their own interests as they see them. The taxes, regulations, and government spending required by the small group's policies hurt most Americans, including most businesspeople.

With regard to oil and, more generally, to energy, a free market, without intervention by the state, would have satisfied the needs of the American people and business without difficulty. Whoever controlled the oil of the Middle East would have needed to sell it. Private entrepreneurs seeking profit would have gravitated to the sources of energy that had the lowest costs and the most security. How much of our need for energy would have been satisfied by oil and how much by alternatives no one can say. But that is not important. What is important is that a noninterventionist foreign policy in the Middle East would not have meant impoverishment of the American economy. Does that mean the policymakers and their industry partners miscalculated? Not really. Although a free market in energy would have taken care of the American people, it would not have necessarily taken care of the interests who profited from the policies that were pursued by the U.S. government. We must assume that the policy elite, Standard Oil, and the other firms that sought U.S. intervention in the region knew what they were doing.

And what were they doing? In general, they were promoting repressive regimes on the condition that they maintain an order favorable to the elite group's interests. That is most clear in the cases of Iran and Israel, although — and here is the connection with the current crisis — it is also true of Saudi Arabia, Kuwait, and other Arabian Gulf states. U.S. intervention in the region has created fertile ground for demagogues and has made an easy target of any leader seen as beholden to the West. And, in the most vicious

---

[5] Joyce Kolko and Gabriel Kolko, *The Limits of Power: The World and United States Foreign Policy, 1945–1954* (New York: Harper & Row, 1972), p. 426.

of circles, the resulting periodic crises have served to justify and sustain the policy.

In Iran, the United States came to the defense of the shah when his power was threatened by the nationalist prime minister Mohammed Mossadegh in 1953. The forces led by Mossadegh nationalized the oil industry and resented foreign interference. The United States joined an international economic boycott of Iran, then sent the CIA into the country to recruit mobs to create disturbances and drive Mossadegh from power. The U.S. government used the excuse that Mossadegh was sympathetic to communists, but knew that was not true. Mossadegh had opposed the presence of Soviet troops in his country after the war and was at odds with the Iranian Communist party. Mossadegh's actual offense was in not pledging fealty to American interests. When the shah was reinstalled, American interests gained their first concessions of Iranian oil.[6]

After 1953 the shah continued his repressive and corrupt regime with the help of the dreaded secret police, SAVAK, trained by the United States and Israel. The shah was one of our constables on the beat. As such, he was favored with billions of dollars of military equipment. When outright military aid was politically unfeasible, the U.S. government turned to indirect methods, such as a rise in the price of oil. The prime mover of skyrocketing prices in the 1970s was that loyal U.S. ally, the shah of Iran — with the support of the Nixon administration, especially Henry Kissinger. Higher oil revenues enabled the shah to buy weapons; in other words, they would be paid for by American consumers rather than American taxpayers.[7]

The Iranian revolution of 1978–1979 was the predictable outcome of years of repression and corruption. And the ensuing anti-American violence was a predictable outcome of years of American patronage. (That violence includes the later taking of hostages in Lebanon.) More than two decades of support for an absolute monarch who put his American mission ahead of the liberty and dignity of his people resulted in a Muslim backlash that still wracks the Middle East. That is not to say that there would have been no Muslim extremism in Iran but for U.S. policy, only that extremists would not see America as the enemy.

Iran is only part of the story. Another part — a major part — is Israel. In a sense, American support for Israel is an anomaly. In the beginning, the oil industry and the foreign policy experts in the State Department

---

[6] See James A. Bill, *The Eagle and the Lion: The Tragedy of American-Iranian Relations* (New Haven: Yale University Press, 1988); Kermit Roosevelt, *Countercoup: The Struggle for Control of Iran* (New York: McGraw-Hill, 1979); and Jonathan Kwitny, *Endless Enemies: The Making of an Unfriendly World* (New York: Congdon & Weed, 1984).

[7] "Don't Blame the Oil Companies; Blame the State Department: How the West Was Won," *Forbes*, April 15, 1976.

opposed that support. They foresaw how it would alienate the Arab masses, and they must have been unsurprised in 1973 when the oil embargo was imposed. Something other than oil drove the decision to support the UN partition of Palestine and the creation of a Jewish state: domestic politics. Only later was it "discovered" that Israel could be a "strategic asset" — not only against the Soviets but also against Arab "radicalism" and in defense of "moderate" — that is, pro-American — Arab regimes. President Truman initially supported partition at the behest of American Zionists, but he had second thoughts after the November 1947 UN vote, when it was clear that partition would produce grievous violence. Those second thoughts were dispelled by Truman's advisers when the Democratic party was shaken badly at the polls in February 1948. In a special congressional election, the American Labor party candidate, Leo Isacson, defeated the Democrat, Karl Propper, in a heavily Jewish district in the Bronx. The key event of the contest was support of Isacson by Henry Wallace, who accused Truman of selling out the Jews. With New York's electoral votes at risk, Clark Clifford and other Truman aides opposed a shift in position on Palestine.

What the United States supported, and pressured other states to support, was the partition of Palestine into Jewish and Arab states. To the Jews, who constituted less than a third of the population, went 57 percent of the land, including the most arable land in Palestine. It is also important to note that Jews had purchased less than 7 percent of the land of Palestine by the end of 1947. The partition was gerrymandered so that the Jews would constitute just over 50 percent of the population. Thus, about half a million Palestinian Arabs were to have what they saw as an alien government imposed on them. Moreover, after the UN vote, the Zionist military forces and underground terrorist groups (Menachem Begin's Irgun and Yitzhak Shamir's Stern Gang) drove hundreds of thousands of Palestinians from their homes, creating the refugee problem that is still with us today. Such tactics continued after Israel's declaration of independence and the 1948 war.[8]

The upshot is that the Arabs were not out of line in thinking they had been treated unjustly. They had been promised independence by the British after World War I but were denied it for the most part. Now something else was to stand in the way of complete self-determination. They did not understand why they should pay for the horrors inflicted by the Nazis.[9]

---

[8] See Edward W. Said and Christopher Hitchens, eds., *Blaming the Victims: Spurious Scholarship and the Palestinian Question* (New York: Verso, 1988); Tom Segev, *1949: The First Israelis* (New York: Free Press, 1986); and Benny Morris, *The Birth of the Palestinian Refugee Problem, 1947–1949* (Cambridge: Cambridge University Press, 1989).

[9] See Evan M. Wilson, *Decision on Palestine: How the U.S. Came to Recognize Israel* (Stanford, Calif.:

As a Jewish state, Israel by definition regards its Arab population as second-class citizens. Since 1948, much pre-1967 land has been confiscated from non-Jewish Palestinians and is owned by the state or the Jewish National Fund and administered via lease by a government authority. (A small amount has been privatized.) While discrimination against non-Jews is prohibited de jure on state-owned land, the state comprehensively plans land use explicitly for the sake of preserving Israel as the state of the Jewish people worldwide. Thus Jewish citizens and noncitizens are officially favored over the 20 percent of citizens who are not Jewish. Jews have access to resources and public services that are denied Israel's Arab citizens. Each Israeli carries an identity card that specifies the "nationality" of the holder: Jew or Arab. The resemblance to apartheid is striking.[10]

Arab — not just Palestinian — resentment of such treatment naturally has been directed at the United States, which was correctly seen as Israel's patron. Dean Rusk has conceded that the American role in the creation of Israel permitted the partition to be "construed as an American Plan."[11] The resentment stimulated by that perception has predictably spilled over to tangential issues.

With a single exception — President Eisenhower's opposition to Israel, Britain, and France in the Suez Crisis of 1956 — the United States has steadfastly supported Israel morally and materially. It has given green lights to Israeli attacks on its neighbors and to repression of the inhabitants of the occupied territories. (The United Nations has been as vehement in opposing that occupation as it has in opposing Saddam's, so the differences in the American response raise disturbing questions.) The United States has increased military and economic aid in the wake of Israel's most egregious actions (the 1982 Lebanon invasion, for example). And it has given Israel free rein to use the aid however it likes. The U.S. position that Israel should not use American aid to build Jewish settlements in the occupied territories has always been toothless.

Perhaps worst of all, the United States has helped establish the myth that Israel is hopelessly surrounded by rabidly hostile Arabs — terrorists by nature — who would delight in driving Jews into the sea. In fact, from the very beginning, the Arab nations have sought to avoid hostilities with Israel, even to the point of selling out the Palestinians.[12] Over the four decades of Israel's existence, there have been numerous offers to make

---

Hoover Institution Press, 1979); and John Snetsinger, *Truman, the Jewish Vote and the Creation of Israel* (Stanford, Calif.: Hoover Institution Press, 1974).

[10] See Sheldon L. Richman, "'Who is a Jew' Matters in Israel," *Washington Report on Middle East Affairs*, March 1990, p. 10. (Chapter 24 of this book.)

[11] Alfred M. Lilienthal, *What Price Israel?* (Chicago: Henry Regnery, 1953), p. 67.

[12] See Simba Flapan, *The Birth of Israel: Myths and Realities* (New York: Pantheon, 1987).

peace. Israel, backed by the United States, has responded with repression in the territories and military force in neighboring states, and none of those acts, interestingly, is ever called "terrorism." Since 1976 the Arab states and the Palestine Liberation Organization have been on record supporting a two-state solution with guarantees of security for Israel. The solution was the substance of a 1976 UN Security Council resolution written by the PLO, a resolution rejected by Israel and vetoed by the United States. (The so-called overnight conversion of Yasser Arafat in 1988 is a myth.) Regardless of who is in power, the Israeli position remains: no talks with the PLO, no Palestinian state, no change in the status of the occupied territories. That is at the heart of Prime Minister Shamir's "peace plan."[13] The Israeli rejection of the PLO, as Shamir made clear in 1989, was "not because of the terroristic character of this organization, but because it desired to establish a Palestinian state."[14] The Palestinians are commanded to recognize Israel's "right to exist," while Palestinian rights are not even to be an issue. Thus, Washington's continuing support of Israel is a guarantee against progress on the most pressing problem in the Middle East.

For several decades, the United States has arrogated to itself the right to manage the Middle East. As a result, it has made America an object of hatred for millions of Arabs and Iranians. The ongoing confrontation with Iraq is only the latest episode. It is but one of the tragedies of American policy. Having allied itself so steadfastly with the forces of repression in the region, the United States cannot now become an honest broker there. Thus, nonintervention finds justification not only in principle and American revolutionary tradition but in empirical reality. It is time to replace political manipulation with an American policy of peaceful commerce with the nations of this troubled region.

---

[13] See Thomas Friedman, "Shamir Faulted on Mideast Remarks," *New York Times*, October 19, 1989, in which Secretary of State James Baker is quoted as saying, "Our goal all along has been to try to assist in the implementation of the Shamir initiative."

[14] Dan Margalit, *Haaretz*, November 29, 1989; quoted in Noam Chomsky, "The Intifada and the Peace Process," Fletcher Forum (Summer 1990): 350.

30
War and Peace in the Middle East: A Critique of American Policy

Middle East Policy, Volume III, Number 4, 1995

Book Review: *War and Peace in the Middle East: A Critique of American Policy*, by Avi Shlaim. New York: Whittle Books/Viking, 1994. 142 pages.

Avi Shlaim, author of the masterly *Collusion Across the Jordan* (1988), has written a short history of Western intervention in the Middle East since World War I, with a special focus on the United States. Unfortunately, in an effort perhaps to gain a large lay readership, Shlaim has skimped too much and diminished the value the book might have had. Too much important material is left out to provide a fair picture of what has gone on in the region. And the omissions tend to prejudice the case against the Arabs and particularly the Palestinians. (It also lacks an index.)

Moreover, Shlaim has an agenda, which is quite obvious at the end of the book. He wants the United States to do more in the Middle East. Informed readers may find themselves asking: Hasn't it done enough already?

Shlaim begins with the collapse of the Ottoman Empire in World War I and Great Britain's remake of the region. He properly emphasizes the imperialist nature of Colonial Secretary Winston Churchill's policy. That fateful policy included the creation of Iraq out of Basra, Baghdad and Mosul; the consequent victimization of the Kurds; and the creation of Transjordan. Of course, Britain's mutually exclusive promises regarding Arab independence and the Jewish homeland stand out as the epitome of Big Power manipulation. Shlaim reminds us of Lord Balfour's immortal words:

> In short, so far as Palestine is concerned, the Powers have made no statement of fact which is not admittedly wrong, and no declaration of policy, which, at least in the letter, they have not always intended to violate.

Many statesmen since have apparently graduated from the Balfour school of diplomacy. (See the record of Henry Kissinger.) Students of government and political science everywhere should have to read Balfour's statement on the first day of class.

Shlaim is quite correct when he writes:

> The post-World-War-I peace settlement is not just a chapter in history but the story of our times. It lies at the root of the countless territorial disputes, denial of some countries' very right to exist, and the numerous wars and struggles for national liberation that have become such familiar features of the policies of the Middle East.

When Shlaim reaches the creation of the state of Israel, he begins to omit material facts. For example, he writes, "The Arab leaders rejected the UN resolution and sent their armies to do battle with the infant state." That statement implies that the Arab states were unified and determined to destroy Israel. Yet his previous book painstakingly demonstrated that the Arabs were disunited and most reluctant to go to war — until they suspected that King Abdullah of Transjordan had territorial designs and may have cut a deal with the Zionists. In *Collusion Across the Jordan*, Shlaim refers to

> a reversal of Egypt's and the Arab League's decision not to send regular armies into Palestine but confine themselves to concentrating troops on the border and extending help to the Arab Liberation Army and Palestinian guerrilla forces. King Farouk [of Egypt] personally took this decision, which upset the Arab League's strategic consensus and forced the other Arab states to follow suit by sending their regular armies into Palestine. The decision arose out of a growing realization that King Abdullah was determined to send his army into Palestine at the end of the mandate whether the other Arab leaders agreed or resisted, and whether they participated in the invasion or remained on the sidelines. It was also clear to the Egyptian and other Arab leaders that whatever the reasons given for the entry of the Arab Legion in Palestine, the *ultimate intention would be to obtain new territory for King Abdullah*. Many suspected that Abdullah would not try to conquer the whole of Palestine by force of arms but would try to reach — and had perhaps already reached — an agreement with the Jews for sharing the spoils. Here lies one of the principal reasons for the reversal of Egypt's earlier stand. [Emphasis added.]

It does the lay reader no service to boil down that revealing story to "the Arab states . . . sent their armies to do battle with the infant state." Couldn't Shlaim at least have added the qualifier *reluctantly*? I should also point out that Shlaim does not mention the carefully thought-out *Jewish* criticism of the Zionist project.

Shlaim's treatment of Nasser is similarly incomplete. Shlaim correctly argues that American policy was hampered by viewing the Middle East through Cold War lenses. The Soviet threat was always overstated. He also properly emphasizes the refusal of the U.S. government to let Nasser buy American arms, which led the Egyptian leader in 1955 to buy them from the Soviet bloc. But the lay reader would benefit from knowing that beginning in April 1955, Nasser's government engaged in secret contacts with Israel, through an American Quaker, aimed at a peace settlement. (See *Middle East Mission*, by Elmore Jackson [New York: Norton, 1983].) Those incipient discussions were badly strained, but not disrupted, when the Israeli government staged a massive attack against the southern Gaza town of Khan Yunis in retaliation for border crossings by Palestinians who had been driven from their homes in the 1948 war. The Soviet arms deal ended the peace initiative. A year later, after Nasser nationalized the Suez Canal, Israel invaded the Sinai, and Britain and France attacked Egypt. Their aim was to unseat Nasser.

When Shlaim gets to the 1967 Six-Day War, he seems in a rush. "The Six-Day War resulted from brinkmanship by Nasser that went over the brink," he states. That's all he writes about the cause of the war. There is surely truth in that statement, but it is woefully inadequate. He might have at least pointed out that Israel engaged in some brinkmanship of its own.

Shlaim handles the rise of Anwar el-Sadat better. He correctly writes that Israeli Prime Minister Golda Meir, backed by President Richard Nixon and Secretary of State Kissinger, rebuffed Sadat's peace overture after he succeeded Nasser in late 1970. Kissinger may have been the main obstacle to peace; he argued that to enter into peace discussions would reward radicals. Sadat's 1972 expulsion of Soviet advisers seemed to mean nothing to Kissinger. The result of his policy was the 1973 Yom Kippur war.

When Shlaim gets to the Iraq-Kuwait crisis, he adopts the Orthodox line in many respects. "Iraq's annexation of Kuwait presented America with a series of challenges-to its interests in oil, to its interests in Saudi Arabia, and to its prestige in the Gulf," he writes. That sentence illustrates what is wrong with Shlaim's critique of U.S. policy in the Mideast. He mistakes the interests of a narrow collection of people for the interests of America. One could forcefully argue that the interests of the vast majority of Americans were never threatened by Saddam Hussein. Even had he invaded Saudi Arabia, he would not have had "the world at his mercy," as Shlaim believes. An analysis done at the time by economist David Henderson demonstrated that even with all the oil under Saddam's control, the maximum cost to the U.S. economy would have been one-tenth of one percent of GDP. (Congress passes legislation that costs that much.) Saddam never threatened to cut off oil to the United States and would have had no interest in doing so. On the contrary, it was the West that cut off shipments of Iraqi and Kuwaiti oil. Moreover, to believe, as

Shlaim apparently does, that Saddam could have jacked up oil prices exorbitantly is to show a lack of understanding of how markets work. Long before he could have brought the West to its knees, a high-price or embargo policy would have set in motion market processes calculated to dilute Saddam's influence. The only reason that did not happen in the oil embargoes of the 1970s is that Nixon's price controls were in place. Shlaim writes that Saddam would have controlled 40 percent of the world's known reserves had he taken Saudi Arabia. But the moment he tried to raise prices, that percentage would have fallen. "Known reserves" is an economic, not a geological, category. It refers to oil that is economical to bring out of the ground at the prevailing price. If the price goes up, reserves that were uneconomical to produce become worthwhile. In short, Saddam's power was grossly overestimated.

In the final chapter, Shlaim becomes confusing. He seems to criticize the New World Order as "a cloak for covering American hegemony in the international system." Fine. But then he faults the United States for not doing more. He faintly praises President Clinton's policy of dual containment of Iran and Iraq. But Shlaim complains that "it does not address the underlying problems of regional unrest, such as the denial of democracy and human rights by authoritarian regimes and the gap between rich and poor." I am curious to know how the United States could address those problems without being hegemonic. Shlaim wants the United States to steer Israel and the Arabs to a formal peace. He wants American troops on the Golan Heights. He wants America to "underwrite" a settlement between Israel and Jordan. (This was written before the peace agreement.) "In short," he writes, "America needs to become much more engaged, to commit resources on a much bigger scale, and to spread them more widely if it is to succeed in forging a comprehensive peace in the Middle East on the anvil of the Israeli-PLO accord."

One might guess from the foregoing that Shlaim is not an American taxpayer. (He was born in Baghdad, grew up in Israel, and lives in England.) But, aside from the added burden he so blithely proposes for those of us who do pay taxes to Washington, how is the United States supposed to pursue Shlaim's program without becoming an overbearing force in the Middle East? And what will the Islamic radicals say when the United States spreads all that money around to promote its interests? It does not sound like a recipe for progress.

Shlaim writes that if the United States does not lead the way, no one will. Yet he also notes that the Oslo Agreement between Israel and the Palestine Liberation Organization "belied the belief that the two sides had to rely on superpower involvement to reach any settlement." (I would argue that the main reason that the "peace process" is essentially stalled is that the United States is involved — on Israel's side.)

Shlaim's wish to see the United States more involved but more evenhanded may be widely shared and well-intended. But good intentions are never enough. A U.S. safety net merely allows the parties to be more careless than otherwise because they will not bear the full responsibility of their irresponsibility. Moreover, the key to peace and prosperity for every country in the Middle East lies in shrinking political society and expanding civil society (the private, volunteer sector). The transfer of money from the United States to those nations' central governments works against that requirement. Giving resources to a central government adds dangerously to the politicization of society. People who would otherwise channel their energies and entrepreneurship into producing economic growth instead devote their efforts to gaining a piece of the power — for if they don't, their enemies will. Thus, so-called foreign aid is corrupting. It does not promote progress. It stifles it.

31

Rethinking the US-Israeli Relationship

Free Association, March 20, 2015

The Benjamin Netanyahu on display in the days before and after Tuesday's Israeli election is the same one who has been in power all these years. Right along, he was there for all to see, so no one should have been surprised by his performance. I seriously doubt that anyone really is surprised. Americans who slavishly toe the Israeli and Israel Lobby line may act surprised, but that's really just their embarrassment at having to answer for the prime minister of the "State of the Jewish People." (If Israel is indeed the State of the Jewish People, it follows that the lobby may properly be called the Jewish Lobby, though that seems to offend some people. The term need not suggest that every person identifying as Jewish is pro-Israel or pro-Likud. I have known religious Jews who are severely anti-Israel and anti-Zionist.)

Democrats especially are in a bind. They can't afford to distance themselves from Netanyahu and alienate Jewish sources of campaign donations, yet they are visibly uncomfortable with his so openly racist fear-mongering about Israeli Arab voters — "The right-wing government is in danger. Arab voters are heading to the polling stations in droves. Left-wing NGOs are bringing them in buses." The Democrats' defense of that ugly appeal as merely a way to get the vote out is disgraceful. (Imagine something equivalent happening in the United States.)

Democrats are also nervous about Netanyahu's declaration that no Palestinian state will be established as long as he heads the Israeli government. (His post-election attempt to walk it back somewhat was not well-received.)

Life was so much simpler for people like Hillary Clinton when Netanyahu didn't say things like that in public. Meanwhile, hawkish Republicans — that's redundant — are unfazed.

For anyone paying close attention, Netanyahu's racism and ruthless opportunism are not news at all. A few years ago a candid video from 2001 surfaced in which he cynically described Americans as "easily moved," i.e., manipulated. The Israelis, he said, can do what they want with the Palestinians because the Americans "won't get in their way." These are the same Americans who are forced to send Israel $3 billion a year in military assistance so that it can regularly bomb and embargo Palestinians in the Gaza Strip prison camp and oppress Palestinians in a slightly more subtle manner in the shrinking West Bank and East Jerusalem.

With Netanyahu, you really do know what you get, which arguably makes him a better choice to run Israel than the left-of-center Zionist Union because the Laborites share most of Likud's beliefs about the Palestinians; they're just more circumspect and therefore more comforting to so-called Americans "liberals." Saying you support negotiations toward a Palestinian state is not the same as actually being for a viable Palestinian state. Palestinians have little left of the walled-off West Bank and East Jerusalem because of state security claims and Jewish-only towns built over the years by the two dominant parties, Likud and Labor. And Gaza is a bombed-out disaster area. (Even for many two-state advocates, justice is not the concern. Rather, demographic circumstances make one state untenable for these pragmatists because out-and-out apartheid, which the world would frown on, would be seen as the only alternative to a genuinely democratic state with a Jewish minority. The one-staters have their own solution to the Palestinian problem, the one used in 1948: transfer.)

The prime minister is a sophist extraordinaire; he says whatever he needs to say to gain his objective of the moment. When he ruled out a Palestinian state before the election, in a bid to shore up his right-wing base, he was interpreted as reversing a commitment he made in 2009, after he had returned to power, the same year that Barack Obama took office. The campaign reversal put Obama and Secretary of State John Kerry in a most uncomfortable position, since they had made the fraudulent "peace process" a top priority, until talks broke down last spring, a failure they pinned at least in part on Netanyahu. Once the election was over and some reconciliation with the U.S. government was required, Netanyahu "clarified" his remarks, saying his 2009 position had not really changed; only the environment had.

> I don't want a one-state solution. I want a sustainable, peaceful two-state solution, but for that, circumstances have to change. I was talking about what is achievable and what is not achievable. To make it achievable, then you have to have real negotiations with people who are committed to peace.
>
> I never changed my speech in Bar Ilan University six years ago calling for a demilitarized Palestinian state that recognizes the Jewish state. What has changed is the reality.

What has changed? Netanyahu probably has a few things in mind. The Palestinians reject a new demand that they formally recognize Israel as the state of the Jewish people (everywhere). Decades ago the Palestinian leadership accepted Israel's existence within the pre-1967-war borders — that is, it relinquished claim to 78 percent of pre-1948 Palestine. (Even Hamas has said it was willing to defer to the secular Fatah and the Palestinian Authority.) But in a goalpost-moving action, Netanyahu recently added the new demand, something he knows the Palestinian leadership cannot accept if it is to maintain legitimacy (or whatever legitimacy it still has). Such a concession would be prejudicial to Israel's non-Jewish Arab citizens and would favor Jews who have never set foot in the country over native-born Palestinian Arabs who were driven out of their ancestral home and who are forbidden to return.

In other words, Netanyahu knowingly placed an impossible precondition on the negotiations. But it is he who has insisted there be no preconditions whatever. When the Palestinians demanded that Israel stop seizing Palestinian-owned land on the West Bank and in East Jerusalem to make room for Jewish-only neighborhoods, Netanyahu refused on the grounds that this was a precondition. (The Palestinians relented and gave talks a chance, no doubt under American pressure.) But it was not so much a precondition as a recognition that the land being seized was precisely the subject of the negotiation. In what universe is it reasonable for two parties to negotiate over territory while one is busy annexing it and building permanent settlements?

It is this sort of thing that exposes Netanyahu's (and most Israelis') bad faith regarding the Palestinians. He sabotages the "peace process," then blames the Palestinians for failing to be an earnest partner for peace. (Now he's trying to sabotage multilateral talks with Iran. See a pattern?)

Netanyahu may also be saying the timing is wrong for a Palestinian state — which would be a rump state completely at the Israeli government's mercy — because ISIS is creating turmoil in nearby Iraq and Syria, and Iran is expanding its influence in the region. The sophistry here is that in fact much trouble in the Middle East can be traced to Israel's injustice against the Palestinians and belligerence toward its neighbors, especially the repeated devastating invasions of southern Lebanon. Ethnic-cleansing, massacres perpetrated by Zionist militias at the time of independence, unrelenting occupation of the West Bank since 1967, the repression and impoverishment of the Gazans, and the routine humiliation of Israel's Arab second-class citizens have created deep grievances that are only made worse by Netanyahu and those who support him.

This of course has spilled over onto the United States, since Democratic and Republican regimes stand by Israel no matter what and no matter how many times its government humiliates American rulers. When former Gen. David Petraeus told a Senate Armed Services Committee in 2010 that the U.S.-Israeli relationship "foments anti-

American sentiment," he was merely repeating what many other officials had acknowledged before. "Meanwhile," Petraeus added, "al Qaeda and other militant groups exploit that anger to mobilize support. The conflict also gives Iran influence in the Arab world through its clients, Lebanese Hezbollah and Hamas." The attacks of 9/11 were in part motivated by anger over America's relationship with Israel. Osama bin Laden's 1996 declaration of war makes clear that this relationship was at the heart of his hostility toward the United States. Mohammed Atta, one of the 9/11 hijackers, joined the cause after Israel's 1996 assault on Lebanon, James Bamford writes in *The Shadow Factory*. (Open discussion of these facts is discouraged by spurious charges of anti-Semitism against anyone who raises them.)

So, again, Netanyahu cites reasons for not making peace that he himself helped create or is now perpetuating. That he is taken seriously in American politics is a testament to the power of the Israel Lobby.

Netanyahu's apparent reelection and the egregious circumstances under which it was accomplished should prompt a reconsideration of the special relationship. Although it should have happened long ago, now would be a good time for the U.S. government to end the relationship and start seeing Israel as a rogue and aggressor nuclear power. (Of course the United States is hardly one to talk.) No more excuses. The Palestinians had nothing to do with the Holocaust. Let's have one moral standard for all.

Not that I think it has a chance of happening, but the U.S. government should cease all taxpayer aid to the Israeli government, stop vetoing UN Security Council resolutions that condemn Israel for its daily violations of human rights, and stop impeding Palestinian efforts to set up an independent country (with membership in the International Criminal Court, etc.). The United States should withdraw from the Middle East and enter into a detente with Iran (which is not developing a nuclear weapon). This would have an immediate dividend: we would not be driven to war with Iran by Netanyahu, the Lobby, and its neoconservative Republican and Democratic stooges in Congress.

Maybe Israeli politicians will act more responsibly if they don't have the American people to fall back on. Probably not. But we know the Palestinians will get no justice under the status quo. Meanwhile, U.S. policy puts Americans at risk. This must stop.

32

US Journalists Consistently Ignore Israeli State Terrorism

Washington Report on Middle East Affairs, May/June 1991

Many people in the media have such a romantic view of Israel that they lose all objectivity. For example, they would have no trouble believing an allegation of an Arab attack on defenseless Israeli civilians. But they act as if Israeli attacks on Arab civilians were impossible.

Syndicated columnist Paul Greenberg has written, "There are terrorists and there are terrorists. There are those who choose their targets carefully for political effect. They're low, but they're several steps above the ones who scrupulously avoid military targets and assault a whole people indiscriminately, like Yasser Arafat's child murderers and Meir Kahane's rhetoric." Greenberg's point is that, except for a fringe character like Kahane, no Israeli would ever "assault a whole people indiscriminately," that when Israel is forced to engage in violence, it is always surgically targeted against the guilty.

This is an article of faith that requires no evidence for most journalists. During the late Persian Gulf war, Iraq's inexcusable Scud missile attacks on Israel brought the predictable outpouring of selective indignation from the news media. Television and newspaper coverage was intense. The networks showed the damage to an apartment house and automobiles, as the mayor of Tel Aviv charmingly reminded American viewers that such is life in Israel.

The ubiquitous Benjamin Netanyahu, Israel's deputy foreign minister, fully exploited the opportunities presented by live television interviews after the attacks. He said they again demonstrated why his country cannot deal with the Palestine Liberation Organization and repeated the canon that Israel is surrounded by hostile countries.

During the war, a National Public Radio newsman could scarcely control his amusement as he reported that Iraq justified the Scud attacks by saying that Israel's military reserve allows no distinction between civilians and soldiers. That journalist's scorn is typical of the double standard that characterizes coverage of Middle East events.

Yet neither Saddam Hussein nor PLO extremists are unique in

overlooking this distinction. The Israelis have been doing the same thing for more than 40 years, with more deadly weapons, in such places as southern Lebanon.

In 1978, after a major Israeli incursion into Lebanon, Chief of Staff Mordechai Gur bluntly told the press, "For 30 years, from the War of Independence until today, we have been fighting against a population that lives in villages and cities." Gur cited as examples of Israel's previous campaigns against civilians the bombing of villages on the east side of the Jordan valley and the shelling of towns in the Suez Canal area in the years after the Six-Day War. These acts of terror drove more than a million and a half Jordanians and Egyptians from their homes.

At the time of the Israeli general's statement, Israel's most respected military journalist, Ze'ev Schiff, wrote, "The importance of Gur's remarks is the admission that the Israeli army has always struck civilian populations, purposely and consciously. The army, he said, has never distinguished civilian [from military] targets . . . [but] purposely attacked civilian targets even when Israeli settlements had not been struck."

This is the policy that Moshe Sharett, Israel's first foreign minister, critically dubbed "sacred terrorism." The doctrine is found in the thinking of Israel's founding prime minister, David Ben-Gurion, and in the military actions approved by both major governing blocs. In 1981, when the Labor Party criticized then-Prime Minister Menachem Begin for his bombing of Beirut, which killed civilians indiscriminately, he responded by listing some of the civilian attacks perpetrated by previous Labor governments. "There were regular retaliatory actions against civilian Arab populations," Begin said.

According to the *Jerusalem Post*, former Laborite foreign minister and ambassador to the UN Abba Eban justified the attacks on civilians by arguing "there was a rational prospect, ultimately fulfilled, that afflicted populations would exert pressure for the cessation of hostilities." This would seem to qualify those Israeli attacks as purposeful terrorism waged against Arab civilians by any reasonable notion, but not by the de facto definition observed by mainstream American media, which inherently excludes Israel.

American commentators seem ignorant of, or blind to, Israeli attacks on civilians — such as those carried out repeatedly in Egypt, Gaza, and Jordan in the 1950s and 1960s, and, with even greater frequency, against civilians in the occupied territories and Lebanon in the 1970s, 1980s and today. Nor do U.S. observers or "terrorism experts" seem to be aware of the abuse of Muslim and Christian civilians during the 1948 war, such as the mass expulsions at gunpoint of the inhabitants of Lydda, Ramle and a large number of other Palestinian villages.[1] It took the full-scale invasion of Lebanon and the ghastly bombardment of Beirut in 1982 to get the media to notice, even briefly. Since then, they have lapsed into their previous pattern.

The power of the biased U.S. media over public opinion was well demonstrated by the coverage of the Scud attacks. The *New York Times* quoted Steven L. Spiegel, a UCLA professor and long-time apologist for Likudist policies in Israel, as saying, "Through television, millions of Americans . . . watched Israelis put on their gas masks . . . and they experienced just about everything the Israelis did. . . . I think many Americans will have a lot more sympathy for some of Israel's security problems after this."

It is also safe to say that Americans would have a lot more sympathy for the security problems of Palestinian and Lebanese civilians if the major U.S. media would provide even a modicum of information and photo coverage of Israeli policies to turn these civilians, through terrorism, against their leaders and each other.

In fact, the media's ignoring of the decades-long Israeli terror campaign against Arab civilians is something more than careless reporting. It betrays a systemic bias which implies that Arab, particularly Palestinian, deaths, no matter how gruesome, matter little, while the endangerment of Israeli Jews is an intolerable crime that takes precedence over all other considerations such as journalistic balance, elementary fair play, and the right of the American public to have access to all of the facts in order to make its own informed decisions.

---

[1] See Benny Morris's new book, *1948 and After: Israel and the Palestinians.*

33

1949: The First Israelis

American-Arab Affairs, Spring 1990.

Book review: *1949: The First Israelis*, by Tom Segev, translated by Arlen Neal Weinstein. New York: The Free Press, 1986.

Edward Jenks, in his book *A History of Politics*, written in 1900, stated, "historically speaking, there is not the slightest difficulty in proving that all political communities of the modern type owe their existence to successful warfare." Tom Segev, in his book about Israel's first year of independence, demonstrates that things have not changed in the twentieth century. If the State is the arrant presumption and imposition that eighteenth-century classical liberalism held it to be, then the state of Israel is the consummate State. It began in 1948 as, and remains today, a manifold imposition from prelude to coda. Segev convicts Israel and its ruling clique of presumption on six counts, involving: Jew versus Arab, veteran resident versus newcomer, European Jew versus Oriental Jew, secular versus Orthodox, Israeli versus Diaspora and farmer versus city dweller. With each pair, the former imposed unconscionably on the latter.

Segev is one of several younger Israeli historians who have examined recently declassified government archives and have begun to revise the stock account of the founding and settling of Israel. The book was met with the predictable howls in Israel because, as Segev writes, it "shattered a firmly established self-image and exposed as mere myths a large number of long accepted truisms." It became a best-seller. Segev summarizes his findings early in the book:

> Thus it became apparent that the Arabs had not always refused to discuss peace with Israel and that Israel has not done all it could possibly do to reach peace with its neighbors at all costs. A large number of Palestinian Arabs were expelled from their homes, not only during the war of 1948–1949, but afterwards as well. It was not the "gathering of exiles" in accordance with the Zionist ideal that was the primary purpose for Israel, but rather its own needs for manpower in agriculture, industry, and the army. Jewish immigrants from Arab countries have been discriminated against, partly as a result of explicit

decisions, and many of them were deliberately stripped of their cultural and religious identity.

All this indicates that the founding fathers of Israel were much less idealistic and more cynical than was commonly assumed. The "good old days" were not so good after all.

The book's strength lies in its almost complete reliance on official records; it contains little polemic. It is model revisionist history. Segev, using quotations and statistics, illustrates the disdain shown by the ruling secular, socialistic, European Jews toward anyone who did not fit their own mold. The "typical new immigrant" was described by one Israeli journalist as "a short little Polish Jew with prominent jaws, accompanied by his little fat wife." (Segev points out that the characterizations of new Jewish immigrants sound almost anti-Semitic.) Yemenite Jews, kept in immigrant camps, were forcibly deprived of their beards and sidelocks. Diaspora Jews were subjected to scare campaigns and lied to about real conditions in Israel so that they would emigrate. (One commando who worked inside Arab countries wrote, "Mass immigration will pour in only as a result of distress. . . . We must consider the possibility of initiating the distress.") Jews who wished not to be farmers were pressured, and in some cases forced, to settle in decrepit agricultural villages.

The attitude toward immigration was contradictory. The governing officials wanted many immigrants for the sake of security and settlement, but not *any* immigrants. Nahum Goldman of the Jewish Agency Executive said that "A State and a nation are entitled to exercise a certain ruthlessness. If we bring in aged people and invalids, other organizations must bear the burden. . . . A more efficient selection is good for the immigration and there can be no ideological objection to it." Itzhak Rafael, saying that he favored "selecting immigrants," acknowledged that he "held up 2,000 visas in Tunis, which had been issued to old people and invalids, and gave an order not to bring them over."

Regardless of age or health, some kinds of Jews were unwelcome by some Israeli officials. Admission of the Karaite community of Egypt was opposed by the chief Ashkenazi rabbi of Jerusalem, who saw its members as a "deadly plague." (The Karaites have long been regarded as heretics because they think the Pentateuch is the only authoritative text.) Similarly, Y. Meir, general director of the Ministry of Health, was "horrified" to learn that the Falashas, the black Jews of Ethiopia, were to be brought to Israel. (In 1985 Israel rescued 8,000 Falashas from the famine in Ethiopia; it is planning for the arrival of more.)

Of course, these impositions pale beside the treatment of the Palestinian Arabs. Losing one's sidelocks cannot compare with losing one's land or life. Segev's document-bound account adds important information to our storehouse of knowledge on this matter. The quotations he has dug out of the archives are particularly enlightening.

The legendary yearning for peace by Israel's leaders, which is incessantly invoked to this day by reporters and commentators, topples heavily before Segev's research. He quotes Foreign Minister Moshe Sharett telling his MAPAI party that "some very creative people" are satisfied with the armistice that ended the 1948 war. These people, Sharett reported, want the leaders "to stop reiterating declarations about our desire for peace, since the Arab world interprets them as a sign of weakness and as an indication of our willingness to surrender. We should say the opposite: We do not need peace."

A second legend is dismembered by Segev: The alleged Arab refusal to negotiate a peace agreement turns out, on closer examination, to be nothing of the kind. (Anwar Sadat was not the pioneer he is reputed to be.) The Arab nations were apparently eager — perhaps overeager, to the detriment of Palestinians — to come to a settlement. But there was no give on the other side. When the Egyptians proposed that the Negev be an independent state, Israel remonstrated that the UN Partition Resolution assigned the Negev to the Jewish state. Yet Israel refused to even discuss giving up the Galilee, which it had seized during the war, although the UN had allocated it to the Arabs. (The UN partition recommendation gave 55 percent of the mandate territory to the Jews and 45 percent to the Palestinian Arabs. After the armistice agreements, Israel had nearly 80 percent.) Thus a chance for an early agreement with Egypt was sacrificed to nationalism.

The reason for the stonewalling is not hard to fathom. A firm objective peace agreement would have undermined the Israeli leaders' expansionist plans. The archives overflow with documentation of their intent to get as much of the land of Palestine — occupied or abandoned — as possible. Only expediency cooled their ardor for the land. Israel's leaders, led by David Ben-Gurion, refused to specify the borders of their new state in the Declaration of Independence or elsewhere on the grounds that doing so would limit their options.

In the course of determining those borders, details such as the rights and dignity of Arabs were rarely allowed to get in the way. The Israeli abuse of Arabs trying to hang on to their villages, homes, and simple belongings was enough to move even Ben-Gurion to say during the war, "I'm shocked by the deeds that have reached my ears." Segev details the widespread murder, pillaging, rape, and uprooting committed by the Israeli troops. The reaction of Aharon Cizling, minister of agriculture, conveys the nature of the conduct: "I often disagreed when the term Nazi was applied to the British. I wouldn't like to use the term, even though the British committed Nazi crimes. But now Jews too have behaved like Nazis and my entire being is shaken." Cizling's candor had its limits, however: "Obviously we have to conceal these actions from the public."

Before, during, and after the so-called War of Independence, Palestinians were pressured or terrorized into leaving their homes. Hundreds of thousands did. Tens of thousands of others who held on through the war were expelled by the army afterwards. Some were removed to Arab countries; others were placed elsewhere in Israel. Why? Two reasons: to isolate the Arabs within Israel and to build villages for Jews. Segev's chapter "Dividing the Spoils" describes how the property left behind was shamelessly allocated to the Israelis.

Palestinians who tried to recover their land or personal property were branded "infiltrators." The refugee problem set off a panicked discussion throughout the country. Most leaders agreed with Ben-Gurion who said in April 1949 that the "government line is that they may not return." Yosef Weitz, head of the Jewish National Fund, proposed harassing the refugees who were near the borders in order to drive them deeper in Arab territory. He was willing to have Israel pay to settle them in the Arab countries, but he wanted no refugees readmitted except to reunify some families. Dov Yosef, military governor of Jerusalem, said "What happened happened, and there's no bringing back the past." When Moshe Sharett, anticipating that Israel might be forced by the United Nations or the United States to accept some refugees, suggested that Israel was willing to take 100,000 back, he set off a firestorm of criticism within MAPAI and among the public. (During negotiations with Egypt, Israel had earlier agreed to annex the Gaza Strip, thinking it contained 180,000 refugees, then backed down when it discovered the number was 230,000.) Sharett tried to calm the opposition by pointing out that since some refugees had already returned, the actual number to be accepted was only 65,000 and that these would be settled where the government wished and not in their own homes. Ben-Gurion, who Segev says "tended to ignore the human tragedy of the Palestinian Arabs," told Weitz, who opposed the plan, that it was "against his [Ben-Gurion's] judgment." Since no peace agreements were reached, no refugee plan, not even this cynical one, was ever adopted.

Sometimes the legal contortions regarding the Arabs were absurd. To ease the confiscation of abandoned property, the Absentees' Property Law was drafted. An absentee was at first defined as one who exited the state. But Moshe Sharett thought this too narrow; it would have left thousands of Arabs who fled their villages for Nazareth free to return home. So the definition was changed to include anyone who had left his "usual place of residence" after November 29, 1947, even though remaining in Israel. This led to the Orwellian concept of "present absentees." The state procured half a million acres under this law. (Eventually the present absentees were allowed to buy new property, but they never regained what they lost.)

The authorities imposed martial rule as Arab territories were conquered. "It was assumed that martial rule would prevail for many years to come. And so it did," Segev writes. Ironically, the legal basis for this rule was the Emergency Defense Regulations put in place by the British during the mandate. Under martial rule the army could seal Arab areas and require Arabs to have permits for entering or exiting the areas. Permits could be denied for "security considerations." Arabs could be deported from their villages; any Arab could be summoned to the police station at any time or confined to his house; administrative arrests could be made at any time without explanation or trial.

Segev writes:

> There were many reports about thousands of people taken from their homes for inspection and identification. Representatives of the military government would gather them in an open field, keeping them there for many hours in the sun, without food, drink, or toilet facilities — men, women and children. When they left their homes, they were ordered to leave the doors unlocked. The houses stood unguarded. When they returned, they often found that the soldiers had stolen household effects, jewelry and cash. These things happened repeatedly. . . . They were a frightened, leaderless people; they caused no danger to state security.

The routine, day-in and day-out humiliation and harassment of martial rule is hard to grasp for people brought up in the security of a constitutionally limited government. It should not have been hard for political and military officials claiming to speak for those victimized by Nazis so recently. What could have made them forget or, more likely, deliberately fail to apply the universal standards of justice? Segev leaves these questions for the reader to ponder. (The treatment described above, though hard to imagine, is not unfamiliar: it happens on the West Bank and the Gaza Strip routinely, and sometimes it even gets into American newspapers.)

When the British emergency regulations were used against Jews in the 1940s, they were denounced bitterly. Segev quotes Menachem Dunkeimann, later justice of the Israeli Supreme Court, who said at the time that they were "a menace to the entire community" and "a violation of elementary concepts of law and justice." Menachem Begin, later prime minister and head of the Likud bloc, objected in 1949 when the Labor government proposed additional emergency regulations, because he thought they might be used against his Herut party. He called the regulations "these Nazi laws" — the same laws that Palestinians continue to be subjected to today, at the hands of the Likud.

Segev is to be admired for his scholarship, his writing, and above all, his courage. His style is reportorial, with little argumentation. But that does not mean the book lacks poignancy. Facts often speak for themselves. Segev at one point discusses the renovation of "an abandoned Arab village on the outskirts of Jerusalem." Government officials looked it over, decided what it needed, and proceeded to establish an immigrant camp there. "The village was now given the name Givat Shaul Bet. In the past it had been known as *Deir Yassin*." This of course was the scene of an infamous massacre in 1948; more than 200 unarmed Palestinian men, women, and children were brutally killed by Begin's Irgun and Yitzhak Shamir's Stern Gang. Some Jews thought it insensitive to build a settlement on the site. In a letter to Ben-Gurion, four scholars, including Martin Buber, said, "Resettling *Deir Yassin* within a year of the crime, and within the framework of ordinary settlement, would amount to an endorsement of, or at least and acquiescence with, the massacre." The government built the settlement anyway. "Several hundred guests came to the opening ceremony [for the new camp], including . . . the Chief Rabbis and the Mayor of Jerusalem," Segev writes. "President Haim Weizmann sent written congratulations. The band of the school for the blind played and refreshments were served."

34

Rabbi Meir Kahane's
Role in Life and Death

Washington Report on Middle East Affairs, January 1991

The murder of Meir Kahane has revealed an interesting aspect of the militant, racist rabbi's career that perhaps even he did not appreciate. In life, and now in death, Kahane functioned as a foil alongside whom others may look more attractive.

In an otherwise worthwhile column in the *Washington Post* on Nov. 11, Walter Reich of the Woodrow Wilson Center wrote that Kahane "expressed views about Palestinians and advocated actions against them, particularly their 'transfer' to Arab countries, that are simply incompatible ... with ... traditional Israeli [standards]. They were, to be sure, compatible with the standards of rhetoric and behavior toward Jews in most Arab countries."

This statement clearly is intended to separate Kahane from Israel's leaders and indeed Israeli society generally. Let's see if they pass historical muster.

If Kahane's proposal for the transfer of Arabs is incompatible with Israeli standards, what are we to make of Joseph Weitz, director of the Jewish National Fund, the organization that acquired land in Palestine? In 1940 Weitz wrote the following:

> It must be clear that there is no room for both peoples in this country.
> . . . If the Arabs leave the country, it will be broad and wide open for
> us. And if the Arabs stay, the country will remain narrow and
> miserable. . . . The only solution is Eretz Israel, or at least Western
> Eretz Israel, without Arabs. There is no room for compromise on this
> point! The Zionist enterprise so far . . . has been fine and good in its
> own time, and could do with "land-buying" — but this will not bring
> about the State of Israel; that must come all at once . . . and there is no
> way besides transferring the Arabs from here to the neighboring
> countries, to transfer them all; except maybe for Bethlehem, Nazareth
> and Old Jerusalem, we must not leave a single village, not a single tribe.
> And the transfer must be directed to Iraq, to Syria, and even to

Transjordan. For that purpose we'll find the money, and a lot of money. And only with such a transfer will the country be able to absorb millions of our brothers, and the Jewish question will be solved, once and for all. There is no other way out.

Weitz uses the T-word four times, eight years before the state of Israel declared its independence. We can go back further. There is a famous statement of Theodor Herzl, founder of the Zionist movement, about "gently" expropriating Arab property and trying "to spirit the penniless population across the border by procuring employment for it in the transit countries, while denying it any employment in our own country. . . . Both the process of expropriation and the removal of the poor must be carried out discreetly and circumspectly."

Nor should we overlook Chaim Weizmann's hope that "Palestine shall be as Jewish as England is English and America is American."

That was the theory. It was faithfully carried out in practice. Before and after the 1948 war, Arabs were dispossessed of their land and belongings and driven mercilessly across the borders. (For details, see Tom Segev's excellent work, *1949: The First Israelis*, and my review in chapter 30.) This was repeated in 1967.

What of the treatment of Jews in the Arab countries? Reich didn't say which country he had in mind, but since the exodus of Jews from Iraq in the early 1950s is well known, let's look at that. Iraq, of course, had a large Jewish community that dated back to antiquity. Despite some bad times, the Jews of Iraq often prospered, especially as the 19th century dawned. The 1839 Noble Words of the Decree introduced a new civil code that applied to everyone regardless of religion or sect. According to Nissim Rejwan, an Iraqi Jew who emigrated to Israel, beginning in 1876 Jews served in the parliament and were appointed to government courts and district and municipal councils. Small numbers of Jews joined the civil service. Jews were free to educate their children and start schools. This is not to say that Jews suffered no discrimination, but the conditions were so favorable that some central European Jews moved to Iraq.

The situation changed with the flourishing of Zionism. A prominent member of the Iraqi Jewish community, Menahem Salih Daniel, confirming predictions of anti-Zionist Jews in the West, wrote in 1922 that Zionism prejudiced the Jews of the Arab world: "If [the Jews of Iraq] espouse so publicly and tactlessly . . . a cause which is regarded by the Arabs as not only foreign but as actually hostile, I have no doubt that they will succeed in making themselves a totally alien element in this country." [See chapter 4.]

The Zionist progress toward statehood, including the above-mentioned aggression against Palestinians, worsened things for the Jews of Iraq. Some Jews left for Israel, but apparently not enough for the

Zionists. They decided to give them a shove, because, as an Israeli agent put it, "Mass immigration [to Israel] will pour in only as a result of distress. . . . We must consider the possibility of initiating that distress." That they did. According to a CIA man in Iraq at the time, Wilbur Crane Eveland, the Israelis transferred weapons to Zionist operatives in Iraq. This was later confirmed by Yigal Allon. "In attempts to portray the Iraqis as anti-American and to terrorize the Jews, the Zionists planted bombs in the U.S. Information Service library and in synagogues," Eveland wrote. The U.S. Embassy was furnished evidence that the terrorism was committed by an underground Zionist organization. The Iraqi government tried to discourage the exodus, going so far as to confiscate the property of fleeing Jews. All but about 5,000 Jews left.

Thus the most celebrated "transfer" of Jews from an Arab country had its roots wholly in Zionism and in a shameful effort that violated the Balfour Declaration's caveat about actions "which may prejudice the rights and political status enjoyed by Jews in any other country."

35

Ambassador Jeane Kirkpatrick Sets Record for Mideast Misinformation

Washington Report on Middle East Affairs, April 1991

"It's not what we don't know that hurts us," Will Rogers is supposed to have said. "It's what we know that ain't so." Could he have had the Middle East in mind?

The person who "knows" the most that ain't so about the Israel-Palestine problem is Jeane Kirkpatrick, former UN ambassador under Ronald Reagan and now a foreign policy pundit. In the *Washington Post* on Feb. 11, Kirkpatrick packed about as much misinformation into one newspaper column as can be imagined. Titled "Roots of Arab Rejectionism," it surely deserves an award.

"The first and most important aspect of the problem," she writes, "is to know when it did and did not begin. The problem did not begin when Israel occupied the West Bank and Gaza after the 1967 war." This is the first and last piece of truth in the column. "It began," she continues, "in May of 1948, when Israel's Arab neighbors — Egypt, Iraq, Syria, Lebanon, Saudi Arabia and Trans-Jordan — rejected the Partition of Palestine and made war to destroy the new Jewish state."

Kirkpatrick is correct, of course, that the problem did not begin in 1967. Who, I wonder, ever said it did? But it didn't begin in 1948 either. It began in the 1920s and even earlier, when Jewish-statehood advocates bought land from feudal landlords (mostly Arabs) in Palestine and had the Palestinian Arab peasants, whose families had lived on that land for generations, expelled. The Palestinians could not even return as employees, because the Zionist movement would not hire Arab labor. By May 1948 many Palestinians, who didn't share the vision of an Arab-free Palestine, had already become victims of massacres and expulsions perpetrated by Zionist paramilitary forces.

The late Israeli historian Simha Flapan writes in his book, *The Birth of Israel: Myths and Realities*, that the Arab nations wanted peace with the new Jewish state and only reluctantly went to the defense of the Palestinians when the atrocities against them could no longer be ignored. The Israelis had made a secret deal with King Abdullah of Transjordan that allowed

him to take the West Bank, which, under the UN partition plan, was to
have been part of the Palestinian state. Israel took the rest of the proposed
Palestinian state, except for the Gaza Strip, which ended up in Egyptian
hands.

It is important to realize that the Arab armies did not attack the Jewish
state, as it was defined in the UN partition plan. The fighting occurred in
the Palestinian part, into which the Israelis had pushed from their UN-
recommended borders in order to realize expansionist ambitions. The
Israeli government had deliberately refused to specify its borders in its
declaration of statehood in order not to foreclose opportunities for
expansion.

When the war was over, Israel had enlarged its territory from 57
percent of mandatory Palestine to over 77 percent and had created
thousands of refugees denied the right to return home. As for the Arabs
who remained in Israel during the war of 1948 and who became Israelis,
they lived under military rule until 1966. (Becoming an Israeli confers no
great benefits on a Christian or Muslim Arab. Being a Jew is what counts.)

This, then, was the problem before 1967: some Palestinians were
refugees, the rest were second-class citizens. That the West Bank and Gaza
Strip have been the focus since 1967 shows, ironically, how far the
Palestinians have been willing to compromise. The two-state solution
essentially abandons the legitimate pre-1967 property claims. Who's
intransigent?

Kirkpatrick goes on to assert the occupied territories did not become
"important to the Arab-Israeli relationship until after Israel's Arab
neighbors had again launched and lost an aggressive war in 1967 against
Israel." Here is a shameless invention of history. Who can deny that
Israel's attack on Egypt started the Six-Day War? Jordan entered the war
only after the attack on Egypt, with whom King Hussein had a mutual-
defense treaty stipulating that an attack on either state would be considered
an attack on both. The Israelis launched a pre-emptive strike? Former
Prime Minister David Ben-Gurion said that he "doubt[ed] very much
whether [Egyptian President] Nasser wanted to go to war." Yitzhak Rabin
has said, "I do not believe that Nasser wanted war."

Finally, Kirkpatrick writes that "as long as Arab governments refuse to
establish normal diplomatic and economic relations with Israel and to
make peace, Israeli governments will feel threatened, will probably be
threatened and will make no concessions. Before there can be talk about
the West Bank, there must be talk between Arabs and Israelis." This is the
position of mainline American apologists for Israel, such as the
Washington Institute for Near East Policy. It could not be more
erroneous. Ironically, Iraq's foreign minister, Tariq Aziz, demonstrated
this. After his failed meeting with Secretary of State James Baker and just

before the Gulf War, Aziz was asked why Iraq doesn't discuss its grievances with Israel. Aziz said Iraq has no grievances with Israel. The issues, he said, are between Israel and the Palestinians. He added that what would satisfy the Palestinians would satisfy the Iraqis. With a war pending, Aziz had no reason to say this other than that it was true.

With two exceptions, the Arabs have no dispute with the Israelis once the Palestinian dispute is resolved. The exceptions, the Golan Heights and Southern Lebanon, are also related to the Palestinian problem.

So it is more than a little absurd for Israel's Deputy Defense Minister Benjamin Netanyahu to say that peace with the Arab nations must come before a settlement with the Palestinians. No informed person seriously believes that this makes any sense at all. It is simply a stalling tactic.

What position will the Bush administration take on this matter? Secretary Baker could advance the prospects for justice and peace simply by acknowledging this reality, which is confirmed by our Arab allies, and not just by Tariq Aziz. Such an action would bring uncharacteristic clarity to the Middle East muddle and could have earthshaking consequences. It would be the kind of shaking the earth could use.

36

Trial Lawyers' Tactics, Ideologue's Agenda

Washington Report on Middle East Affairs, April/May 1992

Trial lawyers have a saying: If the facts don't support your case, argue the law. If the law doesn't support your case, argue the facts. And if neither the law nor the facts support your case, create a smoke screen and obscure everything.

Cynthia Ozick may not be a trial lawyer (she is said to be writing a play about Holocaust revisionism). But she has the old lawyers' strategy down pat. Her Feb. 19 *New York Times* op-ed, "The Territories Aren't Occupied," is a textbook example of how to obscure unfavorable laws and facts.

Ms. Ozick's exercise in obscurantism begins with a dip into history. She asserts that in the 1930s the term "Palestinian" referred to Jews and that those we now know as Palestinians called themselves Arabs. Then she moves further back in history to state that the Romans spitefully came up with the name Palestina (Latin for Philistine) before driving out the Jews. What is the point of all this? She implies it has some parallel with our calling the West Bank "occupied," but that is far from clear.

Ms. Ozick apparently thinks it unimportant that non-Jews with deep roots also lived in Palestine when the Romans came; she has nothing to say about them. As long as we're revisiting history, however, it wouldn't hurt to recall that people lived in Palestine (Canaan) before Joshua and his army committed their bloody pogrom, as recounted in the Old Testament. Today's Palestinians can trace their ethnic and cultural roots back to those people, and all of the other peoples who have lived there before or since, including, of course, the Hebrews of the Bible.

Ms. Ozick's real mission, however, is not historical. It is to challenge the notion that the West Bank is occupied territory. Occupation, she writes, presupposes prior sovereignty. After the fall of the Ottoman empire, there was no sovereignty over the West Bank; thus there can be no occupation. "The unallocated territories known as the West Bank have never had any internationally recognized sovereign status," according to Ms. Ozick.

There are several problems with her analysis. In a narrow, legalistic sense, the formal legitimacy of an independent Palestinian state (independent of other Arab countries as well as of Israel) is inseparable from the legitimacy of Israel. The United Nations in 1947 recommended dividing Palestine into two states, one Jewish, one Arab. Someone who accepts UN authority cannot logically attack the legitimacy of one of the states authorized by the partition (Palestine) without also attacking the legitimacy of the other (Israel). Yet that is precisely what Ms. Ozick does.

She continues that the "partition designating an Arab share was violently nullified by the Arabs themselves. . . . The fact is, then, that for more than 70 years there has never been a *legally acknowledged* claimant to the territories west of the Jordan River." [Emphasis added.] Note that she writes that "the Arabs themselves" nullified the partition. Partisans of Israel never tire of lecturing the rest of us that there is no unified Arab people — until it is convenient for them to invoke it. Here it is convenient. Did all Arabs nullify the partition? No. As historian Avi Shlaim writes in *The Politics of Partition*, different Arabs had different reactions to the idea of partition. The Mufti of Jerusalem and leader of the Arab Higher Committee, Hajj Amin Al-Husayni, opposed the loss of any land. (Some Zionists, such as Yitzhak Shamir, also rejected partition.)

But other Palestinians were willing to accept partition as a second-best resolution. (The first-best resolution would have been for the Western imperialist powers to have practiced laissez faire in the Middle East.) The Mufti's rivals in the Nashashibi family, Shlaim writes, privately "expressed their preference for peaceful partition and peaceful coexistence between the Palestinians and the Jewish communities."

Abdullah, the expansionist king of Transjordan, also supported partition, but only in order to be in a position to grab the Palestinian territory and incorporate it into his kingdom. In this, Shlaim writes, the king had the support of the Zionist leaders, who in secret meetings with Abdullah's advisers had endorsed his aim of "aborting the birth of the Palestinian Arab state envisaged in the UN partition of 29 November 1947." Later in his book, Shlaim points out that "this [the aborting of the state] was the solution urged by the Jews on Abdullah and the basis of his agreement with [Zionist leader] Golda Meir at Naharayhim."

Thus, some Arabs opposed partition, some accepted it, and those who accepted had different reasons for doing so. The people who get forgotten in the grand generalizations are the tillers of the land, the homesteaders, the Palestinian Arabs, who at various times have been used by their fellow Arabs as well as by the Israelis.

By the time of partition, Jews were only a third of the population and owned less than 7 percent of Palestine. (True, the British had stopped land purchases. But that was not unreasonable, considering that the sellers were feudal, absentee landlords who did not have just title and their buyers were specifying that the tillers must be evicted to make way for exclusively Jewish occupancy.)

If no recognized sovereignty was established after the partition resolution it surely was not the Palestinians' fault. The collusion by Israel, Transjordan, and Great Britain cannot be raised against the victims of that collusion. That would make them victims twice over.

Ms. Ozick is right when she says there has been no "legally acknowledged claimant to the territories west of the Jordan." Then again, those in a position to acknowledge legally the Palestinians' claim to their land have had a vested interest in doing otherwise. Should the Palestinians be penalized for that? One thing we know for sure. The Israeli government has no claim to that land.

Ms. Ozick, of course, adds the obligatory misrepresentation of the 1967 and 1973 Arab-Israeli hostilities, which she describes as "wars instigated to wipe out the Jewish state." But no amount of repetition will change the facts. Israel attacked first in 1967, and many Israeli military leaders have since acknowledged that their country had been under no threat. The 1973 war, as Israeli leaders have conceded, was an attempt by Egypt and Syria to regain their occupied territories, not to destroy Israel.

Ms. Ozick's article is one in a long line of attempts to obscure Israel's systematic violation of the Palestinians' natural rights to life, liberty, and property. It should be recognized for what it is.

37

The Christian Right and the ADL: A Controversial Relationship

Washington Report on Middle East Affairs, September/October 1994

The Anti-Defamation League's indictment of the "religious right" as intolerant and even anti-Semitic has in turn drawn criticism from Jewish Republicans and conservatives alike. According to *Washington Jewish Week*, some prominent Jewish Americans have been talking to the Christian Coalition, a prime ADL target headed by Rev. Pat Robertson, about how to respond to the attack. Among them are Marshall Breger of the Heritage Foundation, William Kristol of the Project for the Republican Future, and Matt Brooks of the Republican-affiliated National Jewish Coalition. Americans for a Safe Israel also has weighed in against the ADL. Its chairman, Herbert Zweibon, said that "the greatest friends the state of Israel has in America are the Christian conservatives."

ADL got the controversy started with the release of its report *The Religious Right: The Assault on Tolerance and Pluralism in America*. The reaction from Jews involved in Republican and conservative politics was swift. Marshall Wittmann, the Christian Coalition's Jewish director of legislative affairs, said, "This was liberalism, not Judaism, speaking." He called the report "McCarthyite" and an indication of "incredible intolerance." He added, "It's quite ironic that the ADL, despite all the various anti-Semites out there, would go after people for their political views." He accused the report's authors of using Robertson quotations out of context.

According to a report in *The Forward*, William Kristol, who was Vice President Dan Quayle's chief of staff, said, "It is so shortsighted and self-destructive for a Jewish organization like the ADL to unjustly and gratuitously alienate Christian conservatives." Kristol also said that the ADL is part of the Democratic Party's strategy to "demonize religious conservatives." A spokesman for Kristol, who is the son of Jewish intellectual Irving Kristol, said the Republican strategist frequently consults with Ralph Reed, executive director of the Christian Coalition.

Breger, who was President Reagan's liaison to the Jewish-American community, commented that the ADL report "missed the forest for the trees. It inferred that the religious right is anti-Semitic, and I don't see how you can make that claim on the record." He said the criticism was political because it asserted that "if you hold certain positions on issues such as school choice, gay rights, or child pornography, that means you are intolerant." Zweibon, whose organization opposes the Arab-Israeli peace process, said the ADL report is a "slap in the face" to friends of Israel and indicated "that the ADL has veered off course and adopted a new ultra-liberal agenda that has nothing to do with ADL's stated purposes." He praised the Christian right for standing by Israel when others turned out to be "fair-weather friends."

Elliot Abrams, another former Reagan official, called the report "despicable." "I think that the problem today lies essentially with the Jewish community, because there is a deep-seated fear of Christian evangelical groups," Abrams said. "There is no question that there are people on the Christian right that have shrill tactics and with whom I disagree totally." But he added that the many Jewish Republicans involved with the Christian Coalition have more agreements than disagreements.

Abraham Foxman, ADL national director, stood by the report as "accurate and fair." He said that while "we are not attacking the Republican Party, [Republicans] are attacking us instead of the religious right. It's fascinating." He added that Christian rightist support for Israel does not require Jews to condone its religious intolerance. Foxman and Robertson spoke by telephone after the report was released. The two had a "friendly" debate, Foxman said.

Steve Gutow, executive director of the National Jewish Democratic Council, declared the religious right "very, very dangerous." "When pluralism is challenged," he said, "most of us in the Jewish community are going to stand up and say 'no.'"

A co-author of the report explained that the reaction of Jewish Republicans indicated the GOP's need for fundamentalist support in the coming elections. "Most Republican leaders are starting to circle their wagons," said David Cantor, an ADL senior research analyst. "They can't possibly win without this huge bloc in the short-term." He asserted that Robertson "has clearly made a number of remarks in the last five years that are extremely insensitive or antagonistic toward Jews, and I don't see why people in the Republican Party need to be apologetic for that."

In his foreword to the report, Foxman wrote, "The problem with issuing a critique of the religious right movement is that much of what this movement wants is right. Most of us value strong families, better schools, and a government that upholds its commitment to religious liberty." But he added that the Christian right has created a climate of fear. For example, doctors who perform abortions fear for their safety. "In this way," Foxman wrote, "we proceed down the road to the 'Christian nation,' trumpeted by these prophets of rage." The ADL report did acknowledge the religious right's vigorous support for Israel.

Israeli Deputy Foreign Minister Yossi Beilin's reiteration of his belief that American Jews should use their money to heal their own community rather than sending it to Israel has brought criticism from Jewish American leaders. Beilin more than once has told American Jews that Israel does not need their charity and that Jews in the United States are more threatened by assimilation and intermarriage than Israeli Jews are threatened by Arabs. He recently recommended that fund-raising in the Jewish Diaspora be halted. "There he goes again," said Seymour Reich, head of the American Zionist Movement. Reich told *The Forward* that "what [Beilin] is proposing . . . is divisive, and if carried out, would separate Israel from the Diaspora." Brian Lurie, executive vice president of the United Jewish Appeal, called Beilin "ignorant," but agreed that Israel does not need charity from America.

Beilin recommended the creation of Beit Yisrael, an organization that would promote the Diaspora's connection with Israel and work against assimilation. The organization, he said, should offer every Jewish 17- and 18-year-old a voucher for a trip to Israel. Under Beilin's plan, Beit Yisrael would replace the Jewish Agency and the World Zionist Organization. That plan is opposed by officials of those organizations and is criticized by Prime Minister Yitzhak Rabin. "I regret to say," Rabin said, "that there is a man, a deputy minister, who has seen fit to say things that do not represent the Israeli government."

38

Anti-Zionism: Analytical Reflections

Washington Report on Middle East Affairs, June 1989

Book Review: *Anti-Zionism: Analytical Reflections*, Edited by Roselle Tekiner, Samir Abed-Rabbo, and Norton Mezvinsky. Amana Books, Brattleboro, VT, 1988. 339 pp.

Since the mid-1970s, the Palestine Liberation Organization has expressed its willingness to make peace with Israel on the basis of a two-state solution. In recent months, the PLO has pressed this solution aggressively enough to win recognition from the U.S. government. Since the new Palestinian state would be on the West Bank and Gaza Strip, this is a monumental concession: it appears to forgo all pre-1967 claims, despite the fact that Israeli usurpation of property rights created the original Palestinian refugee problem.

This accommodation by Yasser Arafat and the PLO, helpful as it may be in defusing the Middle East bomb, has overshadowed a fundamental issue: the problem of Zionism. To grasp the difficulty inherent in Zionism, consider this: Zionism would be problematical even if the land the Zionists wanted was uninhabited.

One man who has understood this, and who has worked indefatigably to have others understand it, is Rabbi Elmer Berger. This book is a festschrift in his honor. Few people deserve to be honored for courage and resourcefulness in the service of justice as Rabbi Berger does. For over 40 years he has spoken out and written eloquently against the two-headed perniciousness of Zionism — the violence it has done to the Palestinians and the damage it has inflicted on Judaism. Among his books and articles is the poignant *Memoirs of an Anti-Zionist Jew*. He was a founder of the anti-Zionist American Council for Judaism and later American Jewish Alternatives to Zionism, which he still heads. In an era so lacking in heroes, Rabbi Berger is an inspiration.

The book does him justice. It is indeed a feast in writing, and a suitable introduction to many issues involved in the Palestine/Israel question. It begins with Rabbi Berger's own classic essay "Zionist Ideology: Obstacle to Peace" and includes new essays by Israel Shahak, Sally and W. Thomas

Mallison, Naseer Aruri, Roselle Tekiner, Shaw J. Dallal, Benjamin M. Joseph, Cheryl A. Rubenberg, Ruth W. Mouly, and Norton Mezvinsky. They cover such topics as Zionism as a recidivist movement, the "who is a Jew?" controversy, the anti-Zionist democratic alternative, Palestinian attitudes toward civil liberties, the Israel-South Africa relationship, American efforts for Middle East peace, Israel's Christian supporters, American domestic treatment of Zionists and Palestinians, and Reform Judaism's attitude toward Zionism.

One comes away from this book with a stark sense of the fundamental illiberality of Zionism. As Israel Shahak explains, it was an explicit reaction against the individualistic Enlightenment and an atavistic attempt to restore the stifling ghettos of 18th-century Poland. Zionism's fathers believed Jews could not live normal lives among gentiles — even in free, democratic societies — and propounded a notion of "Jewish people," with national "rights" that rejected the spirit of the age. Zionism, writes Shahak, "can be described as a mirror image of anti-Semitism," since it, like the anti-Semites, holds that Jews are everywhere aliens who would best be isolated from the rest of the world. Moreover, "both anti-Semites and Zionism assume anti-Semitism is ineradicable and inevitable." This attitude among Zionist Jews led to a capitulation to anti-Semitism in Europe, in lieu of a conviction to rally the world's liberal forces against it. Small wonder that some notorious anti-Semites, Adolf Eichmann, for example, have been attracted to the Zionist program. The results have been catastrophic.

Shahak's paper makes much of the last 40 years understandable. Given Zionism's premises, it is unsurprising that Arabs would have been seen as obstacles to be swept away ruthlessly and that the state of Israel would be run ostensibly for the benefit of "the Jewish people," no matter the cost in the lives and liberties of non-Jews. Some of the horrifying results are documented in *Anti-Zionism*. The record of callousness and dishonesty is appalling, all the more so because it was done in the name of Judaism. As Rabbi Berger writes in the first chapter, "Nationalist territorial Zionism's dehumanizing of Arabs has not been in response to or defense against Arab inhumanity to Jews. . . . The source of conflict was always Zionism."

Norton Mezvinsky's account of the early history of Reform Judaism is a needed antidote to the standard accounts of Zionism. If Zionism was an illiberal attempt to roll back the Enlightenment so far as Jews were concerned, Reform Judaism was a glorious embrace of the liberal values of individual freedom and dignity. In 1885, Reform rabbis met in Pittsburgh and adopted a platform that declared Judaism a religious community, not a people or a nation. "We recognize in the era of universal culture of heart and intellect, the approaching realization of Israel's great messianic hope for the establishment of the kingdom of truth, justice, and peace among all men." Its first prayer book omitted the usual references to Jewish exile and the future restoration of Israel. Reform Judaism was, in other words, anti-Zionist. It foretold with perfect accuracy the violence that Zionism would do to Judaism even had there been no Arabs in Palestine. Without Rabbi Berger we'd be less knowledgeable of this "other" — the real — Judaism.

39

Separation, Not Association, Requires Force

The Libertarian Institute, June 8, 2018

Whenever I write about Palestine, Israel, and Zionism — especially when I point out that American Reform Jews en masse gagged on the thought that America was not their "homeland"; they insisted they were Jewish Americans not American Jews — I am lectured on Facebook about how "keeping to one's own kind" is a natural inclination and that inclusion, not exclusion, requires aggression. We shouldn't be surprised, then, that alt-right-types who may dislike Jews nevertheless respect their expressed desire to live among themselves in a Jewish State. Why wouldn't the alt-right take this position? Israel is a (pseudo)ethno-state. It is identitarianism run amok.

As Foreign Policy in Focus (FPF) reports, Richard Spencer, the alt-right leader of "Hail Trump" infamy, told Israel's Channel 2 last year, "You could say I am a white Zionist." FPF went on: "He later described the Jewish state as 'the most important and perhaps most revolutionary ethno-state' — the 'one that I turn to for guidance.'"

What Spencer and his ilk, unlike Israel's supporters, understand is that Israel is an apartheid state — but with a difference. White-supremacist South Africa wanted to separate the whites and the blacks, but they needed the blacks to do society's dirty jobs. In contrast, the Israeli elite and much of the public want the Arab Muslims and Christians to go. The dirty work can be done by the Arab Jews (the so-called Sephardim, though they came not from Spain but from Arab countries; the late Iraqi Jew who turned anti-Zionist Naeim Giladi called them "Islamic Jews") and black African Jews.

But tribalists of all stripes get it wrong, as a glance at history will indicate. It's not association that requires aggression, but dissociation. True, freedom of association entails freedom of dissociation, but historically the liberal struggle has not been over the freedom to stay apart from The Other but rather over the freedom to get together in all sorts of ways.

We have many fictional accounts of warring factions being wracked internally precisely because individual members didn't give a hoot about the prohibitions against interfactional association. It's the old fight between tribalists and assimilationists. Rising generations will always view their elders' taboos with fresh eyes and see that many or most of the old rules are rubbish, existing only to be defied. The writing of such prohibitions into law indicated that the powers that be understood that young (and not so young) people wanted or one day would want to associate commercially and noncommercially with whomever they wished, their parents' stern warnings notwithstanding.

Think of how *Romeo and Juliet* and *West Side Story* resonate with so many of us. Think of the much-beloved *Fiddler on the Roof*. Contrary to popular misconception, that phenomenal Broadway musical — loosely based on Sholem Aleichem's Yiddish stories — is not about the charms of the *shtetls* of the Russian Empire. On the contrary, it is about how suffocating the *shtetl* — a ghetto, after all — was for the rising generation. Young adults rebelled at being told what they had to do and whom they may love and marry. When the Jewish stranger and teacher, Perchik, tells the men of Anatevka that girls also should be educated, he's denounced as a "radical." When he asks the woman he's falling in love with, Tevye's Hodel, to dance with him at her sister's wedding, it's a scandal, though this does not keep the reluctant subversive Tevye from joining Perchik by defiantly dancing with his wife, Golde. Then even the old rabbi joins in (sort of).

When Tevye's youngest marriageable daughter, Chava, falls in loves and wishes to marry the Russian gentile Fyedka, it is too much for Tevye. He lectures his daughter that "you must not forget who you are and who that man is," but *Chavala* pushes back:

"He has a name, Papa."

"Of course. All creatures have a name."

"Fyedka is not a creature, Papa. Fyedka is a man."

"Who said he isn't?" Tevya, the most reasonable man in the village, concedes. "It's just that he's a different kind of man. As the Good Book says, 'Each shall seek his own kind.' In other words, a bird may love a fish, but where would they build a home together?"

"The world is changing, Papa!"

"No! No. Some things do not change for us. Some things will never change."

"We don't feel that way."

"We?"

"Fyedka and I."

When Chava later tells her father, who along with his fellow Jews must leave their village under the tsar's edict, that she and Fyedka are voluntarily leaving, the young man says, "We cannot stay among people who can do such things to others."

In the end, the audacious, yet respectful Tevye — who dares to speak frankly to God — cannot bear to go on if his daughter is "dead" to him, and he subtly relents.

Love defeats fear. This is the man who proclaims at the start of the show, "Without our traditions, life would be as shaky as a fiddler on a roof." This is the man who had prayed to God to keep his children "from the stranger's ways." As he leaves for America (this does not happen in the original stories), Tevye gestures for the symbolic fiddler to follow him to the new world, but it is not really the same fiddler we saw in the beginning, is it?

If you need a real-world example think of the Lovings, the white man and black woman who at great cost defied Virginia's prohibition on interracial marriage and eventually won a victory in the U.S. Supreme Court — in the later 20th century!

Fictional accounts of interfactional romance never strike us as unrealistic because we easily identify with the defiant ones, even in apparently the most unlikely places. In Saddam Hussein's Iraq, marriage between Shia and Sunni was common and uncontroversial. After the U.S. invasion, with its Jacobin rearrangement of power relations, it became impermissible, leading me to quip that Bush's war gave a boost to *same-sect* marriage. Somewhere sometime, a Hatfield married a McCoy, and a Palestinian married a Jew (or "secular Jew"). It wasn't in Israel, however, where civil marriage does not exist, and Jew may not marry non-Jew (and children aren't allowed to read novels about romance between Jew and Arab).

Love (romantic, familial, etc.) trumps difference, fear, hate. We know it. Fear and hate need the state; love and cooperation need only freedom. Demagogues know that one gains power by sowing and reinforcing divisions that otherwise would wither away with each generation.

I could point out that Ludwig von Mises made a powerful case that what initially overcame the fear of The Other was a glimpse of the potential for gains from trade. In the article "Human Society," he wrote:

> The law of association [the mutual gains from trade among parties of unequal endowments] makes us comprehend the tendencies which resulted in the progressive intensification of human cooperation. We conceive what incentive induced people not to consider themselves simply as rivals in a struggle for the appropriation of the limited supply of means of subsistence made available by nature. We realize what has impelled them and permanently impels them to consort with one another for the sake of cooperation. Every step forward on the way to a more developed mode of the division of labor serves the interests of all participants. In order to comprehend why man did not remain

solitary, searching like the animals for food and shelter for himself only and at most also for his consort and his helpless infants, we do not need to have recourse to a miraculous interference of the Deity or to the empty hypostasis of an innate urge toward association. Neither are we forced to assume that the isolated individuals or primitive hordes one day pledged themselves by a contract to establish social bonds. The factor that brought about primitive society and daily works toward its progressive intensification is human action that is animated by the insight into the higher productivity of labor achieved under the division of labor.

Trade brought adversaries together when they perceived the fruits promised by the division of labor. Trade, however, is not just an exchange of goods; it's also an exchange of ideas and other nonmaterial values. Commerce by nature is conducive to trust, toleration, friendship, and more, as scholars have noted. Once the circles of trust begin to expand, there is no stopping the process, as hard as opportunistic tribalists might try.

So, undoubtedly, soon after the first exchange of goods outside the clan or tribe took place, boy met girl; boy and girl fell in love; boy and girl started a family. Well, there went the neighborhood! It's ever been the case.

Zionists, like all particularists, are not only on the wrong side of history; they are at war with human nature.

40

A Glimmer of Hope in Bleak Palestine

The Libertarian Institute, August 3, 2018

The Palestinians' deteriorating conditions in the West Bank and Gaza Strip make even long-term optimism difficult. Neither a one-liberal-state nor two-state resolution seems in the offing because (if for no other reason) either would seem to spell political suicide for any foreseeable Israeli government. The one-staters have a good argument against the two-staters and vice versa. Would it really be easier for an Israeli prime minister to evict 400,000 Israeli Jews from the West Bank (leaving aside the more than 200,000 in formally annexed East Jerusalem) than it would be to agree to one secular democratic state in which non-Jews would soon outnumber Jews if they don't already? I don't see it.

Pessimism is reinforced by the recently passed Nation-State Law, according to which the Knesset made fully de jure what had long been true de facto: that Israel belongs to Jewish people only (whether religious believers or not and wherever in the world they may currently live) and that the minority of non-Jewish Israelis should think of themselves as little more than guests living there at the pleasure of the Jewish supermajority.

"The right to exercise national self-determination in the State of Israel is unique to the Jewish people," the law states. Another part says, "The state will be open for Jewish immigration and the ingathering of exiles." Also: "The state shall act within the Diaspora to strengthen the affinity between the state and members of the Jewish people." And: "The state views the development of Jewish settlement as a national value and will act to encourage and promote its establishment and consolidation."

And we thought laws that specified religious, ethnic, national, or racial groups for special treatment went the way of the dodo bird, at least in western-oriented countries. Israel is officially a throwback to an unenlightened age.

To add insult to injury, Arabic, the language of 20 percent of the population, was demoted from an "official" language to one having only a "special status."

If most of this was already the reigning state of affairs, why was the law passed? It was passed to constrain Israel's Supreme Court. Gone is the wiggle room that the sometimes independent-minded court once had.

The law is now part of Israel's Basic Law, which functions more or less like a constitution. The new law says, "This Basic Law shall not be amended, unless by another Basic Law passed by a majority of Knesset members." In other words, there's no chance in hell of changing it unless Israel's ruling elite want it changed.

With the case for pessimism so strong, we must take whatever good news we can find. Some of us have longed for the emergence of a charismatic Palestinian figure who, while opposing Israeli oppression and settler-colonialism in all its forms, would also defend *individual* property rights and free enterprise while condemning both outside donor aid as dependence-inducing, as well as the corrupt, authoritarian, and unrepresentative Palestinian Authority (PA).

Such a person has indeed emerged: Khaled Al Sabawi. Al Sabawi has quite a story to tell. In 1948, during the Zionists' violent ethnic cleansing of Palestine and establishment of the state of Israel, his father's family was driven from their home and 50-acre farm in the village of Salama, east of Jaffa. The family fled to Gaza, along with many other refugees. Then in 1956, when Israel, Great Britain, and France launched a war against Egypt, the Israeli army invaded Gaza (30 years before Hamas was formed), ransacking and searching the refugees' homes, including the home of Sabawi's grandmother and father. When the soldiers found the grandmother's deed to their home in Salama, they confiscated it and departed. Apparently, that is just what the soldiers were looking for.

When his father, Mohamed Al Sabawi, grew up and earned advanced university degrees, he moved to Canada to raise his family. But then he moved back to Palestine and established a large insurance company in the West Bank and Gaza. His son Khaled, who was born in Kuwait, has now done something similar, graduating from the University of Waterloo in Ontario. After switching from computer engineering to geothermal engineering, he embarked on two entrepreneurial ventures: geothermal energy for the Occupied Palestinians Territories and elsewhere in the Middle East and registration of individual property titles in the West Bank. The latter project is called TABO, the Arabic word for "title deed."

Before the *Nakba*, the 1948 catastrophic ethnic cleansing and the 1967 conquest of the West Bank and Gaza, Palestinians proudly owned homes and land. But much of that land was not registered with the government because under Ottoman rule, that would have made the owners subject to taxation. Some individual parcels were registered in the name of absentee feudal landlords in Beirut and elsewhere, but the residents, that is, the actual Lockean owners, had to pay rent either in cash or kind. (James C. Scott's book *Seeing Like a State* explains how governing elites have long used various forms of registration to facilitate taxation and conscription and generally to keep an eye on the people.)

The immediate problem with unregistered land in the West Bank is that Israel might decide to build Jewish settlements on it. The state has long claimed Palestinian properties in the name of the Jewish people. Israel has already built settlements for 400,000 Jews in Area C, which is the 60 percent of the West Bank it rules directly. (Areas A and B have some degree of internal rule by the PA, which polices the Palestinians on behalf of the Israeli government. International law forbids a country to move population into territory occupied during a war.)

An article about Sabawi in *Forbes Middle East* explained the situation:

> In theory, the land [in the West Bank] is untouchable. After Oslo [the 1990s accords that created the PA], the Palestinian territories were divided into three areas: A, B and C, with just the latter falling under direct Israeli control. Al Sabawi works only in Area A, a zone officially under PA administration, but leaves nothing to chance. "If Israel tries to circumvent the agreement, they'll go after land without title deed, because once you have proof of ownership of your land it's very difficult for anyone to put their hands on it," [he says].
>
> And Al Sabawi is out to keep it that way, securing proud Palestinian land with the papers to prove it.

So his TABO project has the admirable objective of preventing more Israeli settlements on land that Palestinians legitimately own. He and his team work to track down the last owners of properties or their heirs and to plot the boundaries. *Forbes* reports that "after identifying land for sale from Palestinians who possess inheritance documents but no official papers, Al Sabawi sets about obtaining approval from relevant family members, before determining the borders in a manner more accurate than the 'this olive tree to that one' approach."

"We have to walk every corner of the land with a GPS machine, the head of the village council and every single neighbor," Al Sabawi said. His work has ruffled feathers, and that may seem unsurprising until you learn that "the challenge did not come from Israel; it came from the Palestinian Authority."

As he says in his TED Talk:

> For our outspokenness [that is, his criticism of the PA], however, we paid a heavy price, one that I never imagined. For our criticism of their leadership, individuals within the Palestinian Authority abused their power and suspended all of the title deed transactions of TABO. Think about this for a moment. To punish us for our freedom of expression, powerful individuals within the Palestinian Authority went out of their way to stop and suspend the registration of Palestinian land, thereby

preventing the protection of Palestinian land from Israeli settlement expansion.

In a testament to Al Sabawi's determination, the project has made progress, nevertheless. First, he and his team sued the PA for its abuse of power in the Palestinian High Judicial Council — and won. With that obstacle cleared, they moved ahead.

Forbes says:

> Three years on from TABO's launch, the initiative has enabled 250 families, both resident and in the Palestinian diaspora, to own 371 plots of land. Of TABO's sales so far, 30% have been generated by the diaspora. And the cost falls far short of the million-dollar price tag hanging from land just minutes away. TABO offers plots for between $13,900 and $32,000, with interest-free payment financed through the company for up to four years.

That was three years ago. The figures are higher now. Al Sabawi says that TABO has protected more than a million square meters of land, paved over 10,000 meters of roads, and helped more than 400 families to acquire 600 properties.

While the PA has obstructed TABO, so has the Israeli government, which harasses, interrogates, and detains Al Sabawi and his team when they try to travel to the West Bank.

Overcoming these hurdles has been an astonishing achievement. When Al Sabawi appeared on Al Jazeera's television show *The Cafe*, host Medhi Hasan said, "Sabawi believes corruption is rife inside the Palestinian Authority and says foreign aid has stunted an independent Palestinian economy." On the program, Sabawi noted:

> The Palestinian Authority today has essentially become a subcontractor of the Israeli occupation. When Oslo was created in 1993, and Israel was bearing the economic burden of occupation. It was very expensive, but when the Palestinian Authority was created it essentially started policing the Palestinian cities. But who paid for the bill? All the donor states, the United States, Canada and the entire international community, but Israel fully maintained its occupation. Israel still controlled borders, airspace, water, and pretty much all aspects of life for the Palestinian people, but brought in the Palestinian Authority to manage these cities. So it's been about 20 years of occupation management, and that's taken us back significantly, and what it's created is this entity that's become, you know, focused more on its self-interest than the interests of the Palestinian people. . . .

> [T]he Palestinian leadership . . . hasn't served to push Palestinian liberation forward whatsoever. As it stands today, the Palestinian Authority is completely anti-democratic. It has no mandate for the

Palestinian people. The people that go and negotiate with Israel, the Palestinian leadership that goes to negotiate with Israel, has no mandate from the Palestinian people. They do not represent them.

Al Sabawi rejects the conventional wisdom that donor aid is indispensable to economic development:

As it stands today, about 40 percent of the GDP of the Palestinian territories is accounted for by donor aid. The Palestinian people, as a result of it, also in the Palestinian Authority, have become the highest recipients of foreign aid in the world per capita. In addition to that, there's an enormous dependence on the Israeli occupation. Ninety-five percent of our energy comes from Israel; 80 percent of our imports come from Israel; 90 percent of our exports go towards Israel. The Palestinian economy is a sub-economy.

Sabawi clearly sees the perverse consequences of so-called aid:

It compromises the political and economic independence of the Palestinian people. So if the Palestinian people take an independent road or elect their own government, as they eloquently did in 2006 [in Gaza], so the 80 percent voter turnout, then the donor aid was cut off and the Palestinian people were punished for exercising their democratic rights[,] for being democratic. And just one small point, the situation now, economically, is far worse than it was before. The PA . . . is forcing Palestinian banks to give 50 percent of their deposits as loan facilities for the Palestinian people. Why? Because OPIC, the Overseas Private Investment Corporation, which is an American foreign policy organization, came and provided loan guarantees for Palestinian banks, for a push to drive the Palestinian economy to be more debt-based. Now debt has accumulated to $3 billion, consumer debt for Palestinian people. . . . The Palestinian Authority has created further dependent victims of the Palestinian people as opposed to confront[ing] the Israeli occupation.

Champions of liberty can only hope that Al Sabawi inspires a new generation of Palestinian liberators, one that is dedicated to individual freedom and autonomy through private property and free enterprise.

Libertarian Institute Original Articles

The later essays in this series are available in Sheldon Richman's archive at the Libertarian Institute:

https://libertarianinstitute.org/articles/sheldon/
https://libertarianinstitute.org/articles/tgif-shimon-peres-and-911/
https://libertarianinstitute.org/articles/tgif-shabbats-with-zade/
https://libertarianinstitute.org/articles/tgif-abused-jews-iraq/
https://libertarianinstitute.org/articles/tgif-anti-semitic-law-israel/
https://libertarianinstitute.org/articles/tgif-separation-association/
https://libertarianinstitute.org/articles/tgif-why-palestine-matters/
https://libertarianinstitute.org/articles/tgif-kushner-plan/
https://libertarianinstitute.org/articles/tgif-deal-of-the-century/
https://libertarianinstitute.org/articles/tgif-dehumanizing/
https://libertarianinstitute.org/articles/tgif-a-glimmer-of-hope/
https://libertarianinstitute.org/articles/tgif-defining-anti-semitism/
https://libertarianinstitute.org/articles/tgif-invidious-conflation/
https://libertarianinstitute.org/articles/tgif-palestinian-refugees/
https://libertarianinstitute.org/articles/tgif-trumps-delusions-persist/
https://libertarianinstitute.org/articles/tgif-art-of-smear/

Acknowledgments

These essays, stretching back more than 30 years (and having since undergone some editing), benefitted from encounters, in person and/or in print, with many people. They include, first and foremost, my late grandfather Samuel Richman, a tolerant and joyous Orthodox Jew and the lone critic of Zionism whom I knew or knew of during my first quarter-century. After him, I learned much from Alfred M. Lilienthal, Rabbi Elmer Berger, Imad-ad-Dean Ahmad, Noam Chomsky, Roy A. Childs Jr., Leonard P. Liggio, Edmund Hanauer, Allan C. Brownfeld, David Hirst, Ilan Pappé, Gilad Atzmon, Shlomo Sand, Avi Shlaim, Janet McMahon, Anne Joyce, Ted Galen Carpenter, Ben White, Leon Hadar, Rachelle Marshall, Norman G. Finkelstein, Israel Shahak, Moshe Menuhin, Yehoshafat Harkabi, Mattityau Peled, Miko Peled, Lenni Brenner, Norton Mezvinky, Edward W. Said, Christopher Hitchens, Hanan Ashrawi, Ramzy Baroud, Gideon Levy, Ernest Renan, Simha Flapan, Anthony Saidy, Philip Weiss, Stephen P. Halbrook, Thomas A. Kolsky, Jack Ross, Jeremy R. Hammond, Tom Segev, and Benny Morris, among others.

I also profited immeasurably from hours of spirited, civil Millian argument with my late brother, Marc P. Richman, though he could not have disagreed with me more.

My thanks to Mike Dworski and Grant F. Smith for their assistance with the production of this book.

Finally, this book would not exist but for the yeoman efforts of Scott Horton of The Libertarian Institute.

About the Author

Sheldon Richman is the executive editor of The Libertarian Institute, senior fellow and chair of the trustees of the Center for a Stateless Society, and contributing editor at Antiwar.com.

He is the former senior editor at the Cato Institute and Institute for Humane Studies, former editor of *The Freeman*, published by the Foundation for Economic Education, and former vice president at the Future of Freedom Foundation. In the late 1980s and early 1990s he was a columnist for the *Washington Report on Middle East Affairs*.

Richman is also the author of "'Ancient History': U.S. Conduct in the Middle East Since World War II and the Folly of Intervention," *America's Counter-Revolution: The Constitution Revisited, Separating School & State: How to Liberate America's Families, Your Money or Your Life: Why We Must Abolish the Income Tax*, and *Tethered Citizens: Time to Repeal the Welfare State* and a contributor to *The Concise Encyclopedia of Economics*.

He keeps the blog Free Association at SheldonRichman.com.

Made in United States
Cleveland, OH
06 December 2024

11406343R00115